Advance praise for Both Sides of the Table

"Raw, authentic, and emotional...These autoethnographies of educators who teach about and live with disabilities, or care for those who do, will break your heart. They offer hope that through personal stories we might create a sense of belonging for all touched by disability. These heartfelt and candid stories provide important insights that help us love more fully those who need us, provide assistance to those who are caregivers, teach more practically those interested in disabilities, open up the world of research to those who seek to understand experience deeply, and change the world...A thoughtful and penetrating resource for classrooms, practitioners, and those living with disabilities and their loved ones."

—Carolyn Ellis, Professor and Chair of Communication, University of South Florida;
Author of *Final Negotiations: A Story of Love, Loss, and Chronic Illness*;
The Ethnographic I: A Methodological Novel about Autoethnography;
Revision: Autoethnographic Reflections on Life and Work;
and *Handbook of Autoethnography*

"Disability has always provoked stories—stories of 'what happened,' stories that attempt to answer the how, when, and why of disability. The stories here, however, have a larger 'point to make,' talking back to dominant ways of thinking and knowing about dis/ability. Thus, while we create stories to know and to be known—in story we also insist on the authority of our own (and other's) experience. Deftly constructed like lines in a poem, in *Both Sides of the Table* Smith allows one story to speak to another, as the other nods back in shared understanding.

More than an anthology, however, *Both Sides of the Table* is a 'gentle manifesto.' In an era dominated by calls for 'evidence-based practice,' the field of education has been increasingly loathe to take risks. Although telling one's story is inherently risky, taking those stories seriously, ceding to their inner-authority, and allowing them to dislodge our taken-for-granted assumptions and ways of knowing involves an equally profound and existential risk. These are the risks that we as readers are invited, indeed, compelled to take in *Both Sides of the Table*. In putting story in the service of social transformation, Smith pushes the field to move beyond its current sense making about research, dis/ability, and inclusion to embrace a more radical and far-reaching conception of belonging."

—Beth A. Ferri, Associate Professor and Coordinator
of the Doctoral Program in Special Education, Syracuse University

Both Sides of the Table

Disability
Studies in
Education

Susan L. Gabel and Scot Danforth
General Editors

Vol. 12

The Disability Studies in Education series is part of
the Peter Lang Education list.
Every volume is peer reviewed and meets
the highest quality standards for content and production.

PETER LANG
New York • Washington, D.C./Baltimore • Bern
Frankfurt • Berlin • Brussels • Vienna • Oxford

Both Sides of the Table

Autoethnographies of Educators Learning and Teaching With/In [Dis]ability

Edited by Phil Smith

PETER LANG
New York • Washington, D.C./Baltimore • Bern
Frankfurt • Berlin • Brussels • Vienna • Oxford

Library of Congress Cataloging-in-Publication Data

Both sides of the table: autoethnographies of educators learning
and teaching with/in [dis]ability / edited by Phil Smith.
pages cm. — (Disability studies in education; vol. 12)
Includes bibliographical references.
1. People with disabilities—Education—United States—Research.
2. Disability studies—United States. 3. Education—United States—
Biographical methods. 4. Ethnology—United States—Biographical methods.
I. Smith, Phil, editor of compilation.
LC4031.B68   371.9—dc23   2013013005
ISBN 978-1-4331-1452-6 (hardcover)
ISBN 978-1-4331-1451-9 (paperback)
ISBN 978-1-4539-1152-5 (e-book)
ISSN 1548-7210

Bibliographic information published by **Die Deutsche Nationalbibliothek**.
Die Deutsche Nationalbibliothek lists this publication in the "Deutsche
Nationalbibliografie"; detailed bibliographic data is available
on the Internet at http://dnb.d-nb.de/.

Cover art by Ruth Salles
Cover design by Phil Smith

© 2013 Peter Lang Publishing, Inc., New York
29 Broadway, 18th floor, New York, NY 10006
www.peterlang.com

Printed in the United States of America

This book is for Mom and Pop, who never got to see it. Thanks for all you gave me. I'm still trying to make you proud (or piss you off—sometimes it was hard to tell the difference, hey?).

Table of Contents

Acknowledgments ix

Section 1: Introducing Autoethnography
    Introduction: What Dis Is, Why Itz Here/*Phil Smith* 3
    Chapter 1: Why Autoethnography?/*Phil Smith* 15

Section 2: Living With Disability—Stories by Labeled People
    Chapter 2: Who knew school could be so cruel?: Tales of a Learning
        Disabled Student at an Institution of Higher Learning/*dené granger*37
    Chapter 3: The Bad Apple/*Michael Peacock* 53
    Chapter 4: Autistethnography/*Elizabeth Grace* 89
    Chapter 5: This Closet/*Phil Smith* 103

Section 3: Living Alongside Disability—Stories From Family Members
    Chapter 6: I Am Not of This World, and Yet I Am in It: A Daughter's/
        Disability-Studies-in-Education Alien's Log Of a Journey Through
        Hell/*Alicia Broderick* 121
    Chapter 7: Listening: A Star Is Born!/*Bernadette Macartney*...............137
    Chapter 8: Help Wanted/*Casey Harhold*..155
    Chapter 9: Picture This: Snapshots of My (A)typical Family/
        David Connor..167
    Chapter 10: An Open Letter to Wyatt/*Erin McCloskey* 185
    Chapter 11: That's OK, They Are Beautiful Children/*Kathleen
        Kotel* 199
    Chapter 12: A New Chance to Matter/*Liz McCall* 213
    Chapter 13: Being an Albee/*Lynn Albee* 231

Section 4: What's It All Mean? Reading Lives, Creating Futures
    Chapter 14: What Do These Stories Tell Us About Education and
        Autoethnography?/*Phil Smith* 247
    Chapter 15: Looking to the Future/*Phil Smith*....................................263
About the Contributors...279

Acknowledgments

My friend, colleague, collaborator, and co-conspirator, Dr. Jackie McGinnis, gave me the time and space to write over a long hot summer. Her work mattered a lot—and I know it wasn't easy (oh, how I know). I think I still owe her a martini. Or eight. I know she'll go to heaven. I'm headed the other way.

Liz McCall had the idea for this book, and propelled me into making it happen. Scot Danforth and Susan Gabel gently and ably urged me on with their wonderful editing and leadership skills. The folks at Peter Lang have been SO patient with me.

Ibby Grace reminded me what was important. My gratitude is large.

Liat Ben-Moshe said some extraordinary things at just the right time. Her writing and thinking have informed mine in powerful ways, and will for a long time.

Folks think students hang out with teachers to learn from them. Wrong: teachers hang out with students to learn from *them*. Casey Harhold, Lori Harvard, Michael Peacock, and Christie Routel have taught me much over the course of years. Jessica Bradley, Kevin Dorn, Billy Milburn, Sarah Radu, and Ruth Salles are others that have taught me things in the last year or two that I needed to know (and didn't always know that I needed to know).

Ruth Salles is also a great artist. What a cover! What a gift!

Corinne Glesne started me on this journey 15 years ago. I've spent my life since then paying it forward, learning how to give what I have received (undeservedly) to others.

Kim retaught me about living. For realz.

Marilla, of course. And Sara. For the reasons you know.

Section 1

Introducing Autoethnography

Introduction

What Dis Is, Why Itz Here

Phil Smith

This Book Is Liz's Fault

One fall afternoon, a couple of years ago, I was working on my computer at the university, responding to an email from a student with an advising question. I heard a knock at my office door, turned around, and found a tall woman with short red hair standing at the door. "Liz!" I said. "Come in!" I turned my desk chair around to face her, and pulled out a chair for her to sit down at the table.

Liz was one of my graduate students, taking a second class with me, this one about families with members with a disability. With a quick smile, ready laugh, and a keen, ironic sensibility, she had made an impression on me the previous fall when she had taken an introductory course in education and disability studies. She had great questions, good answers, and written a terrific paper a year ago. I was glad to have her back in class.

Liz and I exchanged pleasantries, and then she got down to business. "I have an idea for a final project in your class," she said, and then smiled, almost sheepishly. "But it's a paper, not one of those other kinds of projects." I encouraged students to represent their learning and knowledge in creative ways, outside the boundaries of typical graduate course student papers. They could make a video, or sew a quilt, or make a painting. One student made a wooden bowl. Others created sculptures, performed music and dance, and took photographs.

"That's OK," I laughed. "If I were going to do something creative for one of my classes, I'd probably do something written, too. What do you have in mind?"

She leaned on the table. "Well, I have an idea—its about families, and disability—but I don't know if its possible to write about—if its something you'd allow. I don't know if its academic enough, you know? If it's the kind of thing you're looking for—if its what you want."

"Why don't you tell me what you have in mind, Liz," I said. "You should know by now that I'm open to interesting ideas."

"Well," she said, looked up, and breathed out. "I write a lot, you know." I knew that Liz had a blog in which she wrote about what was going on in her life. Pretty interesting stuff.

She went on, looking down. "Well, there's this story that I've been trying to write. Its about—it started with my father-in-law. He committed suicide. And then a couple of years later, my father—he committed suicide too."

I looked at her. "Wow," was about all I could manage.

"Yeah," she said, and chuckled. "Wow. And then my stepdad committed suicide too." She rushed on. "So I've been trying to write about it—how it affected me, and the rest of my family. Do you think that would be something that I could write about—kind of a story—for your class?"

"Liz, I think that would be a great project. In fact," I said, and turned to face the bookshelves over my desk. "In fact—now where is that?" I scanned the line of books that stretched across the room. "There it is!" I stood up, reached, pulled down a blue paperback, and turned back to Liz. "I just finished reading this book over the summer. It's by Carolyn Ellis, called *Final Negotiations: A Story of Love, Loss, and Chronic Illness* (1995a)."

I put the book on the table between us, and leafed through it. "In it, she described her experience caring for her partner, who was dying with a chronic illness. It's a kind of research—autoethnography—in which the researcher writes about their own life as a way to understand the way that culture does certain things—in Ellis's case, its about relationships, among other things. But the way she writes about it—" I looked up at Liz. "It reads more like a novel than a traditional piece of research."

I looked down at the book, and then back at Liz. I was getting excited by the idea. "I think you could do the same thing, Liz. You could write about your experiences with suicide in your family—write about it in the form of a short story, maybe—and draw connections to how the systems of services for families and people with psychiatric disabilities did—and maybe didn't—meet their needs. Call it an autoethnography, and—shazam!—its research. You could get it published."

I sat back, thinking. I'd had an idea for a paper I wanted to write for a couple of years, an autoethnography about my own experience living with disability, tying it to how it had changed my thinking about education. Maybe...

I sat up, leaned on the table, and looked at her with a goofy grin. "Liz, I am really glad you came in to see me this afternoon. How would you like to write a chapter for my next book?"

Questions and Theories and Subjectivities

We learn about and begin to make sense of the world through the tales that we tell—stories that we tell ourselves about the world, about ourselves; stories that others tell us; stories that we perform, create, and imagine. Ellis (2004) pointed out that "Stories are the way humans make sense of their worlds" (p. 32). We create stories in order to understand who we are, and what we are, and how we are, in the world.

As I've gone about my work over the past couple of decades—as an educator, critical ethnographer, support broker, teacher educator, writer, and disability studies scholar—I've had the opportunity to listen to the stories of other teachers and teacher educators who work with people with disabilities and their families. Many—the most interesting, to me—were stories of their own experiences with disability, or the disability of someone close to them. I began to wonder to myself: how has the experience of living with a disability, either personally or for someone close to them, made an impact on how teachers and teacher educators understand and create teaching and learning? This book is a beginning answer to that question. Or maybe its not so much an answer, as a way to open up a new set of questions, a new set of ideas, a new way of looking at this thing we call disability.

This book is founded in post, critical, and disability studies perspectives—ideas that I'll take a (brief) stab at unpacking. By disability studies, I want to mean an interdisciplinary, bricolagic exploration of ways in which disability plays out in social and cultural contexts. Here, as elsewhere, I understand disability as a socially constructed enterprise, and the study of it as being intentionally, explicitly, and unabashedly interdisciplinary in approach (Smith, 2010).

This kind of disability studies is multiple, plural, poly—opposed to essentialism. It looks at disability through social model lenses—again, not a single way of understanding disability phenomenon. The social model of disability that I value is one placed in firm opposition to medical models, in which disability is essentialized. In medical models, people with disabilities are intentionally and explicitly Othered—through that process, they are "deprived of visibility, uniqueness, subjectivity, voice, and knowledge" (Krumer-Nevo, 2012). Othering occurs in such a way that what could be understood as difference is translated as being lesser, inferior, deficit (Krumer-Nevo, 2012). Formal Othering processes of labeling and sorting, developed by Eugenicist pseudo-science and extended through special education taxonomic procedures for creating difference, meet the needs of Eurocentric, ableist, racist culture and ideology (Smith, 2008a; 2012).

The process of Othering is an artifact of ableism, which I have defined elsewhere as

> the persecution and discrimination of people with so-called disabilities by the dominant, normate culture. In the case of people with disabilities, it creates Others in order to support and advance the social, economic, and cultural goals of the normative. (Smith, 2010, p. 8)

Ableism is the ideological spawn of the dominating discourse of modernist, positivist Cartesian, Eurocentric culture and science.

The disability studies scholars in this text look at disability as it manifests itself in educational contexts. Disability studies in education (DSE) is a field that wants

> ...to deepen understandings of the daily experiences of people with disabilities in schools and universities, throughout contemporary society, across diverse cultures, and within various historical contexts. More specifically, and within the realm of praxis, DSE works to create and sustain inclusive and accessible schools. (Connor, Gabel, Gallagher, & Morton, 2008, p. 441–442).

Disability studies in education is not aligned with, supportive of, or exemplified by, special education. Far from it: DSE scholars, at the barest minimum, critique special education practices and policies, and often are in direct and defiant opposition to it as an institution and an ideology. Many of the teachers and teacher educators writing in this volume would describe themselves as inclusive educators. Like inclusive education, disability studies in education "is the antithesis of special education" (Underwood, 2008, p. 2).

This book, and my writing in it, is founded in post and critical work. I've described these social cartographies elsewhere in more detail (Smith, 2010). That being said, I align my thinking with that of Patti Lather (2010), and

increasingly find post and critical "traditions" (if such a word can be used) to
be a place of messiness, following post and after structuralism, post-
structuralism, modernism, post-modernism, critical, and post-critical
theoretical/practical constructs. What lies there, it seems to me, is the place
of "-ish," a kinda sorta not-quite growing organic way of thinking and
understanding, trying hard to avoid being elitist and abstract; and trying hard
to be resistant, intersectional, and queer. It's a topography of justice, a
landscape of sustainability, a space of doubt and what-the-heck-is-going-on-
here infidelity. In it, perhaps the only thing that can be said to be certain is
that "education is always political and teachers are unavoidably political
operatives. Teaching is a political act—there's no way around it" (Kincheloe,
2008, p. 164). A fun and scary place, both at the same time—kinda like a
Steven King novel. Pull up a chair.

My scholarship in the field of disability studies in education has been
diverse and varied, as those who've read my work know. An important
strand of this work—arguably the most important weaving, at least from my
perspective—has led me to an exploration of ways in which research can be
represented (Smith, 2001a; 2001b; 2006a; 2006b; 2007; 2008b). It is this
path in my work that this book mostly follows. I come to this work as an
educator, a teacher educator, the parent of a young woman with a disability,
and most importantly, as someone who identifies as a disabled person.
I also identify myself as white, middle-class, queer, cis-male, and hearing.
(In this book, I will use both person-first language as well as language that
puts the disability first. This is explicit and intended. Person-first language
has become a norm in the field of supporting students with disabilities, to
indicate that they are, literally, a person, not the disability. When referring to
myself, however, I put the disability first, in alliance with the thinking that
disability is an identity, one which I seek to assert and reclaim, and also to
remind the reader that disability is socially constructed, created to oppress
those who are not seen as normal by a dominant, ableist hegemony.)

In the next chapter, I'll look more closely at what autoethnography is. At
this point, though, it seems appropriate to talk briefly about the kind of
autoethnography that you'll find in this book. The autoethnographies in this
text are in alignment with the mix of research writing that Richardson and St.
Pierre (2005) refer to as creative analytical practices; it is a kind of research
that is "unruly, dangerous, vulnerable, rebellious, and creative" (Ellis &
Bochner, 2006, p. 433). Denzin (2006) calls this kind of autoethnography

"evocative or emotional" (p. 420) and, with others, performative (Denzin, 2011). It is a kind of research that wants "to change the world by writing from the heart" (Denzin, 2006, p. 422). It is the sort of autoethnography that is opposed to what Anderson (2006) calls analytic autoethnography, which Ellis and Bochner (2006) describe as another kind of realist ethnography, in which the reader "is a detached spectator... cut off from... body and emotions. There's no personal story... Knowledge and theory become disembodied words on the page" (p. 431).

The kind of autoethnography you'll find in this book is about stories. They invite you (sometimes by twisting your arm) to be part of them. You'll do as much work reading them as the authors did writing them—reading and writing are inseparable. They're opinionated, emotional, personal, exciting. They're a new way of thinking about research. If that's the kind of stuff that interests you, read on.

What This Book Is About

This book looks at the stories of educators, and how their experiences with disability, personally and in the lives of those who are close to them, have made an impact on their understanding of disability. It uses disability studies and critical theory lenses to understand the autoethnographies of educators and their personal relationships with disability.

Both Sides of the Table is divided into four sections. The first, "Introducing Autoethnography," includes this introduction, as well as the first chapter, "Why Autoethnography?" in which I outline the meaning of autoethnography, describing what autoethnography is, or might be, or might become. The chapter outlines the kind of performative autoethnographic work that will be exemplified in this book, how and why that work has come into being, what it looks like, and its impact on understanding society and culture, and, ultimately, disability. I look briefly at the history of autoethnography, how autoethnography fits into the larger tradition of qualitative and ethnographic research, critiques of autoethnography, and how autoethnography has explored disability and teaching. I also look at how autoethnography can function as a means for creating social justice and change, and the riskiness involved in doing autoethnographic work.

In the second section, "Living With Disability—Stories by Labeled People," disability studies scholar dené granger tells stories about her life in school and college and relationships and medication, in her chapter, "Who

Knew School Could Be So Cruel?: Tales of a Learning Disabled Student at an Institution of Higher Learning." As a graduate student, working on a doctorate, she writes about the meaning of learning disability—how it affects her research and writing, how it impacts the way her colleagues and mentors look at her and understand her. She applies for food stamps. She takes medication to help her pay attention, then stops taking it, and then starts again.

Elizabeth Grace—an assistant professor and talented writer—penned a chapter that she calls "Autistethnography," about growing up as a person with autism. Her wonderful stream-of-consciousness writing, told tongue-in-cheek and with tremendous honesty, is a terrific story, about life, and learning, with occasional not-random forays into baseball, dodecahedrons, librarians, freeing frogs, and Linus Pauling.

Graduate student and educator Michael Peacock, in his self-described "cheeky" chapter, "The Bad Apple," describes the process of becoming a white, gay, male teacher. On the road to being an educator (a role he didn't always know that he wanted to become), while traveling and studying around the United States, he discovers he has trouble sleeping, becomes an alcoholic, and is diagnosed first with a panic disorder and agoraphobia, then depression, and finally bipolar disorder. In between, he spazzes out, and merrily performs to and with music. His chapter reflects his gradual acknowledgment of his disability, and its impact on him as a pre-service educator.

Next up is my own autoethnography, "This Closet," in which I talk about living with major recurrent depression. Although I can't imagine living without the darkness that sometimes comes to visit me, it has led me to harm myself physically, spending time in jail, and has had a powerful impact on my relationships. The end result? More questions than answers; an existential wondering about what is real and not real in my life, in my memory. I explore the meaning of recurrent depression as it is socially constructed, and how it has changed my career.

The third section of the book, "Living Alongside Disability—Stories From Family Members," describes the life stories of a number of educators who have family members that live with a disability. The first chapter in this section, by teacher educator and disability studies scholar Alicia Broderick, is aptly titled "I Am Not of This World, and Yet I Am in It: A Daughter's/ Disability-Studies-I Education Alien's Log of a Journey Through Hell." Alicia's father, admitted to the hospital to undergo surgery, ends up dying in the Intensive Care Unit from complications. She juggles caring for her mother at home (she has her own disabilities), fighting with physicians and other professionals at the hospital who lack empathy and any understanding of her disability studies perspective, trying to communicate to the rest of her family, and her own ethical and emotional dilemmas.

The next chapter is by Bernadette Macartney, also a teacher educator and another disability studies in education scholar. Entitled "Listening: A Star Is Born!" McCartney describes raising her daughter Maggie Rose, juxtaposing her inclusion in the loving fabric of a caring family with the unwillingness of most medical and educational professionals to see her as anything except a collection of symptoms and deficits.

Educator and researcher Casey Harhold describes her relationship with her grandmother in "Help Wanted." Casey was a care-provider for her Grandma, who experienced a seizure disorder, bipolar disorder, and other disabilities. She talks about the impact her grandmother's disabilities had on her family, and how it has affected her teaching and learning and life.

David Connor, a teacher educator, disability studies scholar, and book author, describes the many members of his extended family who have experienced disability in their lives, in a chapter titled "Picture This: Snapshots of My (A)typical Family." Written as a set of portraits—framed photographs arranged, perhaps on the top of a piano, or on a mantle—he describes his relationships with uncles with psychiatric disabilities and attention deficit disorder; cousins with dyslexia, speech impairments, growth abnormalities, and intellectual disabilities; his mother with physical disabilities; and other relatives with Cornelia de Lange Syndrome and significant disabilities. David questions the notion of the typical or normal family, and explores the impact of difference and the Other on his work as a scholar and researcher, on himself as a gay man, and as the member of an extraordinary and diverse family.

Erin McCloskey—a researcher and author—speaks directly to her son in her chapter, "An Open Letter to Wyatt." In it, she describes the quirky parts of her son that she loves, but that other people understand as symptoms. She also discusses her conflicted role as mother, special educator, student (in which she spent as much time unlearning as she did learning), teacher, and teacher educator. And she talks about a seminal moment, in a school meeting for her son, in which the disparate identities that she embodies came together.

Kathleen Kotel writes about her own life, as well as the birth and early life of her daughter, Talia, who has Down syndrome, in a chapter entitled "That's OK. They Are Beautiful Children." She looks at her early experiences with disability, and then later experiences as an educator. Then she talks about her reactions in discovering that her daughter has a disability, as well as the conflicts and learning that she experienced as a result—experiences that she cannot separate, that merge along a continuum of growth.

Liz McCall is an experienced writer, graduate student, and a teacher of students with emotional and behavioral disabilities. In her chapter, "A New Chance to Matter," she describes what it was like for her to watch her father get swallowed up by psychiatric disability, and the unwillingness of the mental health and correctional systems to provide him (and her) with the kind of supports he needed to live a life of value. She writes about the impact this set of events had on her—as a person, a family member, and a teacher.

Lynn Albee writes about her hilarious, caring, and wonderfully zany family—a cast of characters with an off-balance, unusual sense of humor and joie-de-vivre—in her chapter, "Being an Albee." Her brother, David, has been labeled as a person with autism—but in the context of the rest of her family, the difference between Autism and Albee begins to be hard to define or categorize. Her descriptions of people and events in the context of a supportive and open community call into question the meaning of disability, and the meaning of humanity.

The last and fourth section of the book is entitled, "What's It All Mean? Reading Lives, Creating Futures." In it, I and the other authors in this book look back on the stories that we've told, reflect on what they mean and what they've taught us, and think ahead to the future. In the penultimate chapter, "What Do These Stories Tell Us About Education and Autoethnography?" the other authors in this book and I talk about the meaning of autoethnography and disability, and what we've learned about them by writing them into being. The chapter is written in the form of a scripted performance text. I asked the book's authors to respond by email to a series of questions, and then framed their answers into an imagined in-person symposium. The chapter reflects the resulting conversation.

The final chapter, entitled "Looking to the Future," is an autoethnographic description of a conversation between my daughter, Marilla, and myself, reflecting on what I've learned as a result of editing this book. It takes my thinking about autoethnography, research as a whole, education, and disability, coupled with scholarship by Illich, Aronowitz, Prakash and Esteva, and Ben-Moshe, and extends it into the future. It is a proposal (or perhaps a gentle manifesto) for what research, education, disability, and a utopian revolutionary politics of social transformation could and should look like.

This, then, is the book *Both Sides of the Table: Autoethnographies of Educators Learning and Teaching With/In [Dis]ability*. It looks at disability from multiple perspectives—people with disabilities, and family members of people with disabilities. It explores ways in which disability plays itself out in schools, and in communities, viewed by people who are educators and teacher educators. The title, *Both Sides of the Table*, refers to the context in which educators find themselves in Individualized Education Plan (IEP) meetings in schools. There, educators often sit on the other side of the table from people with disabilities, their families, and their allies. In this book, in these chapters, the authors assume roles that place them, literally, on both sides of IEP tables. They inscribe new meanings—of relationships, of disability, of schools, of what it means to be an educator and a learner.

It's a whole new story about education and disability. It's a whole new way of researching about education and disability. I think this is one of the first of many such stories. This story is a beginning glimpse of the future—of education, of disability, of research. I hope you'll welcome this future, as I do, with anticipation and open arms.

References

Anderson, L. (2006). Analytic autoethnography. *Journal of Contemporary Ethnography, 35*, 373–395. doi: 10.1177/0891241605280449

Connor, D., Gabel, S., Gallagher, D., & Morton, M. (2008). Disability studies and inclusive education: Implications for theory, research, and practice. *International Journal of Inclusive Education, 12*, 441–457.

Denzin, N. (2006). Analytic autoethnography, or déjà vu all over again. *Journal of Contemporary Ethnography, 35*, 419–428. doi: 10.1177/0891241606286985

—— (2011). *Custer on canvas: Representing Indians, memory, and violence in the New West*. Walnut Creek, CA: Left Coast Press, Inc.

Ellis, C. (1995a). *Final negotiations: A story of love, loss, and chronic illness*. Philadelphia: Temple University Press.

—— (2004). *The ethnographic I: A methodological novel about autoethnography*. Walnut Creek, CA: Left Coast Press.

Ellis, C., & Bochner, A. (2006). Analyzing analytic autoethnography: An autopsy. *Journal of*

Contemporary Ethnography, 35, 429-449. doi: 10.1177/0891241606286979

Kincheloe, J. (2008). Afterward: Ten short years—Acting on Freire's requests. *Journal of Thought, 43*, 163–171.

Krumer-Nevo, M. (2012). Researching against othering. In N. Denzin & M. Giardina (Eds.), *Qualitative inquiry and the politics of advocacy* (185-264). Walnut Creek, CA: Left Coast Press.

Lather, P. (2010). *Engaging science policy: From the side of the messy.* New York: Peter Lang.

Richardson, Laurel, and Elizabeth Adams St. Pierre (2005). Writing: A method of inquiry. In N. Denzin & Y. Lincoln (Eds.) *Handbook of Qualitative Research* (3rd ed.) (pp. 959–78). Thousand Oaks, CA: Sage.

Smith, P. (2001a). Inquiry cantos: A poetics of developmental disability. *Mental Retardation, 39*, 379–390.

——— (2001b). MAN.i.f.e.s.t.o.: A Poetics of D(EVIL)op(MENTAL) Dis(ABILITY). *Taboo: The Journal of Education and Culture, 5* (1), 27–36.

——— (May, 2006a). Looting the ludic: metaph(l)o(o)r(mat)s uv dis{ease} able tease stud {ease}. 6th Annual Disability Studies in Education Conference, East Lansing, Michigan.

——— (2006b). Split------ting the ROCK of {speci[ES]al} e.ducat.ion: FLOWers of lang(ue)age in >DIS<ability studies. In S. Danforth & S. Gabel (Eds.) *Vital questions facing disability studies in education* (pp. 33–61). New York: Peter Lang.

——— (May 2007). An OUT(in)lan{dish} po(l)em/it-ics uv DISability stud tease in ed DUCAT ion. Third International Congress of Qualitative Inquiry, Urbana, IL.

——— (2008a). Cartographies of eugenics and special education: A history of the (ab)normal. In S. Gabel & S. Danforth (Eds.), *Disability and the politics of education: An international reader.* New York: Peter Lang.

——— (2008b). an ill/ellip(op)tical po—ETIC/emic/Lemic/litic post® uv ed DUCAT ion recherché repres©entation. *Qualitative Inquiry, 14*(5).

——— (ed.) (2010). *Whatever happened to inclusion? The place of students with intellectual disabilities in education.* New York: Peter Lang.

——— (2012). Why disability studies must not use statistical analysis. Paper presented at the 8th International Congress of Qualitative Inquiry, University of Illinois—Champaign, Champaign, IL.

Underwood, K. (2008). *The construction of disability in our schools: Teacher and parent perspectives on the experience of labeled students.* Rotterdam: Sense Publishers.

Chapter 1

Why Autoethnography?

Phil Smith

"… all ethnography, is self-ethnography" (Goldschmidt, 1977, p. 294).

"I am an instrument of my inquiry: and the inquiry is inseparable from who I am" (Louis, 1991, p. 365).

"Stories are gifts" (Goodall, 2002, p. 386).

"There is always a story going on" (Stein, 1935, p. 118).

"I am part of the story" (Dillow, 2009, p. 1345).

"experience is the stories people live" (Clandinin & Connelly, 2000, p. xxvi).

…we are, as Walter Fisher expresses it, *homo narrans*—humans as storytellers (Goodall, 2010, p. 28).

…the world we see is about the way we see (Matthews, 1984, p. 20)

We understand the world through stories that we tell ourselves about the world and about ourselves. As Denzin (2010a) says, "We are all storytellers…" (p. 10). We create stories in order to understand who we are, and what we are, and how we are, in the world.

One way to understand the world is through statistics, a kind of numbering of the world. But the numbering of people is a dangerous thing, creating taxonomies of difference and privilege (Smith, 1999; Smith, 2012; Smith & Millstead, 2012). In fact, for me, "a number is a story not worth telling" (Kibel, 1999). A kind of story that *is* worth telling is autoethnography. Autoethnography is a betweener approach to understanding: "it operates within the interstices—and blurs the boundaries—between art and science" (Rolling, 2008); it is a "vehicle of emancipation" (Spry, 2001, p. 708) from traditional structures of identity and inquiry.

This is a description of what autoethnography is, or might be, or might become. It is partial, situated, incomplete, multiple—like an autoethnographic sketch, it is a way "...of leaving open other possibilities without imposing artificial closure on the final product... open for interpretation" (Rambo, 2007, p. 533). It is "...for more than personal release and discovery, and for more than the pleasures of the text. It is not a text alone" (Jones, 2008, p. 206).

Autoethnographers are a kind of postmodern, bricolagic griot (Stoller, 2002): telling the fictions/truths of the peopled world through stories of their own lives, their own bodies, as seen through the lens of their own vision. And "...it resists clarity. It is radically uncertain..." (Denzin, 2010a, p. 36). It is an impossible thing to do. It is the only thing to do.

Simply, autoethnography is a kind of self-writing (Murav, 2003)—by which I mean not simply a writing about the self, but a writing *of* the self—a making and performing of me-in-culture. Some place it in the traditions of anthropology and the social sciences, outside of description and performance (Chang, 2008). While the autoethnography described here begins in those traditions, the one imagined here is in closer alignment to a performative mode, one in which "...writers become ethnographers of their own lives, moving back and forth between self and other, self and history, self and social structure..." (Denzin, 2010a, p. 30).

Autoethnography "...points to an intersection between autobiography and ethnography..." (Chiu, 2004). Reed-Danahay (1997) says that

> It synthesizes both a postmodern ethnography, in which the realist conventions and objective observer position of standard ethnography have been called into question, and a postmodern autobiography, in which the notion of the coherent, individual self has been similarly called into question. (p. 2)

More formally, autoethnography might be defined as "...a self narrative that critiques the situatedness of the self in relation to others in social contexts..." (Morimoto, 2008, p. 30). Carolyn Ellis, who has played an important role in developing and describing this genre of writing and researching, describes it as "...research, writing, story, and method that connect the autobiographical and personal to the cultural, social, and political...autoethnography claims the convention of literary writing" (2004, p.xix). She places it in a growing discourse within the broader tradition of qualitative research, in which "...researchers seek to tell stories that show bodily, cognitive, emotional, and empathetic social complexities of concrete moments of lived experience" (Ellis, 2004, p. 30).

Pinning autoethnography down like this, though, may be dangerous, for it is "...a blurred genre, it overlaps with, and is indebted to, research and writing practices in anthropology, sociology, psychology, literary criticism, journalism, and communication..., to say nothing of our favorite storytellers, poets, and musicians" (Jones, 2008, p. 208). It keeps wanting to change itself. This is much like the identity that autoethnography seeks to uncover—always changing, never single, its position hiding from both self and other. You look at it, and it is gone, or changed, or moved, or it was never there, or was never an it—all by or through or with the act of looking.

Understanding identity is an important focus of autoethnographic work, an approach to answering the questions: "Who am I? Who am I becoming?" (Diggs & Clark, 2002, p. 371). It is a way of understanding the self—of writing the self—as a way to understand culture (Bochner, Denzin, Goodall, Pelias, & Richardson, 2007). The exploration of identity is often done in the context of negotiated relationships, in which the understanding of self is done within the experience of being "...in the company of others, who have their own individual or collective understandings of our identity (or identities)..." (Diggs & Clark, 2002, p. 371). Ellis (2010) came to understand "...that the self and other are intertwined and that you can't know one without the other" (p. 244). Identity—and autoethnography—is a making, a transforming, a place from which to stand and draw a sketch of the self-in-relation (Rambo, 2007).

Autoethnography is also a way of understanding culture, by looking at "human beings as universal singulars" (Denzin, 2010a, p. 12): seeing ways that individuals perform the socio-cultural contexts within which they find themselves. But autoethnography looks at culture in a specific way: "it seeks to understand how power and ideology operate through and across systems of discourse, cultural commodities, and cultural texts" (Denzin, 2010a, p. 24). Outsider researchers (more traditional ethnographers) may miss the details or nuances of lived experience that autoethnographers, as insider researchers, can capture (Erickson, 2010).

The person who speaks in autoethnographic narratives is an I, a me, and it is about my and mine—it is "…an ongoing conversation between the 'I,' the acting subject, and the 'me,' the actor's perception of self as object…" (Rambo, 2007, p. 538). Not THE I—it is AN I, one of many– a very particular first-person singular. Autoethnography is a kind of storied conversation between an I and an audience (Berry, 2006). Rather than looking at Others, autoethnography looks at the self, critically, Othering the I (Goodall, 2000).

Autoethnography as the Performative

Autoethnography is, perhaps, seen best as a performative I rather than a narrative I, one which creates "…a vigilant, a curious, a questioning knowing… uncertain, ungrounded, and thus fragile tellings…" (Jackson & Mazzei, 2008, p. 314). A performative autoethnography tries "…to critically interrupt dominant narratives by offering a performance that breaks normative patternized behaviors and remakes a transgressive coperformance with others in sociocultural contexts and histories… the autoethnographer seeks to construct a plural sense of self…" (Spry, 2009, p. 604). This performative narrative is embodied: "language is always coming from our bodies" (Corroto, Weems, Rambo, Poulos, Foster, & Lockford, 2007). Autoethnography as performance is not as concerned with accuracy, objectivity, fact, or an ever-elusive Truth as it is with storying, evoking, and feeling social and cultural experiences (Wall, 2008). As such, "performative writing expands the notions of what constitutes disciplinary knowledge" (Pelias, 2005, p. 417). It broadens the idea of what it means to know, and how it is we come to know, about various facets of our world.

Denzin (2011) describes performative ethnography (of which autoethnography as performance is one variant) in this way:

> We are in a postexperimental moment, performing culture and history as we write it… culture becomes a dramatic performance. Performance texts are situated in complex systems of discourse where traditional, everyday, and avant-garde meanings… all circulate and inform one another. Performance ethnography simultaneously creates and enacts moral texts that move from the personal to the political, the local to the historical and cultural." (p. 19–20)

And yet autoethnography is about the use and exploration of the multivocal subjective voice, in which the researcher and subject of regard are the same. Subjective voice is multiple, reflecting the many selves within each human identity, and offers a way to explore the social and cultural constructions of identity. It is principally a process/tool/method for exploring identity, relationships, and situated human experience (Olson, 2004). Ellis (2009) describes the place from which she as an autoethnographer speaks:

> I am both the author and focus of the story, the one who tells and the one who experiences, the observer and the observed, the creator and the created. I am the person at the intersection of the personal and the cultural, thinking and observing as an ethnographer and writing and describing as a storyteller. (p. 13)

Autoethnography does this by placing the story of the person within the context of all stories, all experiences: "every person is like every other person, but like no other person. The autoethnographer inscribes the experiences of a historical moment, universalizing these experiences in their singular effects on a particular life" (Denzin, 2003, p. 268). Here is the place that autoethnography finds its home, in which "the writer refuses to make a distinction between self and other..." (Denzin, 2003, p. 269).

Autoethnography offers a way to describe self and others, within relationship, through written sketches and layered accounts (Rambo, 2005). Because autoethnography provides an opportunity to describe hidden or inside knowledge that might be otherwise inaccessible, it can be particularly useful for exploring topics with sensitive cultural or social qualities (Philaretou & Allen, 2006).

Autoethnographies are very specific kinds of narratives—they are stories. Ellis again: "I call myself a writer—not a reporter—which means I focus on the construction of stories and their meanings rather than on the collection, organization, verification, and presentation of evidence" (2009, p. 14). These stories are made things, and the things that they are and do should be understood as made up and written down, one possible perspective or making. Autoethnographers recognize that "realism is an ideology. It involves the belief that the world, a thing, can be accurately, objectively recorded, painted, photographed, transcribed, performed" (Denzin, 2011, p. 159). Autoethnographers, mostly, adopt another ideology: that stories are created, made up. This does not mean that they don't reflect truth; far from it. Instead, the kinds of stories autoethnographers tell are perhaps *more* truthful, because they include the author's subjective understandings—a kind of knowledge thought to be outside of realistic narratives.

This storying and storied process should be understood to be never settled, never final—it is "a starting point" (Kidd & Finlayson, 2009, p. 984). It is always versioned,

> ...constructed from my current position, one that is always partial, incomplete, and full of silences, and told at a particular time, for a particular purpose, to a particular audience... all of us constantly reframe and restory our lives, attempting to arrive at a version that presents these lives as changing, yet continuous and coherent... (Ellis, 2009, p. 13)

Elsewhere, Ellis points out that autoethnography offers us opportunities "...to understand the meanings and significance of the past as incomplete, tentative, and revisable..." (2004, p. 30).

Poet William Matthews describes the meaning of these kinds of stories in "A Happy Childhood":

> It turns out you are the story of your childhood
> and you're under constant revision...(p. 35)

I think Matthews would say that the writing of the story of one's self is in an act of revision. As is the living of it; and what is the difference between the living of it and the storying of it?

So, is autoethnography True with a big T? This begs, of course, the question of the nature of such Truth. Leaving that aside, Owen, McRae, Adams and Vitale "conceive of truth as *a* rather than *the* "rhetorical device" to use for evaluating personal research and believe that demanding factual, historical truth-of-life research is faulty and problematic" (2009, p. 178). Autoethnography aligns itself with a small-t truth that is multiple, informed by the subjective, and culturally constructed.

Autoethnography: Making Meaning, Performing Culture

Autoethnography is, in part, a way to understand and explore culture; but that understanding is from a particular standpoint, a specific vantage: it is "...the study of a culture that involves the self" (O'Byrne, 2007, p. 1381). Ellis (2008) describes her autoethnographic work as being about, at least in part, "... the joy of figuring out through writing what my life is about and what it may mean" (p. 1317). What life is about is always situated in a cultural context, and so all autoethnography is at least partially about culture, even if unacknowledged.

As such, autoethnography has been used to express and explore a variety of issues, across a variety of cultures and contexts. It crosses boundaries that are hard to see and understand; one example is that between autoethnography and memoir (Goodall, 2006).

Because autoethnography is always already a performance of lived experience as seen from the vantage of a single subjectivity, it can never be objective. This is not a bad thing; it acknowledges the subjective experience of being human. It allows for the living of fiction. In a way, it is a kind of transliteration of experience, of life. In her poem "Artemis," Olga Broumas describes the impact of this kind of transliterative making of meaning, which she calls "a politics/of transliteration..." (1977, p. 24).

This sort of commitment, this kind of politics, is a political commitment to the explication of lived experience, a learning-through-story for the self and audience. It is a way of coming to see multiple meanings inherent in what might otherwise be understood as single events, single contexts. This is a quantum life, in which objects and people are in more than one place at a time, doing more than one thing simultaneously, outside of common sense and the appearance of reality. Autoethnography allows for understanding experience as multiple all-at-the-same-space-time transliterative quantum life-states.

Lau (2002) speaks to this kind of transliterative quantum autoethnography when she writes a "text which is not one," which she sees as a feminist mirroring, opposed to linearity. In this multiple text, she writes, it is possible to explore how "meaning might exist, in part, in the spaces between the dominant narratives", in the space of "intertextuality" (p. 246). This space she describes with words like multivocal, fragmented, multilayered, fluid, multivalent—text(s) as collage, many-in-one. This kind of text is a "denial of singular meaning" (p. 256).

Disability and Autoethnography

A variety of autoethnographies address disability issues. In his introduction to a forum about self-representing disability, Couser (2000) proposes that such autoethnographies might be a means "to explore the positive ways in which identity and life narrative are shaped by disability, the ways in which disability may create culture. (And, in a sense, self-representation by people with disabilities itself constitutes a form of disability culture)" (p. 308).

One researcher explored what it meant to live with a mother with intellectual disabilities (Ronai, 1997). Another talked about her relationship with a daughter with intellectual disabilities, looking at violence, sexuality, and families (Rogers, 2009). Shuman (2011) also described her role as a mother of a child with disabilities, with regards to empathy and alignment to other parents of children with disabilities.

Others have looked at fatness, thinness, and weightism within physical education and kinesiology (Morimoto, 2008); stuttering (Weinreb, 2008); and chronic illness and the death of a loved one (Ellis, 1995a; 2004). Another looked at the impact of a stroke (Kelley & Betsalel, 2004). Blindness has also been explored in autoethnographic work (Pfau, 2007). Clare (2003) described the impact of staring—gawking, she calls it—on her life as a disabled woman.

Chouinard (1995/1996; 2010) talked about her long struggle to obtain workplace accommodations, again as a disabled woman. Richards (2008) used his own medicalized life as a way to explore the ways in which autoethnography can talk back to normative representations of disability and illness. Malthouse (2011) wrote about the impact on her relationship with her mother, who experienced Alzheimer's dementia.

Some explored living with a parent with a psychiatric disability (Foster, McAllister, & O'Brien, 2005); a child with a psychiatric disability (Schneider, 2005); and an eating disorder (Kiesinger, 1998; Mukaia, 1989; Tillman-Healy, 1996). In fact, the exploration of psychiatric disability, psychiatric survival, recovery, and "mental health" in autoethnographic work is a not-uncommon theme (Gallardo, Furman & Kulkarni, 2009; Isaac, 2007; Kidd & Finlayson, 2009; B. Smith, 1999; Weems, 2006). Brooks (2011) wrote about her performance of and experience with Obsessive-Compulsive Disorder, and its impact on her relationships.

Wyatt (2008) described his somewhat difficult and distant relationship with his father, who (almost parenthetically) had a physical disability as a result of polio. Ward (2008) talked about living with a mother who had post-polio syndrome; Lindemann (2010) also described living with a father with paraplegia, and ways in which disability is distinctly gendered. Atkins (2008), a woman with a rare neuromuscular disability, described the ethical decision-making process that she and her lesbian partner engaged in regarding pre-natal testing for their planned children.

Valente's (2011) work looked at d/Deaf culture and life, from a between perspective, locating himself in neither/and oral deaf and Deaf worlds. He used multiple lenses to uncover and unpack his life, drawing on traditions that range across. His writing mixed styles, genres, and voices in a bricolagic, interpenetrative word movie that owes its heart to comic books and good storytelling.

Teaching and Autoethnography

Teachers, like others, "...are persons making meaning" (Diamond, 1992, p. 69)—yet the meaning that they make is too often not given importance or value. Autoethnography offers a way for them to outline their meaning, and to give it legitimacy—it "...can evoke the meaning that events have... and... reveal the process and structure of... knowledge" (Diamond, 1992, p. 72). Autoethnography provides a process for educators to understand, interpret, analyze, and explicate their stories, and the means to communicate them to others in ways that give them legitimacy.

Some have described the work of Torres (1998), Grant (1999), deMarrais (1998), and Rogers (1998) as belonging to (and at least partially creating) the genre of critical personal narrative and autoethnography in education (Burdell & Swadener, 1999). These works, they assert,

> are multivocal and question previous assumptions of empirical authority, while also interrogating the construction of subjectivity... much of their content draws from critical theories, in that they embody a critique of prevailing structures and relationships of power and inequity in a relational context. (Burdell & Swadener, 1999, p. 21)

Clearly, it reflects a continued turn toward the political.

Warren (2011) suggests that autoethnography offers an opportunity for educators to think about and act on their teaching, to create a truly reflexive pedagogy; it is about moving "from 'what I believe about teaching' to 'why I believe what I believe about teaching'" (p. 139). This kind of teaching allows educators to perform a way of being in the classroom that is increasingly critical. Wilson (2011) also found that autoethnography has the potential to create reflexive practice, and to understand ways in which culture plays out, in, and through education.

Goode (2007) uses autoethnography to discuss issues in the teaching of English literature related to inspiration and creativity. Rodriguez (2009) describes her experiences as a Latina professor facing resistance from her

White students. Wamsted (2011) also explores racial tensions, from the perspective of a white teacher working with black students. Dressman (2006) looks at resistance, too, in this case that of in-service educator-researchers towards her critical questioning of their values and beliefs in relation to the communities in which they work. Woods and Henderson (2002) used autoethnography to critique the Reading Recovery approach to literacy intervention, noting that it conflicts with much current literacy research.

Cook (2012) uses autoethnography in her college sociology classes to enhance engagement, encourage critical thinking, and as an assessment tool. Vasconcelos (2011) looks at relationships between teachers and students. Averett and Soper (2011) also look at student and teacher relationships, using a feminist perspective, in higher education.

Critiquing Autoethnography

Critiques of autoethnographic approaches have included suggestions that it is "...non-evaluative, allows for anything goes, encourages self-therapizing, lacks objectivity and generalizability, promotes self indulgence and privileges marginalized voices while excluding voices in the mainstream..." (Moriomoto, 2008, p. 31). Morimoto responds to these critics, pointing out that

> ...historically marginalized voices ought to be celebrated for expanding the conversation... autoethnography... deliberately challenges the illusion of researcher objectivity. Furthermore, it does not seek to produce findings or generalizability, but to illuminate the privilege and position of the reader/audience relative to the author and the culture at large. Lastly, autoethnography challenges what counts as knowledge, making the case for first person knowledge and life experience as data... (2008, p. 31)

Sparkes (2002) responds to the charge that autoethnography is self-indulgent by noting that such an assertion reflects

> a misunderstanding of the genre in terms of what it is, what it does, and how it works... Autoethnographies can encourage acts of witnessing, empathy, and connection that extend beyond the self or the author and thereby contribute to sociological understanding in ways that, among others, are self-knowing, self-respectful, self-sacrificing, and self-luminous. (p. 222)

Autoethnographic work is, by definition, an insider approach to research.

Insider research has numerous challenges (as well as opportunities) (Voloder, 2008). Critics describe this approach as based in narcissism and self-indulgence (Chang, 2008). Others suggest that autoethnographers "...may take the habitual too much for granted, underreporting some of it. And they may be blind to aspects of their own privilege. They may have their own axes to grind, their own self-deceptions" (Erickson, 2010, p. 117).

Morse (2009) argues that autoethnography is not balanced, or fair, that it encourages voyeurism, that it is unethical. Like other emerging approaches, autoethnography challenges notions of validity and reliability (Lewis, 2009). Those who support autoethnography assert that it "...is more authentic than traditional research approaches, precisely because of the researcher's use of self, the voice of the insider being more true than that of the outsider..." (Wall, 2006, p. 155). And some suggest that usual understandings of validity are not applicable to autoethnographic work (Wall, 2006). Instead, argues Denzin (2010a), autoethnographers have other criteria for determining the value of their work. They are, he says, bricoleurs, and "the bricoleur tests interpretations against the most severe criteria of all—does it work or not—; that is, does it advance a social justice initiative?" (p. 36).

Ellis (2009) describes three kinds of critiques:

1. Autoethnography isn't sufficiently realist and it tries to be too aesthetic/literary...
2. Autoethnography is too realist...
3. Autoethnography isn't sufficiently aesthetic... (p. 231)

She is not terribly worried by (or about) these criticisms, seeing them as evidence that autoethnography has become sufficiently important to warrant criticism. To this, I would add that the critiques that she notices are so completely contradictory that they don't stand as any kind of unified argument in opposition to the genre.

Autoethnography as an Agent of Social Justice and Change

Clearly, the autoethnographic process of understanding self in relationship with others can be used to explore and understand broad social issues (Corroto, Weems, Rambo, Poulos, Foster, & Lockford, 2007; Hughes, 2008; Morimoto, 2008; Patton, 2004) and create opportunities for social change and emancipation (Denzin, 2010a; Glowacki-Dudka, Treff, & Usman, 2005; Wall, 2006). In fact, this may be its central purpose: it "...redresses social injustices and imagines a radical democracy that is not yet" (Denzin, 2010a, p. 15). Autoethnography exposes the political nature of experience and research:

> performative writing starts with the recognition that individual bodies provide a potent database for understanding the political and that hegemonic systems write on individual bodies. (Pelias, 2005, p. 420)

Autoethnography is a way to talk back to dominating stories about the world and people; it "...is a useful vehicle for injecting personal knowledge into a field of expert voices... [and] resisting dominant discourses... " (Wall, 2008, p. 50). Importantly, autoethnography is a way of speaking outside and against the dominant, hegemonic culture: it "is a form of critique and resistance that can be found in... texts that identify zones of contact, conquest, and the contested meanings of self and culture that accompanies the exercise of representational authority" (Neumann, 1996, p. 191). Its use of personal narrative and story aligns it with critical race theory (Morimoto, 2008) and feminist theory (Olson, 2004; Wall 2006), tying together theory and narrative to create wider understanding of specific issues. It can be seen "...as a social project that helps us understand a larger relational, communal, and political world of which we are a part and moves us to critical engagement, social action, and social change" (Ellis, 2009, p. 229). It "...can tell, teach, and put people in motion. It is about autoethnography as a radical democratic politics..." (Jones, 2008, p. 206). Specifically, autoethnography is one medium

> ...through which fictionalized and nonfictionalized social life—the human condition—can be portrayed symbolically and aesthetically for spectator engagement, reflection, raising critical consciousness, and for purposes of social action. (Denzin, 2010a, p. 50)

It should, perhaps, come as no surprise, that autoethnography has ideological, value, and political meanings—all knowledge-making endeavors do, after all (Denzin, 2010a; Smith, 1999). Denzin (2003) aligns autoethnographic research with performance approaches, and notes that this kind of meaning-making creates a space for "...a series of tools for countering reactionary political discourse... a way of being moral and political in the world" (p. 258). Within this discourse, he seeks to create a

"...civic, publicly responsible [auto] ethnography that addresses the central issues of self, race, gender, class, society, and democracy" (p. 259)—to which I, of course, would add the issue of [dis]ability. Through his conception of performance autoethnography, both education and democracy become "pedagogies of freedom" (p. 262). Such a performance text, argues Denzin (2010a), is

> political,
> emotional,
> analytic,
> interpretive,
> pedagogical,
> local, partial,
> incomplete,
> painful to
> read,
> exhilarating. (p. 95)

Ellis (2009) places autoethnography squarely in the realm of social justice, pointing out that "...good ethnographies always have included the other, and they always have involved critical engagement, social problems, and social action" (p. 233). In this way, say some, "individually written autobiographies are illusionary: we write them in relation to powerful discourses producing our subjectivity" (Phillips, Harris, Larson, & Higgins, 2009, p. 1456).

Autoethnography as Risk

Doing autoethnography—living it, writing it, performing it—is risky: emotionally, professionally, psychologically, personally (Ellis, 2010). Because, as Denzin (2010b) writes, "cops are everywhere" (p. 265): the policing practices of academia and research that

> ...tell us not to write out of the personal, not to be political, not to be experimental, or performative, or to write autoethnography. They tell us to keep the personal at home, to keep it quiet, in the closet, act as if it never happened (Denzin, 2010b, p. 265).

The forces of positivism are still active, and continue to hold enormous power, in social science research. Kincheloe and Tobin (2009) point out that

"Challengers to such power," like, for example, autoethnographers, "are irrational and disruptive 'episto-paths'" (p. 526).

As a result, autoethnography is a kind of "rogue narrative," because it

> opposes the ruling bodies of the reigning empire—applied and social scientific methods of inquiry... it becomes a form of inquiry that does not merely write up the research but is itself the story of discovery. Autoethnography contends with proprieties in social roles and acts of research, interrogating and thus disrupting the insistence of authoritative and abstract analyses, and allowing new interpretive stories to be insinuated into any discourse. (Rolling, 2008, p. 841)

It transgresses, pushes the boundaries of the nature of research, of what counts (numerative pun definitely intended). It steps outside scientism's hegemonic understanding of analysis, knowledge-making—about who can make it, and why, and how. Because of that, it holds dangers for those who write it into being—unaccepted by tenure and promotion committees, ignored by journal editors, criticized by conference reviewers, those who make it and do it will find it hard to build a career from it.

Which is, in part, why this book exists.

It is in th-is/ese context(s) that the authors, in the chapters that follow, tell their stories, as teachers, as family members, and as people with disabilities.

References

Atkins, C. (2008). The choice of two mothers: Disability, gender, sexuality, and prenatal testing. *Cultural Studies–Critical Methodologies, 8*, 106–129. doi: 10.1177/1532708607310791

Averett, P., & Soper, D. (2011). Sometimes I am afraid: An autoethnography of resistance and compliance. *The Qualitative Report, 16*, 358–376.

Berry, K. (2006). Implicated audience member seeks understanding: Reexamining the "gift" of autoethnography. *International Journal of Qualitative Methods, 5*(3), 94–108.

Bochner, A., Denzin, N., Goodall, H., Pelias, R., & Richardson, L. (2007). Let's get personal I: First generation autoethnographers reflect on writing personal narratives. Third International Congress of Qualitative Inquiry, University of Illinois at Urbana-Champaign, Urbana, IL.

Brooks, C. (2011). Social performance and secret ritual: Battling against obsessive-compulsive disorder. *Qualitative Health Research, 21*, 249–261. doi: 10.1177/1049732310381387

Broumas, O. (1977). *Beginning with O.* New Haven, CT: Yale University Press.

Burdell, P., & Swadener, B. (1999). Critical personal narrative and autoethnography in education: Reflections on a genre. *Educational Researcher, 28*(6), 21–26.

Chang, H. (2008). *Autoethnography as method*. Walnut Creek, CA: Left Coast Press.

Chiu, J. (2004). "I salute the spirit of my communities:" Autoethnographic innovations in Hmong American literature. *College Literature, 31*(3), 43–69.

Chouinard, V. (1995/1996). Like Alice through the looking glass: Accommodation in academia. *Resources for Feminist Research, 24*(3/4), 3–10.

—— (2010). "Like Alice through the looking glass" II: The struggle for accommodation continues. *Resources for Feminist Research, 33*(3/4), 161–177.

Clandinin, D., & Connelly, F. (2000). *Narrative inquiry: Experience and story in qualitative research*. San Francisco: Jossey-Bass.

Clare, E. (2003). Gawking, gaping, staring. *GLQ: A Journal of Lesbian and Gay Studies, 9,* 257–261.

Cook, P. (2012). "To actually *be* sociological": Autoethnography as an assessment and learning tool. *Journal of Sociology, 48*, 1–14. doi: 10.1177/1440783312451780

Corroto, C., Weems, M., Rambo, C., Poulos, C., Foster, E., & Lockford, L. (2007). Let's get personal II: Second generation autoethnographers reflect on writing personal narratives. Third International Congress of Qualitative Inquiry, University of Illinois at Urbana-Champaign, Urbana, IL.

Couser, G. (2000). The empire of the "normal": A forum on disability and self-representation—Introduction. *American Quarterly, 52*, 305-310.

deMarrais, K. (Ed.). (1998). *Inside stories: Qualitative research reflections*. Mahweh, NJ: Lawrence Erlbaum Associates.

Denzin, N. (2003). Performing [auto] ethnography politically. *The Review of Education, Pedagogy, and Cultural Studies, 25*, 257–278.

—— (2008). *Searching for Yellowstone: Race, gender, family, and memory in the postmodern West*. Walnut Creek, CA: Left Coast Press.

—— (2010a). *The qualitative manifesto: A call to arms*. Walnut Creek, CA: Left Coast Press.

—— (2010b). Writing as transformation. In N. Denzin & M. Giardina (Eds.) *Qualitative inquiry and human rights* (pp. 243–246.) Walnut Creek, CA: Left Coast Press.

—— (2011). *Custer on canvas: Representing Indians, memory, and violence in the New West*. Walnut Creek, CA: Left Coast Press, Inc.

Diamond, C. (1992). Accounting for our accounts: Autoethnographic approaches to teacher voice and vision. *Curriculum Inquiry, 22*, 67–81.

Diggs, R., & Clark, K. (2002). It's a struggle but worth it: Identifying and managing identities in an interracial friendship. *Communication Quarterly, 50*, 368–390.

Dillow, C. (2009). Growing up: A journey toward theoretical understanding *Qualitative Inquiry, 15*, 1338-1351. doi: 10.1177/1077800409339581

Dressman, M. (2006). Teacher, teach thyself: Teacher research as ethnographic practice. *Ethnography, 7*, 329–356. doi: 10.1177/1466138106069524

Ellis, C. (1995a). *Final negotiations: A story of love, loss, and chronic illness*. Philadelphia: Temple University Press.

—— (1995b). The other side of the fence: Seeing black and white in a small, southern town. *Qualitative Inquiry, 1*, 147–167.

—— (1996). Maternal connections. In C. Ellis & A. Bochner (Eds.), *Composing ethnography: Alternative forms of qualitative writing* (pp. 240–243). Walnut Creek, CA: AltaMira Press.

—— (2004). *The ethnographic I: A methodological novel about autoethnography.* Walnut Creek, CA: Left Coast Press.

—— (2008). Do we need to know? *Qualitative Inquiry, 14*, 1314–1320. doi: 10.1177/1077800408322681

—— (2009). *Revision: Autoethnographic reflections on life and work.* Walnut Creek, CA: Left Coast Press.

—— (2010). Telling moments in an autoethnographer's life. In N. Denzin & M. Giardina (Eds.) *Qualitative inquiry and human rights* (pp. 243–246.) Walnut Creek, CA: Left Coast Press.

Erickson, F. (2010). Affirming human dignity in qualitative inquiry. In N. Denzin & M. Giardina (Eds.) *Qualitative inquiry and human rights* (pp. 112–122). Walnut Creek, CA: Left Coast Press.

Foster, K., McAllister, M., & O'Brien, L. (2005). Coming to autoethnography: A mental health nurse's experience. *International Journal on Qualitative Methods, 4*(4), 1–15.

Gallardo, H., Furman, R., & Kulkarni, S. (2009). Explorations of depression poetry and narrative in autoethnographic qualitative research. *Qualitative Social Work, 8*, 287–304. doi:10.1177/1473325009337837

Glowacki-Dudka, M., Treff, M., & Usman, I. (2005). Research for social change: Using autoethnography to foster transformative learning. *Adult Learning, 16*(3/4), 30–31.

Goldschmidt, W. (1977). Anthropology and the coming crisis: An autoethnographic appraisal. *American Anthropologist, 79*, 293–308.

Goode, L. (2007). Telling tales out of school: Connecting the prose and the passion in the learning and teaching of English. *Qualitative Inquiry, 13*, 808–820. doi:10.1177/1077800407304465

Goodall, H. (2000). *Writing the new ethnography.* Walnut Creek, CA: AltaMira Press.

—— (2002). Narrative heat. In A. Bochner & C. Ellis (Eds.) *Ethnographically speaking: Autoethnography, literature, and aesthetics* (pp. 377–387). Walnut Creek, CA: AltaMira Press.

—— (2006). *A need to know: The clandestine history of a CIA family.* Walnut Creek, CA: Left Coast Press.

—— (2010). *Counter-narrative: How progressive academics can challenge extremists and promote social justice.* Walnut Creek, CA: Left Coast Press.

Grant, C. (Ed.). (1999). *Multicultural research: A reflective engagement with race, class, gender and sexual orientation.* Philadelphia, PA: Falmer.

Hughes, S. (2008). Toward "good enough methods" for autoethnography in a graduate education course: Trying to resist the matrix with another promising red pill. *Educational Studies, 43*, 125–143.

Isaac, C. (2007). By their own hand: Irreconcilable silence. *Qualitative Inquiry, 13*, 1209–1220. doi: 10.1177/1077800407308820

Jackson, A. & Mazzei, L. (2008). Experience and "I" in autoethnography: A deconstruction. *International Review of Qualitative Research, 1*, 299–318.

Jones, S. (2008). Autoethnography: Making the personal political. In N. Denzin & Y. Lincoln

(Eds.) *Collecting and interpreting qualitative materials* (3rd ed.) (pp. 205–245). Thousand Oaks, CA: Sage.

Kelley, H., & Betsalel, K. (2004). Mind's fire: Language, power, and representations of stroke. *Anthropology and Humanism, 29*, 104–116.

Kibel, B. (1999). Outcome engineering. Presentation to the Vermont Division of Developmental Services, Waterbury, VT.

Kidd, J., & Finlayson, M. (2009). When needs must: Interpreting autoethnographical stories. *Qualitative Inquiry, 15*, 980–995. doi: 10.1177/1077800409334200

Kiesinger, C. (1998). From interview to story: Writing Abbie's life. *Qualitative Inquiry, 4*, 71–95.

Kincheloe, J. & Tobin, K. (2009. The much exaggerated death of positivism. *Cultural Studies of Science Education, 4*, 513–528. doi: 10.1007/s11422-009-9178-5

Lau, K. (2002). This text which is not one: Dialectics of self and culture in experimental autoethnography. *Journal of Folklore Research, 39*, 243–259.

Lewis, J. (2009). Redefining qualitative methods: Believability in the fifth moment. *International Journal on Qualitative Methods, 8*(2), 1-14.

Lindemann, K. (2010). Cleaning up my (father's) mess: Narrative containments of "leaky" masculinities. *Qualitative Inquiry, 16*, 29–38. doi: 10.1177/1077800409350060

Louis, M. (1991). Reflections on an interpretive way of life. In P. Frost, L. Moore, M. Louis, C. Lundberg, & J. Martin (Eds.), *Reframing organizational culture* (pp. 361–365). London: Sage.

Malthouse, M. (2011). An autoethnography on shifting relationships between a daughter, her mother and Alzheimer's dementia (in any order). *Dementia, 10*, 249–256. doi: 10.1177/1471301211407626

Matthews, W. (1984). *A happy childhood*. Boston, MA: Little, Brown and Company.

Morimoto, L. (2008). Teaching as transgression: The autoethnography of a fat physical education instructor. *Proteus, 25*, 29–36.

Morse, J. (2009). The PI as participant. *Qualitative Health Research, 19*, 1655.

Mukaia, T. (1989). A call for our language: Anorexia from within. *Women's Studies International Forum, 12*, 613–638.

Murav, H. (2003). Fictions of Jewish self-writing in the post-Soviet era. *Symposium, 57*, 175–185.

Neumann, M. (1996). Collecting ourselves at the end of the century. In C. Ellis & A. Bochner (Eds.), *Composing ethnography: Alternative forms of qualitative writing* (pp. 172–198). Walnut Creek, CA: AltaMira Press.

O'Byrne, P. (2007). The advantages and disadvantages of mixing methods: An analysis of combining traditional and autoethnographic approaches. *Qualitative Health Research, 17*, 1381–1391. doi: 10.1177/1049732307308304

Olson, L. (2004). The role of voice in the (re)construction of a battered woman's identity: An autoethnography of one woman's experiences of abuse. *Women's Studies in Communication, 27*, 1–33.

Owen, J., McRae, C., Adams, T., & Vitale, A. (2009). truth troubles. *Qualitative Inquiry, 15*, 178–200. doi: 10.1177/1077800408318316

Patton, T. (2004). In the guise of civility: The complicitous maintenance of inferential forms of sexism and racism in higher education. *Women's Studies in Communication, 27*, 60–87.

Pelias, R. (2005). Performative writing as scholarship: An apology, an argument, an anecdote. *Cultural Studies–Critical Methodologies, 5*, 415–424. doi: 10.1177/1532708605279694

Pfau, H. (2007). To know me now. *Qualitative Social Work, 6*, 397–410. doi: 10.1177/1473325007083353

Philaretou, A. & Allen, K. (2006). Researching sensitive topics through autoethnographic means. *The Journal of Men's Studies, 14*, 65–78.

Phillips, D., Harris, G., Larson, M., & higgins, k. (2009). Trying on — Being in — Becoming four women's journey(s) in feminist poststructural theory. *Qualitative Inquiry, 15*, 1455–1479. doi: 10.1177/1077800409347097

Rambo, C. (2005). Sketching Carolyn Ellis, purple diva of autoethnography. *Studies in Symbolic Interaction, 28*(1) 3–14.

——— (2007). Sketching as autoethnographic practice. *Symbolic Interaction, 30*, 531–542. doi: 10.1525/si.2007.30.4.531.

Reed-Danahay, D. (1997). Introduction. In D. Reed-Danahay (Ed.). *Auto/Ethnography: Rewriting the self and the social* (pp. 1–17). Oxford, UK: Berg.

Richards, R. (2008). Writing the othered self: Autoethnography and the problem of objectivication in writing about illness and disability. *Qualitative Health Research, 8*, 1717–1728. doi: 10.1177/1049732308325866

Rodriguez, D. (2009). The usual suspect: Negotiating white student resistance and teacher authority in a predominantly white classroom. *Cultural Studies <=> Critical Methodologies, 9*, 483–508. doi: 10.1177/1532708608321504

Rogers, C. (2009). (S)excerpts from a life told: Sex, gender and learning disability. *Sexualities, 12*, 270-288. doi: 10.1177/1363460709103891

Rogers, L. (1998). *Wish I were: Felt pathways of the self*. Madison, WI: Atwood Publishing.

Rolling, J. (2008). Contesting content, or how the emperor sheds his old clothes: Guest editor's introduction. *Qualitative Inquiry, 14*, 839-850. doi: 10.1177/1077800408318297

Ronai, C. (1997). On loving and hating my mentally retarded mother. *Mental Retardation, 35*, 417-432.

Schneider, B. (2005). Mothers talk about their children with schizophrenia: A performance autoethnography. *Journal of Psychiatric & Mental Health Nursing, 12*, 333-340.

Shuman, A. (2011). On the verge: Phenomenology and empathic unsettlement. *Journal of American Folklore, 124*, 147-174.

Smith, B. (1999). The abyss: Exploring depression through a narrative of the self. *Qualitative Inquiry 5*, 264–79.

Smith, P. (1999). Drawing new maps: A radical cartography of developmental disabilities. *Review of Educational Research, 69* (2), 117–144.

——— (2012). Why disability studies must not use statistical analysis. Eighth International Congress of Qualitative Inquiry, Urbana, IL.

Smith, P. & Millstead, K. (2012). Rejecting analytic statistics in (dis)ability studies in education. 12th Annual Second City International Conference on Disability Studies in Education, New York, New York.

Sparkes, A. (2002). Autoethnography: Self-indulgence or something more? In A. Bochner &

C. Ellis (Eds.) *Ethnographically speaking: Autoethnography, literature, and aesthetics* (pp. 209–232). Walnut Creek, CA: AltaMira Press.

Spry, T. (2001). Performing autoethnography: An embodied methodological praxis. In *Qualitative Inquiry, 7*, 706–732. doi: 10.1177/107780040100700605

——— (2009). Bodies of/as evidence in autoethnography. *International Review of Qualitative Research, 1*, 603–610.

Stein, G. (1935). *Lectures in America*. New York: Bantam Books.

Stoller, P. (2002). The griot's many burdens—fiction's many truths. In A. Bochner & C. Ellis (Eds.) *Ethnographically speaking: Autoethnography, literature, and aesthetics* (pp. 297–307). Walnut Creek, CA: AltaMira Press.

Tillmann-Healy, L. (1996). A secret life in a culture of thinness: Reflections on body, food, and bulimia. In C. Ellis & A. Bochner (Eds.), *Composing ethnography: Alternative forms of qualitative writing* (pp. 76–108). Walnut Creek, CA: AltaMira Press.

Torres, C. (1998). *Education, power, and personal biography: Dialogues with critical educators*. New York: Routledge.

Valente, J. (2011). *d/Deaf and d/Dumb: A portrait of a deaf kid as a young superhero*. New York: Peter Lang.

Vasconcelos, E. (2011). "I can see you": An autoethnography of my teacher-student self. *The Qualitative Report, 16*, 415–440.

Voloder, L. (2008). Autoethnographic challenges: Confronting self, field and home. *The Australian Journal of Anthropology, 19*, 27–40.

Wall, S. (2006). An autoethnography on learning about autoethnography. *International Journal on Qualitative Methods, 5*(2), 142–160.

——— (2008). Easier said than done: Writing an autoethnography. *International Journal on Qualitative Methods, 7*(1), 38–53.

Wamsted, J. (2011). Race, school, and Seinfeld: Autoethnographic sketching in black and white. *Qualitative Inquiry, 17*, 972–981. doi: 10.1177/1077800411425153

Ward, S. (2008). Does anyone see me? Playing host to the uninvited guest of post-polio syndrome. *Qualitative Inquiry, 14*, 360–383. doi: 10.1177/1077800407309327

Warren, J. (2011). Reflexive teaching: Toward critical autoethnographic practices of/in/on pedagogy. *Cultural Studies–Critical Methodologies, 11*, 139–144. doi: 10.1177/1532708611401332

Weems, M. (2006). Numbers. *Qualitative Inquiry, 12*, 389–397. doi: 10.1177/1077800405280660

Weinreb, Al (2008). Hottentot b-b-blues. *Ethnography, 9*, 123–131. doi: 10.1177/1466138108088950

Wilson, K. (2011). Opening Pandora's box: An autoethnographic study of teaching. *Qualitative Inquiry, 17*, 452–458. doi: 10.1177/1077800411405432

Woods, A. & Henderson, R. (2002). Early intervention: Narratives of learning, discipline and enculturation. *Journal of Early Childhood Literacy, 2*, 243–268.

Wyatt, J. (2008). No longer loss: Autoethnographic stammering. *Qualitative Inquiry, 14*, 955–967.

Section 2

Living With Disability—Stories by Labeled People

Chapter 2

Who Knew School Could Be So Cruel? Tales of a Learning Disabled Student at an Institution of Higher Learning

dené granger

My first memory of a dyslexic moment, prior to a diagnosis, is from first grade, when our first graded assignment was returned to us. I was quite pleased with my 76, as I couldn't even count that high. Patiently completing the assignment, I double- and triple-checked my work. My care was evident in the fact that I was one of the last ones to complete the assignment. It was one of those worksheets where we had to fill in the blanks using a word-bank. Then I saw my peers' grades. I didn't realize that we had to copy the words letter for letter, exactly as they appeared in the word-bank. If I had known that, things would have been different.

*

Probably near that same year, I asked my mother how to spell "maw-maw." I was writing a letter to my grandmother, and my mother told me she wasn't sure how to spell it: Try m-a-w-m-a-w; does that look right? She wasn't sure. It didn't look right to me at all, but I didn't understand how to translate a French sounding alphabet to my English frame of reference for spelling.

I shouldn't have been surprised. In Southwest Louisiana, a lot of people still speak French, and my great-grandparents did not speak English. When my mom was a schoolgirl, speaking French at school was against the rules.

Many teachers would use this as an excuse to bully students. Some would hit the student's hand with a ruler, sometimes leaving welts. I've also read stories of students forced to recite poems in English, and publicly ridiculed for the perceived incompetence that comes with being bilingual. Gloria Anzaldúa experienced this kind of harassment on the border, in south Texas, for speaking Spanish at recess and for trying to teach her teacher how to pronounce her name. In college, she was required to take a remedial speech course to cure her of her accent, and her Spanish-speaking mother welcomed this, as she was "mortified" that Anzaldúa "spoke English like a Mexican" (1987, p. 53–54).

I think my mom had an easier time than Anzaldúa did. She had one teacher who called on her to answer a question, but my mom didn't know what the English word was, so she asked the teacher if she could answer in French. Teachers that spoke French outside of school would usually refuse to speak French with any student, even denying the ability to speak or understand French, but this teacher allowed my mom to answer in French.

Separate from this story about bilingual teachers in Louisiana, but not too far, in Syracuse, New York, where I moved for graduate school, the Border Patrol's "practices evoke the same fears as a new immigration law in Arizona — that anyone, anytime, can be interrogated without cause" (Bernstein, 2010). One officer interrogated a Chicana friend of mine in Syracuse, and later returned to ask her to translate for him, to interrogate another passenger. She didn't understand why he wouldn't admit to knowing Spanish, because he clearly understood her. She told him, "Ask your mother"; "wild tongues can't be tamed, they can only be cut out" (Anzaldúa 1987, p. 54)

And another Syracuse friend, a resident of the Onondagan Nation (a Native American Nation), had a group of friends from the nation, in full Native humor, turn a crass joke into an informal greeting. They decided to print sweatshirts with this greeting and wore them to their high school Their sweatshirts were confiscated by his high school principal because she feared that it might be a new gang symbol.

We shouldn't be surprised. President Theodore Roosevelt encouraged an English-only citizenry as part of the reactionary U.S. nationalism that followed WWI. In this political climate, schools in Louisiana forbade the use of books that contained any language other than English, and forbade teachers from using any other language in their classrooms. During this same time, Roosevelt moved to standardize the English language. One of his first moves in doing so was through an executive order, distributed in newspapers, listing several word spellings that were going to be standardized across all White House communications. It was a way to unify the people. "C-o-l-o-u-r" now signified "foreigner."

*

In sixth grade, our social studies teacher gave us the opportunity to get some major extra credit points if we colored the Aztec calendar. The only requirement was that the calendar had to be comprised of at least four colors. The Aztec calendar is considered the most accurate calendar ever created. It is round, at its center is the sun, and in the concentric circles around the sun are intricate images that represent different deities. Some of my peers colored the sun one color, a couple of rings other colors, received full credit. I stayed up late that night, coloring, studying, respecting the details. I used lots of color that was consistent across each small image of the deities, but as I was coloring along, I marked the white space outside the calendar to make sure I was using the right colors. With all this "mess," as my teacher called it, my calendar didn't deserve full credit. Whenever I walk away from a sour discussion with a teacher, I think of this moment.

*

When I was in junior high, I have this memory of a kid at school, like many others, who had a broken locker. It's not as if my school lacked funds, but anyone with any experience of school lockers knows that each locker requires its own caress. Some lockers wouldn't open if you put in the *right* combination. Sometimes you had to be really precise with the number combination you used. Some lockers required that you bang on them with a folded fist in the top left corner; some would get stuck in the bottom left corner, requiring that you pull on the lock with a little more force; others would open at any moment you lift the lock. Every year, we had to learn how our new lockers opened, what degree of pressure needed to be placed where, or how we might need to turn the dial. One particular day, a kid tried beating in his locker, pulled on the lock in such a forceful way that his fingers slipped past the lock that refused to open, then yelled, "Stupid locker!" as he threw his fist at the locker for one last try.

This was a moment when I began politicizing my learning disabled identity. Of course it was common to hear a kid scream "stupid locker" as they punched it. Anything broken had to be stupid, and violence against the stupid has historically been justified. Intellectually disabled people die in restraints every year, in school buses, in time-out rooms, in their beds in institutions, as if the authorities believe that these folks must have superhuman strength (Coalition Against Institutionalized Child Abuse, 2010). As if you need a certain IQ to be able to feel physical violence, or recognize the difference between hateful and loving words. Our pain is not read as pain, and this violence is never questioned.

*

I was in the 11th grade when I squirmed my way into an honors English course for the first time, and I happened to be in class with my best friend. Hanging out in the hallway, getting distracted from our assignments, we got into a conversation about dyslexia. It was the usual, "What does that poster look like, are the letters reversed?" I turned back to, "I just think different," which is an impossible position to defend, so I slid to, "I just need extra time." I didn't want to explain how much labor goes into reading. Besides, I can be quite comfortable with how I read, but what's a brain doing, thinking about its own brain anyway? That almost doesn't make sense. But in all of her persistence, her own frustrations and fears built. My best friend told me "You're using your dyslexia as a crutch."

She was afraid that I might do better than her, which would mean that she was stupid. I was the special ed. kid, she knew it, most peers knew it, but none of them knew what that meant. All they knew was, if I could beat them at their own game, they were in trouble. She needed my failure to prove her success. I can't blame her. That's what we get in this competitive market and this meritocracy.

*

When it was time to go to college, I was left trying to decide between larger state schools and a beautiful small liberal arts college. While my parents supported my decision to go to college, I was mostly left to my own devices when deciding. My options were far more expansive than theirs were. Even though I read all the advice I could, I had no idea how I was suppose to make a fully informed decision. I ended up picking that small liberal arts college— not even knowing what a liberal arts college was. I knew the small class sizes would save me. After all, I always depended on teachers who took the time to get to know me.

I searched for scholarships, not knowing that was an ambitious way of paying for school. I found plenty of scholarships for various disabilities, but none of which were specific to learning disability. My grades were good, but not good enough. There were some scholarships geared for students in my GPA range, but all of them required intense community involvement—which I did not have time for, considering the immense amount of time my studies required. As far as I can tell, there are no funding structures that refuse to support the myth of meritocracy.

As it turned out, my math skills were outstanding, giving my SAT scores the competitive edge that I needed to get a scholarship from my liberal arts college. In talking to my parents about loans to pay for school, they kept asking me, "Are you sure?" I didn't know how to be sure. I had no conception of the amount of money I needed to pay for school. I just knew that I wanted to build the armor I needed to make positive changes in this world, so I started out with big loans and work-study hours.

By the end of my first year, I could not manage to hang onto the 3.0 GPA required to keep the scholarship. No amount of study time would curb the schooling structures that prevented my success. During my second semester that first year, I used a public speaking course assignment to practice arguing for an exception to their rules. My professor was stunned by my ability to grab the attention of my audience. Even so, I could not bear to bring myself to have a meeting with the scholarship committee. I knew I would be brought to tears before I could even open my mouth, so I wrote a letter and asked some professors to put in a good word for me. The scholarship committee, as impressed as they were with my efforts and my professors' recommendations, refused my appeals—my grades just were not good enough.

*

When I went to college and began having conversations with new people about my name, I had to explain the accent mark. One friend made me a card and wrote my name with the accent placed as I suppose I taught her how to place it. I went home for a visit that first semester, and pulled out my birth certificate to double check my accent. As it turns out, my certificate has "DENE' ANGELE GRANGER." In those days, the typewriters didn't have accents. I wonder how many other people have lost their accents on their birth certificates. Then, I pulled out my Christmas stocking with the accent placed in the opposite direction than what was written in my card. I told my friend how to spell my name the wrong way. My college diploma also has my accent placed the wrong way.

I stopped using my accent in the fifth grade, after one of the only teachers who ever confidently pronounced my name correctly on the first day of class, recognized that there was supposed to be an accent mark, and asked me which way it was supposed to go. After I told her, performing an unwavering answer, she asked if I wrote my name with my accent. With a lot less assurance, I told her, "yes." Then she went on to tell me, "as long as you're consistent." I am not sure if my teacher corrected the accent on some paper or if I came to realize that I could not remember which direction I told her; either way, I stopped using my accent and the teacher never asked about it.

It wasn't until I came to graduate school that I learned how to spell my name *right*, when I had a gentle professor who asked, "Dené, does your accent go this direction?" I knew she knew the answer to her own question. But still, it's easy to forget all over again. When I order take-out, people ask for my name and usually ask how to spell it. If I give them that spelling, they won't pronounce it right. I usually tell them, "Spell it how you want to." Most of them don't go for that suggestion, but the ones who do know how to pronounce it.

Under the usual spelling conventions, I technically have several names: dene, Dene, Dené, dené, Denè, & denè. And if I had to choose one, I hate to say it, but I would choose "Dené." I hate to say it because it makes me think that if it really came down to it, I'd choose the normates way of naming over my own, and my college diploma would no longer be mine. But if I really had a choice, I would rather collect different ways of writing my name.

*

My first introduction to the drug Adderall was in college. As part of the paperwork to go to college with accommodations, I had to see a new kind of professional, one who diagnosed me with ADD. As part of the test, I had to push a key on a keyboard on the right for capital letters and a button on the left for lower case—something like that. I have anxiety about my ability to recall right and left, so the test was hard. I walked out thinking, "This test was not made for a dyslexic."

But by the time I was a sophomore in college, I really struggled with school, so I tried my friend's ADD medication and quickly got a prescription. I did this, despite the fact that I saw friends deal with Adderall addictions. I was careful about how I used it. I planned my whole day around it. I scheduled five-hour blocks of time, in between two heavy meals, and a cigarette break every hour. I made sure I never took this kind of speed two days in a row, because if I did, it would have a drastic impact on my ability to eat. I was vulnerable to migraines, which had always structured my eating habits. I had a pill and a plan, and I couldn't have made it through without that.

*

I didn't know how to separate my narrative of my experience with schools from the research I was reporting for a paper in a sociology of education class. My teacher warned me that I would get a letter grade off if I did not follow the rules dictated in the syllabus: our papers had to be divided in two halves, research and personal narrative. After discussing my dilemma with her, she told me, as so many have before and since: I have to be fair; I didn't give other students an opportunity to alter the assignment, so I can't let you.

I imagine that my teacher was worried about the assignment, and how other students might also want to alter the assignment. I can't help but think that it's just another excuse. It's not like she would alter the syllabus next semester, to reflect any more flexibility than she had then. Maybe I offered a convincing argument for altering the assignment, but she was afraid that I would miss the point, so I had to be kept on a short leash.

I could not divide the personal narrative from the research into two halves of the paper. I couldn't have asked the research questions I was asking if I hadn't had a personal narrative to contextualize its existence. So I deployed a back-and-forth form that clearly distinguished the two ways of speaking. She took a letter grade off anyway. Perhaps she didn't understand how her form could not work for me and my stories and my research.

Disappointed in the ways in which my grade failed to represent the value of my work, the inventiveness of the material, the contributions this labor brought into class discussions, feeling absolutely cheated, I shared my work with a trusted professor. Since he had not seen a description of the assignment, his diplomacy was cautious. He postulated: perhaps with your use of colloquialisms, she did not think you articulated your point well enough? But my maw-maw understood. She kept a copy of this paper in her cigar box of treasured belongings.

*

I lived with one of my best friends from college for about a year. I have vivid memories of her doing work on one paper. So many drafts. Her room was consumed with it, and it followed her everywhere she went. She couldn't help but chase down rabbit holes that would take her into forbidden territory. All the while, I would find out some years later, she sat next to me, watching me read the same sentence over and over. We are both dyslexic but we never talked about it. The silence was not heavy. I felt no elephant in the room, and didn't even realize how much we didn't talk about *it* until I started my graduate work, and started talking to her about what I was doing.

*

Shortly after I graduated from college, I discovered that I had Irlen Syndrome or Scoptic Sensitivity Syndrome - which explained the regular migraines with which I had been living (Irlen.com, 1998). When I was in high school, I went through various rounds of chronic migraine medications. Doctors told me that I was going to have to take a pill every day for the rest of my life. But as it turns out, my brain and my eyes don't talk to one another very well about certain light frequencies. Making it hard to follow lines of text across a page, without skipping lines, or without repeating lines. When I put prescription tinted glasses on, I knew what it was like to read without my eyes straining to find the warmth of those dark letters amongst a glowing, glaring, white page. When I put the glasses on, I learned that I didn't know what it was like to be without a headache.

For the first time since middle school, I actually finished the books I started reading. I actually read in my spare time. For pleasure. I could read for hours without my eyes burning and straining, without the letters going blurry. So I gave up my Adderall when I found my glasses.

*

In getting ready for graduate school, once again I made a serious search for scholarships. In spending a day at the University of Texas Regional Foundation Library, which houses an extensive catalogue of grants and scholarships, I found a couple of new scholarships for learning disabled students going to college, but nothing for graduate students. If I wanted to teach in special education classrooms, I could get funds, but nothing for someone who wanted to disrupt normative ways of thinking about learning disability. I got into Syracuse University, but without any funding. I was told that my grades and GRE verbal scores were not competitive enough. Again, loans saved me.

During my second semester of graduate school, not having any faith in my ability to get scholarships, and feeling as though I could not risk compromising one day of contributing to class discussions, I did not apply for scholarships. Absolutely scared of how impossible it would be to keep up with my schoolwork and have time for a job, I went on a serious job search. Not having any sense of the hiring cycle, I got a late start. Again, loans saved me.

By second semester my second year, I finally got my first job offer. Since I was a special ed. kid studying the politics of learning disabilities, someone thought a TA position in an undergraduate class for special education teachers would be a good place for me. I could not imagine teaching them about all my deficiencies and abnormalities. I knew I needed to protect myself and my work from that kind of insult, and I refused. Not fully understanding what kind of position that left me in, I ended up having to confide in a professor: even if I did land my dream job, if I were to take out another round of loans, I probably would not be able to afford the loan payments. I decided that, if I could not get funding, I would take a year off. Miraculously, funding came out of the woodwork, with enough to hold me over for another two years. No one told me that I could maintain full time status with an assistantship and keep my loans in deferment if I took one less class. My schoolwork and mental health suffered tremendously, but at least I had financial security for the first time.

*

I used to cry because I didn't think that *they* would let me in to grad school. With every assignment I turned in, during the first couple of years of undergraduate work, I feared losing a scholarship. In the second half of undergraduate work, all of my papers were turned in with the fear of not getting into graduate school. I worked so hard at every detail, even though this labor was usually overlooked. Everything mattered because the only way

I was going to get in was by the skin of my teeth.

I made it in, close to toothless. My first semester of graduate school, when I had to start my first round of disclosure conversations in a new place, I cried all the way to school, thinking about all the times I succeeded when I was told I would fail, all the times I proved them wrong, got into places I'd always been told I'd never go. When I got to school, I had to have conversations with strangers who would later decide if I got to stay here, at my prized institution. I had to tell them how I'm "bad with words" which makes me "not able to learn," or about how I'm going to have to turn in another paper late, or about the ways school has terrorized me, to explain why I hadn't finished my stack of incompletes, as if the official "time and a half" extension matters when the semester is still three and a half months long, especially as a graduate student.

When I got to school, with my red face, they would sometimes ask, "Are you okay?" and I had to say, "Yes, but today, I have to confess, with me, you do not know what you're getting yourself into." One asked me "But why does that make you cry?" I could not say, "Because I know, beloved teacher, one day you will deny me." They say, "But I care about you, stranger." They have no idea that they had already decided that this stranger does not belong.

Sometimes, when school haunts me, I start to wonder to myself, "What the in the world do you think you're doing here?"—so far away from family and home and the sun, adding to my absurd debt for college years I already can't afford, feeling like I'm the only one trying to talk about the learning disabled experience, drilling my body into the ground. I could hardly hang out with friends without thinking about school: it was always there, eating my attention. Some of my work is intense. Sometimes an hour of writing brings out so much emotion that I spend the rest of the day recovering. Along with stress from the Office of Disability Services—being promised that I'd get audio versions of my readings on time but continually getting them late, or getting books with chapters or every other page missing—sending me into panic mode. I was in perpetual fear of the rejection of my voice and all its quirky ways, the fear of being perceived as unintelligible, the fear of people recognizing my incredibly tiny short-term memory. I still managed to put so much of myself in my work, it's scary.

I understand that it is important to learn how to be a vulnerable observer (Behar, 1997) and how potentially powerful this marginalized space is (hooks, 1990). And I do this work because I can't imagine doing anything else. But with all of this, it's not really conducive to putting school to rest—to being able to sleep at night without dreaming about class discussions or writing papers, and it's certainly not conducive to maintaining one's mental health.

*

I went through most of my first year of grad school without Adderall. I sustained myself. I had a few dramatic moments, in trying to get my readings in audio format. But by the end of the first year, I knew I needed something more. As life altering as my glasses were, it was not enough. So, I went back to my amphetamines, my Adderall, my speed. After a few months of cutting my prescription, and taking Adderall "as needed," I confided to a friend about having a hard time with school, and keeping on task. She asked me, "Well, have you been taking your pills?" I explained how I didn't want to take them as prescribed, because I was nervous about my friends and watching their addictions. I knew the dangers. I knew not to trust those doctors. I know that the bottle says take it every single day, but I know that amphetamines build up in your system, and if they build up, I'd have to start taking more. But then what happens when they lower your prescription, or when they don't know how to counsel you on the addiction that they created, or they refuse your prescription, and they refuse to tell you to your face? But I said, "What the hey, I can try that for a little while, see how it goes." Something has got to change. And, I didn't know what else to do.

For a while, I would take Adderall five days a week, as if any graduate student works just five days a week. But what started to happen was, those days when I didn't take it, it was really hard to get going in the morning. A day off of Adderall turns into a day out-of-the-world. Most mornings, I'd be in bed with an empty belly that needed to be wrapped up and held tight, knees tucked into my chest. When I finally emerged, I'd have to be careful not to sit up too quickly or else I'd give myself a head rush. Sometimes my knees would wobble when they felt the full weight of my body. When my stomach is that empty, it can be hard to eat, like thirsty roots in dry soil that refuses any water. The thought of some foods made me nauseous. My partner learned how to feed me when I couldn't any more.

By the time I finished with my second year of graduate school, I started writing a paper, "A tribute to my dyslexic body, as I travel in the form of a ghost" (2010). Then, the day after my birthday, a dear uncle passed away, far too early in his life. I flew to Louisiana for the funeral and when I got back into town, I took a long bath and I cut my hair. I had five years of dense dreadlocks. After the water weight left them, they were 1.25 pounds.

I didn't tell anyone I was going to do it, and I hadn't planned the event any more than the other, impulsive "it's time to cut this" moments of weakness. Everyone from school commented on how nice it looked, some with a little too much excitement; perhaps I was more comfortably white in my dark olive summer skin, or more comfortably girly in my old sneakers and cute curls and *clean* look. One professor was stunned speechless by how differently she perceived me. Another student commented on how my style seemed so much more *chic*. When I walked through the library to buildings across campus, I no longer commanded the attention I once had. I posted a photo with my new haircut a few days after, as a way of saying what I wasn't ready to say out-loud.

I remember being surprised by how small I was, but how familiar it was to comb my fingers through hair that was now short and thick, although thinner than I could have possibly remembered. After cutting my hair, on a second stop to the beer store, a friend asked me, "Now dene, people don't cut their hair for no reason, what's going on? Was it the funeral or is there something else?" He knew the face of crisis, better than I had at that moment. Even in this time, the cruelties of school could not leave my mind.

*

I stopped taking days off of Adderall. Growing less capable of sustaining my own life, I kept at my work, with all the persistence I could muster. And I never took more Adderall than what was instructed on the bottle. Before, I thought it was really impossible for my body weight to fluctuate, but at my worst, I lost a little more than ten pounds in a month—a tenth of my body weight. I learned from anorexics which protein drink was most acceptable for an empty belly. I worked incessantly: listening to books for hours, playing free-cell, biting my nails and cuticles until they bled, making scabs and scars while picking at ingrown hairs and blackheads.

Sometimes I checked my email obsessively, reading anything that seemed rationally interesting. No matter how much work I did, it was never enough, and no matter how much I wanted to get the work done, my body wasn't going to let me. I started having panic attacks in anticipation of going to school, or even meeting friendly people from school. My partner learned to calm me down with tea, to anticipate by packing lunch, to feed me encouraging words, and offer me cigarettes on the porch before getting into the car to drive me to school.

I learned that I couldn't keep doing this to myself. I know why a balanced life is important. But isn't that always a challenge? I got good at escaping the world with TV on the Internet, and playing Tetris. I was never big on watching TV, but, suddenly, I watched a lot of it. I started closing out everyone I love. Just that question, "How are you doing?"

*

During a run one morning, I began imagining myself, or some self of mine, as my own mother—not the mother that gave birth to me, but the part of me that is my own mother, who cleans up after me and feeds me and sends me to bed on time and who will always be the first to remind me that tomorrow is another day, and that I tried my best, and that is everything I could do. I also imagined myself, or maybe another one of my selves that is a child, who loves school and singing schoolyard songs, and who needs to be reminded about brushing my teeth, whose eyes are just so big from an incredible eagerness to explore.

I also imagined some other self that knows the normate scripts all too well. I remembered those times, after hours of reading, being frustrated, not going very far or fast - at this point my pace could be pretty close to eight pages of reading an hour. Painfully slow. I could have said, "Excellent work, you deserve to close your books and go to the lake." But instead I'd force myself to read on until I couldn't see through my tears any more. Sometimes I would let myself fall apart for a few minutes. That mantra, "Humility breeds strength," kept me plugging along until my self-doubt would slip away.

There have been countless days when I was bad at getting myself to school on time, leaving without lunch. I'd push myself into reading and writing until right before it was time to go to school—if I was actually an employer, this would be abuse. I know I have some privilege; I could walk into a room and there would be nothing about my visible embodiment that systemically gets constructed as unintelligible. Even as I was driven by fear to do my readings in a way most students would never experience, I managed to make smart-enough comments in class discussions—smart-enough to catch the attention of professors and students alike, but not smart-enough that I could recognize it. How is it that a student, who has so much potential, after 21 years of schooling, can still feel absolutely incompetent when it comes to school? Schools are cruel places to live, and they have never been safe.

Teachers worry about how to motivate students and instill values that will help them navigate these treacherous waters. Others can kick us when we're down, or fail to add nutrients to the soils powering the fruits of our labor. And others know how to smile at us, but still never understand how their words leave wounds that will not heal. All the while, it is so easy to forget how much we must make ourselves vulnerable by just showing up to class.

And still, after all this, a professor can find it appropriate to ask me: "Given your experience in schools, how do you find yourself fitting in here?" as we begin a conversation in which I must explain why it is that I have so many incompletes. She worries whether or not I feel as though my teachers have been unkind; she wants to know that she has done good by me, but still can't imagine how there was nothing either of us could have done to prevent this conversation. I have been made to believe that I should accept the normate's ways of doing school, or else I'm a failure, a pitiful student who, just three or four years ago, could not walk into a professors office and say, "I am dyslexic," without crying. And who, in the year of this writing, has to sit through 30 minutes of tears because I am made to feel as if I need to ask for mercy, because this system was designed to keep me out. While I get to hear about how I have been oppositional, as if it is possible to survive under this double bind (Frye, 1983), behind closed doors (Fine, 1994), in any other way. As if I am the stranger that does not belong. Of course. Nothing I haven't heard before. Just another day in the neighborhood.

*

In the year of this writing, I make my way to the Onondaga County Department of Social Services to apply for food stamps. The sign on the door instructs me to find the blue form. After walking around the whole office for five minutes, I wait patiently at a desk that holds a sign reading something like "bring all your questions to the information desk, not here," so that I can ask "where is the information desk," so I can ask "where are the food stamps forms." As my partner and I sit, filling out the forms, under glaring lights, the only reprieve I get from the static coming out of the intercom system is when they call the next person up to one of their desks. Feeling on edge from all the sensory overload I experience, I can't believe how difficult it was to navigate the office, and to get relevant information on what kinds of assistance we might qualify for. Afterwards, my partner comments, "I can't believe how stupid I felt through that whole process." I am thankful that I wasn't the only one.

References

Anzaldúa, Gloria. (1987). *Borderlands / La Frontera: The new mestiza.* San Francisco: Aunt Lute Books.

Behar, R. (1997). The vulnerable observer. In *The vulnerable observer: Anthropology that breaks your heart* (pp. 1–33). Boston, MA: Beacon Press.

Bernstein, N. (2010, August 30, 2010). Border sweeps in north reach miles into U.S. *New York Times,* pp. A1.

Coalition Against Institutionalized Child Abuse. (2010). *Deaths in facilities.* Retrieved January 28, 2012, from http://caica.org/RESTRAINTS%20Death%20List.htm

Fine, M. (1994). Working the hyphens: Reinventing the self and other in qualitative research. In N. Denzin, & Y. Lincoln (Eds.), *Handbook of qualitative research* (pp. 70–82). Newbury Park, CA: Sage Publication.

Frye, M. (1983). Oppression. In *The politics of reality: Essays in feminist theory* (pp. 1–16). Trumansburg, New York: Crossing Press.

hooks, b. (1990). "Choosing the margin as a space of radical openness" and "postmodern blackness". In *Yearning: Race, gender and cultural politics* (pp. 145–153). Toronto: Between the Lines.

Irlen, H. (1998). *Irlen.* Retrieved January 28, 2012, from http://irlen.com

Chapter 3

The Bad Apple

Michael Peacock

Throughout my life
    they have told me
    I should
    trend toward
    becoming a teacher
No one ever told me that I
    couldn't become a teacher
And still
    I've heard the words:
    "You should be a teacher,"
    lodged in hives
    so many times
        unable to listen to
    them
But to satisfy
    "the separate choices of thousands of bees…
    [a] kind of voting mechanism…
    more reliable than single-handed
    evaluation by the queen" (Pratt, 1998, pp. 203–204)
Who am I to say…?

Drones combing through Rapunzel's divine golden hair
    "belonging in the otherworldly realm of the sun," (da Silva, 2004, p.
    279)
    absorbing the heat, the light
Prescribed to be

"a daughter like a flower,
in a tower" (Sondheim, 1986)
outside,
out there,
outcast,
                generally anxious

Zoom in on the beehive behavior
                Control-upswipe
                Control-plus
                Control the bow up
                        giù arco
                                "The maestro took bow after bow" (Coslow,
                                1939)
        slowly typing away like journalists
        hopped up
                on obsolete technology,
        frantic, compulsive combing,
        tracing paths,
        orbiting around,
        weaving
        as Sleeping Beauty spindled—
                — work so hard I'd collapse from exhaustion,
        "carrying out the occupations of a young girl
        in a normal manner" (Robert & Powell, 1969, p. 49)
        prior to sleeping a sleep
        a hundred oceans wide

Frequency, severity, and duration
        to assess
        in writing
        the progress of the beehive behavior
                and that SOUND!
Brezhnev-era underground rock 'n' roll bees
                The Apples of Discord: LIVE!
        swapping bootleg tapes with
        microbiologist bees

to "explore the overlap between a
committed... self
and an autonomous, agentical self" (Howell, 2010, p.358)
with telescopic guitars,
making music and observing all that is
cometic angelic phosphorescence
Wearing homemade hexagonal corsages,
    sweating the small stuff;
        bees poking fun at geometry
            how hilarious—a pentacontagon!
        the period
        after-over-foraging
        competing against hyphenation

Zoom out of the beehive behavior
        Control-downswipe
        Control-minus
        Control the bow down
          sull'arco
"'I [want] control of the comb,'" (Watkins, 1969, p. 240)
        Rapunzel lashes
        moments before the sorcerist
        sorts her out,
        beladder-braids her

Bouncing, frenetic
        now-seemingly-not-orbiting,
        weaving through an invisible barrage
            of machine gun fire
           rifle gun fire, tear-gas canisters (Kifner, 1970, p. 1)
        now defenseless against geometry
          April 26, 1937: the bombing of Guernica
            Spanish Civil War... World War II...
      "spazzing out"
        And that SOUND!
Gymnopédie
        da-dee-da da-dee-da do-da-dee daaaaa

"the festival, one in which the participants performed…
        'unarmed…' men of all ages…
[dancing] associated with Apollo
and commemorated [war] victories" (Jensen, 1994, p. 237)
            Eris' bellicose apple
Three beats as "unofficial" as *Waltzing Matilda* (Whitmer,
2005, p. 5)

    Three syllables: Rapunzel
down the clinically significant ladder
to get
outside—
        out there—
only to get back inside
some other place
prescribed to be
        clean as a princess:
        "having things, being cool,
        …and having heart" (Copes, Hochstetler, Williams, 2008, p.
        260)
Pollen and nectar expected
    parenthetical: (obedience; remedy; sustenance)

Forget the beehive metaphor,
        moral of the fairy tale,
        Eve's damned apple
            Snow White's somnolent apple
                Eris' bellicose apple
                    Iduna's thanatic apple (Fontenrose, 1983, p.
                    56)
        the sweetness of the honey I didn't even mention
I've heard those words so many times
Unable to listen

1.7% of adults in the United States
        identify… as gay or lesbian (Crary & Tang, 2011)
Do they engage in homosexual activities

that we find repugnant and immoral?
Are you going to hell?
A demon in their eyes,
          "detestable" (NIV, Lev. 18:22)
                    Faggot
And yet,
          people
                    straight and serious,
          clean, disinfect, make appearances
How our identities are simultaneously ubiquitous and formless
          concrete answers to abstract questions earthquaked
                    on a network of flimsy seismographs

Not long before my grandfather died,
          lying consciously in a well-lit
          ground-floor single-occupancy room
          on a bed of tubes and cords,
          under beeping and buzzing monitors,
          he said he *knew* the marriage between my husband and me
          could be accepted one day
We "received [his] blessing" (Hardwig, 2009, p. 43)

I came out to my grandmother
          when I was fifteen,
          and she broke the news to my grandfather
The last male Peacock
          to pass on the family name
They never disowned me or disrespected me
I make them proud
I don't know if
          a straight person can understand
          what it feels like
          to be humbled by such an experience

300,000 gay male teachers (Crary & Tang, 2011; Coopersmith, 2009)
          and I will be one of them,
          compelled to avoid

divulging details about in-my-life
"Here teacher, pupil, home, and community share
　　　common middle-class standards and values" (Finder, 1955, p. 199)
"Passing" as a straight man
　　　in everyday life
Invisible ink messages
　　　an ersatz identity
　　　chiseled into me beyond habit
　　　to the detriment of my integrity:
　　　　　　"Among dominant groups of men,
　　　　　　the circuits of social embodiment
　　　　　　constantly involve the institutions on which their
　　　　　　privileges rest" (Connell & Messerschmidt, 2005, p. 852)
And yet,
　　　I benefit from privileges,
　　　clean, disinfect, make appearances,
　　　crediting things I say or do,
　　　omitting things I won't say or don't do
Oh, "how men sometimes simply
　　　have to show up to reap [the] benefits" of (Messner, 2011, p. 5)
　　　　　　a white-male education
Vivid
　　　beyond neckties and Standard English
Vivid
　　　beyond valid identification
Vivid

Boxed-in nucleus colony
　　　of parenthetical bees (soldiers)
　　　headed by a queen
Remember the beehive metaphor:
　　　"Tho' Physick liv'd, whilst Folks were ill,
　　　None would prescribe, but Bees of Skill;
　　　Which, through the Hive dispers'd so wide,
　　　That none of 'em had need to ride,
　　　Waved vain Disputes; and strove to free
　　　The Patients of their Misery;

Left Drugs in cheating Countries grown,
And used the Product of their own,
Knowing the Gods sent no Disease
To Nations without remedies." (de Mandeville, 1724, p. 15)

The reverend Lorenzo Langstroth
         invented
         "the first really practical
         movable frame" for bees
"'I wanted control of the comb.'" (Watkins, 1969, p. 240)
Not to isolate the bees
         or make them
         disappear,
         but figure out how
         they multiply (Langstroth, 1852, p. 49)
How to figure them out…
         and give more −scriptions
Transcription:
         do you copy that?
Conscription:
         we recruit, you comply
Description:
         use my words
Proscription:
         you don't exist anymore and I own everything that was ever yours

Looking at the time, having it
Measuring cups ready
         a prescription,
         doctor's orders,
                  "the baker is not what I had in mind" (Sondheim, 1983)
Paper folding with words, letters
         for recipe precision
"Traces of objects into the body that—like food or medicine—"
         have an effect on my universe (Jordan, 2010, p. 19)
A pre-heating oven
         "fingernail pink" (Powell & Persico, 1996)

      laughing at its ability
      to earn a degree
Baking the smell of what was cooked the night before,
      absorbing the heat, the light,
      laughing at its ability
      to assess
One turn
      Bent at the elbow, looking into the face
One turn
      Pinch—375 degrees—pull
One turn
      Pinch—180 degrees—flatten
         Dimensionality, positionality, exteriority, *a posteriori*-ity
The opposite of being
      never designed
      as an outcome

That face-cheek muscle
      grimace-gliding
         the alliterative couplet...
      for fermata
        and that SOUND—
           grunt buzzing-hum-din dint-in-the-normal
      drone in my ears,
      wisdom teeth lodged into lobes,
      aspects of my life
A tautological morosophy:
      we can learn a lot about ourselves
      from learning about ourselves.
"All good knowledge is found in searching" (de La Perrière, 1545, p. 214)

Toddler-me's intense attraction,
      how strange to want to race
      with no one
      to sit across the room from the TV
      to the theme of *Kelly & Company*
         parenthetical: (seventeen-year local morning talk show)

The pleasure of sit-wiggle-dancing
Unable-to-put-my-own-shoes-on-me
Third generation:
>   Grandpa's stubborn-as-a-Peacock obduracy,
>   intractable
Mom pleaded,
>   competing against hyphenation
>   to stop curling my toes,
>   to fit my feet in

A few years later
>   I screamed, "I love you, Whitney!"
I knew she could hear me
>   Whitney Houston, Pine Knob, 1986
This was my first standing ovation
With thanks
>   the concert was linked to my "pretend bias"
I could have been labeled
>   a "no bias" or a "real bias"
>   parenthetical: (I lost a chance at winning a spelling bee
>   because of "bias")
Magic could have been crushed by an
>   ability
>   to make inferences
>   based on supporting evidence (Tullos & Woolley, 2009, p. 110)
I wanted my mom to rent Pine Knob for me
>   for my own concert
A perfectly reasonable request
An alternative venue was arranged, however
In the basement of our apartment
>   my entire world could see me
I flung myself around a pole,
>   squirmed about the floor,
>   hair spiked sky-high,
>   front teeth missing
It was "the gayest thing ever seen,"
>   preserved on videotape,

Mom shook her head,
giggling with tears in her eyes
and said, "Oh, shit!"
That's how normal days should be

My second grade teacher asked me
to walk around
and help my classmates
("I am able," he thought)
"High-quality teacher-child
relationships
foster children's achievement" (O'Connor & McCartney, 2007, p.
361)
I learned to write in cursive slightly earlier than some of my peers
One of the taller boys who was in my Cub Scout troupe
couldn't make his lower case fs
properly
Transcription
He was always nice to me
Invited me to a pool party
I felt
empowered to help
I remember that rainy October day in 1988
That was my first experience as a teacher
Vivid
beyond prismatic explosions
Vivid
beyond symphonic shivers
Vivid

Spencerian capital Ws are so impressive
to see in old documents,
old account ledgers,
flowery mundane correspondence
that sounds just like
love letters,
elegant impressions of business,

even ladies had a special prescription
Wooing, wowing,
      even the ampersands have flowers,
      "ornate by modern standards" (Eaton, 1985, p. 261)
How do they consistently look
      so beautiful?
They aren't upside-down capital Ms;
      they're closer to high Hs, tall Ts, or full-figured Fs
Spencerian script,
      older, grander than the Palmer Method, (Yoffe, 2009)
      made for a different pen,
      for a different purpose
The Palmer Method,
      no left-handedness allowed,
      built for speed
            Conscription
Write it, read it
      Write it, read it
            Write it, read it
Locomotive, industrial,
      methodical,
            a crude pencil could do it
I've never seen a fountain pen that wasn't behind glass

I am able
      to disappear in letters
      or anything very close to
      them
Auditory imagery: "melopoeia"
      mental imagery: "phanopoeia" (Pound, 1960, p. 42)
            hieroglyphic, "[encoded, secretive]" (Bergal, 1985, p. 121)
      "mystical revelations" (Dexter, 1975, p. 51)
Uncalculated scribbling gibberish
      even though I don't get Cy Twombly
Ideograms, syllabaries, and fonts
      even though I don't get Ezra Pound
But, I was *caught*!

Spazz
The Letter People sang to me
Writhing and buzzing,
  my neck contorted,
  straight and serious
"Tall teeth," I chanted
    the alliterative couplet...
  "Tall *teeth!*" (Barnes, 1974)
My left pointer finger
  massaging my *depressor anguli oris* –
    that face-cheek muscle
  Proscription
My right hand, cubism
  even though I don't get Picasso
Cometic angelic phosphorescence
  even though I don't get Kepler
The blunt orange crayon
  orbiting around
  one of the countless
    dittos, dittos, dittos
The sharp green crayon
  weaving onto Mr. T.'s scalp
  the laurel wreath
A barrage of tall blank-paper-white teeth

The Letter People,
  illuminated
  manuscripts for the abecedarian
Or like emblem books:
  "above all the figure is
  essential for comprehension;" (Saunders, 1986, p. 648)
  symbolic expressions of allegories,
  engraved words of wisdom and woodblockspirations
The Letter People,
  self-explanatory anthropomorphized
  consonants and vowels
Their likenesses reproduced:

inflatable toys
trading cards
          parenthetical: (I still have them)
coloring book pages
          dittos, dittos, dittos
TV programs
8-tracks and records
Unintended apostolicity from kindergarten curricular materials,
          genuflect in mind,
          tremulating in hand;
                    you have a witness!
I grind my teeth
Clenched,
          fingernails dig calluses into my palm
          like Joe Louis' fist (Graham, 1986)
My fingers harden and curl like ribbon bows on both hands:
                    parenthetically
          the left hand
          giù arco against my philtrum
                    Paganini's bow gliding down
                    for fermata
                              "Is that with two fs?" (Mann, 1999)
          "The maestro took bow after bow…
                    When from the balcony way up high," (Coslow, 1939)
          the right hand playing an invisible keyboard
          my eyes bulge and look upward
Sull'arco—up bow my heart rate,
          my pulse a scherzo

I disappear

Orbiting around

Where am I *not* alone?
In a partly cloudy paroxysmal burst of lightning
That's where!
          Epileptic? Epicycloidal?

"The motion in the epicycle would also
need to be non-uniform" (Aiton, 1975, p. 255)
        Spirographs
        on a network of flimsy seismographs
                wheels with orbiting dots on carts
Tympanic temporalis thunder—
        and that SOUND!
Convulsant
        The sounds of the *actual* muscles in my head!
This is when I know I'm at my best!

And it's the most embarrassing thing that I do

"If it did not pose a real challenge
        to accepted norms...
        and have the capacity to provoke
        the uninitiated—
        it would not belong" (Varnedoe, 1994, p. 18)
And I refuse to "spazz out" in a room
        where I am not alone!
The shame,
        the "odds"
        twice felt and remembered
Vivid
        beyond bloody noses
Vivid
        beyond barfing in public
Vivid
I couldn't imagine "spazzing out"
        out there,
                (a description of a perception or a place or a kind of person)
        out*side*
                (variously other, neither, beyondness)
"There's no escaping the jaws of the alien this time." (Temperton, 1982)
Would finding a real name for "spazzing out"
        change the persistence of the behavior?
Would "spazzing out" become a less fruitful means of contemplation

once a name has been given to it?
    Description

Orbiting around
    breathing heavily
I will vocalize a punctuated low
    grunt buzzing-hum-din dint-in-the-normal,
        susurrous succor
    competing against hyphenation,
    "expressive of a mind which has reached
    the gelatinous mildewy stage in the mortification
    of all healthy and courageous thought" (Thoreau, 1910, p. 165)
    falling down an adrenaline dream well
Butterflies
    orbiting around
    in my stomach,
    a torus connected to my Adam's apple,
Butterflies
    doing
    work so hard I'd collapse from exhaustion
    like
    drones combing through Rapunzel's divine golden hair

My second grade classmate asked me,
    "What are you doing, Peacock?"
Opprobrium hum,
    echoing whale song
        shame
    a hundred oceans wide
    that "constitutes a shock effect…
    which, like all shocks,
    should be cushioned
    by heightened presence of mind" (Benjamin, 2003, p. 525)
Twenty-five residual years ago,
    and still
        "'brake fluid'" (Auerhahn & Leonard, 2000, p. 601)
    I remember that halt expression

            that face-cheek muscle
        witnessing "spazzing out"
"[Benjamin] Franklin had accidentally discovered a
            tenderizing technique, one still used by the meat industry
            today, whereby an electrical current helps an animal's muscles
            to relax and modifies the effects of rigor mortis." (Riely, 2006, p. 24)
We were making lemon juice
            invisible ink messages

It worked

"Colin Powell went before the United Nations…"
                the laurel wreath
            "to make his case for war…
            [and] cover Picasso's *Guernica*,
            usually displayed at the entrance of the Security Council,
            with a blue cloth" (Hansen, 2004, p. 391)
To clean, disinfect, make appearances
            disappear like
            invisible ink messages

It worked

"To remake the [Eisenhower Corridor…]
            money in some budgetary cookie jar…
                for months… draped in drop cloths,
            looked like a Jackson Pollock retrospective.
The hammering and sawing seemed to go on
            forever.
The corridor… was being painted fingernail pink…
It turned out the paint number had been
            transposed
            on the work order, and
[T]he hallway had to be redone." (Powell & Persico, 1996)

That worked, too

I used to sit on the
      underside of the playground slide
      flipping through a miniature Japanese dictionary
I saved and borrowed
      allowance money
      and with gleeful abandon
      purchased as many foreign language dictionaries as I could
I didn't understand
      grammatical terminology well enough at the time
      to formulate my own sentences
            parenthetical: (Is *consider* ever a reflexive verb?)
But, I loved sitting in the bookstore floor
      to fit my feet in
          criss-cross applesauce
      hidden between the empty travel and reference sections
      "spazzing out"
            parenthetical: (had I known the library gave that stuff out for
            free…)
Writing systems fascinated me most;
      understanding the other
      languages' mechanics was secondary
To be so up close and personal
      with foreign calligraphy
I've never seen a fountain pen that wasn't behind glass
      and I didn't initially consider
      that a computer had produced such wonderful music
      mimicked after some virtually unknown
      calligraphers' hands
Thousands of symbols,
      each with their own story
      as interesting as a fictional account
They made a children's television show about the letter T
         "Tall teeth!" (Barnes, 1974)
      complete
      with puppets and toys and
            dittos, dittos, dittos
         even though I don't get Walter Benjamin

with color schemes and jingles and—
 "spazz," "spazz," "spazz"—
  even though I don't get Andy Warhol

My fifth grade teacher gave me an award,
 a certificate:
  "everybody is too good now, really" (Warhol, 2003, p. 747)
 for writing to one thousand using Japanese characters
I inspired a classmate
 who seemed to join
 a previously nonexistent race
And then it became war
 insomuch as a war could happen in 1991
How strange to want to race
 counting to one thousand
  in writing
I don't think I'll ever understand that,
  that's how normal days should be
 but if that day comes
 I will think to thank that classmate
 for whatever wisdom results

In middle school
 they passed out
 bags with hygiene products and information
 to keep us
 clean, disinfect, make appearances
 better than they were
And the kids on the bus drank the mouthwash to get drunk
And the kids on the bus took a lighter to that faggot's hair
 for having a fairy tail
And the kids on the bus were abused at home
And the kids on the bus,
 and the kids on the bus,
  and the kids on the bus...
"The separate choices of thousands of bees... (Pratt, 1998, p. 203)

I was hospitalized when I was seventeen,
Psychotic
     a recovering addict since my first prescription
At the time
     "protective effects against suicidal thoughts,"
     the "odds"
     half as likely,
          Iduna's thanatic apple (Fontenrose, 1983, p. 56)
     the "trend toward an increased risk of self harm
     is paradoxical" (Curtin et al, 2005, p. 1148)
Doctor's orders
     "None would prescribe, but Bees of Skill" (de Mandeville, 1724, p. 15)
What is *paradox*?
     Side effects oppose
     intended therapeutic effects
Dimensionality, positionality, exteriority, *a posteriori*-ity
The opposite of being
     never designed
     as an outcome

Prescriptions are labels,
     the breath behind your ear
"I know it may not fix the hinges,
     but at least the door [stops] its creaking" (Crow, 2002)
Two choices:
     either you like it or you do not
Frequency, severity, and duration
Wheels with orbiting dots on carts
     tracing epicycloidal paths,
     "belonging in the otherworldly realm of the sun," (da Silva, 2004, p. 279)
     breathing heavily

Back to the juvenile psychiatric ward
     on the eighth floor
We were in a support group

Most of us victims of self-harm
"Ripening bananas
     [exhibiting] blue luminescence…
     develop strongly luminescent blue halos
     around senescence associated dark spots." (Moser et al, 2009, p.
     15539)
Oh, to instill glory for children
     thinking tenebrous thoughts…
       dittos, dittos, dittos
And they all signed my pillow when I left
For nine days they saw me as the elder,
     wearing a thrift store blazer that
     hadn't been dry
     cleaned
They didn't seem to notice that I was there, too
     wrist under hospital band
That was my second experience as a teacher

"The underlying trials were
     never designed
     to assess
     suicidality
     as an outcome
     but to satisfy
     regulatory agencies
     about efficacy." (Lucas, Schubert, & Halpern, 2010, p. 1149)
       no statute of limitations

Before I dropped out of high school during my senior year
     there was a day
     I don't remember
       whether I went back to school or not
In between hazes
     Vivid
       beyond driving around aimlessly after midnight
     Vivid
       beyond getting lost

Vivid
I think I remember sitting in a history class,
        most people seemed too afraid
        to ask where I had been
"We like each other a lot,
        and we span time together.
We just don't touch
        each other, all right?" (Gallo, 1998)
But, when one or two people did ask,
        loud enough for
        others
        to hear,
        I told them I was sick—
                had been sick
I think I remember going to my locker,
        not remembering the combination
        to get it to open,
        after walking in between buildings
        where my legs would daily lock at the knees
        barely able to breathe, crawl, or talk
No one, including me, knew I was having panic attacks
I think I remember that day,
        leaving my locker,
        still full of textbooks and probably a book bag,
                a close approximation to running to my car
        and left
        alone
This may have been a dream, however
"It's very difficult to keep the line between the past and the present.
        You know what I mean?
                It's awfully difficult." (Maysles, Maysles, & Froemke, 1975)

You can thank me for becoming
        a part of
        a "nationally representative sample" (Vaughn et al, 2011, p. 203)
Don't worry, I got my GED
        and discovered ways to get myself

into and through university
to earn a degree
I was terrified of attending college
in my home state
"the gelatinous mildewy stage" (Thoreau, 1910, p. 165)
for fear of coming into contact
with anyone I knew from high school
Meanwhile, prescriptions came and went,
baggage and laundry lists and diagnoses
depressed and panicked in Detroit
like Joe Louis' fist (Graham, 1986)
and too many familiar landmarks to mention
balking the severity of a 6.8 magnitude earthquake in Seattle
on a network of flimsy seismographs
fireworks shooting off the Space Needle
the frisson of a new year
a witness to tropical storms in Largo
snapping pictures of toppling palm trees
and double rainbows
to sit across the room from the TV
watching the Twin Towers fall
seasonally affected in Fairbanks
She-Ra—Princess Aurora's Crystal Castle
the borealis screensaver in the sky:
"people stare
arranging and changing placing
carefully there a strange
thing and known thing here" (Cummings,
1970, p. 175)
so cold we froze bubbles in mid-air
post-traumatically stressed and bipolarized in Iowa City
not a stitch of corn to be found
The International Dada Archives available online
da-dee-da da-dee-da do-da-dee daaaaa
a witness in Minneapolis to a fiftysomething figure
a pentacontagon
hopped up

on crystal meth
and the kids on the bus
and Mary Tyler Moore's bronze
frozen flung-hat on her fingers (Gillen, 2002)
All of the bugs that hit
the windshields of cars, pickups, airplane wings, and moving trucks
You may not notice
them
Until I thought I'd reached home,
covered in squished insects,
the instinct to scrub and scrape
clean, disinfect, make appearances
Disappear
Astounded at how many of
them
I'd gathered along the way

"Compared to the hell on wheels that I used to be.
Is that with two fs?" (Mann, 1999)
A recovering addict since my first prescription
"Did I find you, or you find me?" (Byrne, 1982)
Throughout my life
I've been prescribed more than several medications
on the FDA black box warning list
"No one knows the physiological or
psychological consequences/" (Shearer & Bermingham, 2008, p.
711)
long-term side effects
Patient
trapped in a darkened room
illuminated
by ghastly faces,
crying faces,
faces
covered in a slime (Oursler, 2009)
"frightfully… elegant aspic…
the whole decorated dish"

the alliterative couplet…
"various elements coated with
or molded in jelly" (Child, 2011, pp. 544–545)

And yet,
I've never been diagnosed with a sleeping disorder:
insomnia
"Language is not the only realm
in which one builds theories." (Premack & Woodruff, 1978, p. 518)
I've struggled with sleep
sleep deprivation, over-sleeping:
no moderation
Restlessness, drowsiness
unable to
to formulate my own sentences
I'm a consumer of prescriptions:
no real solace
Katzenmusick vs. caterwaul; (Coates, 2005, p. 648; Spitzer, 1945, p. 504)
no statute of limitations
pots and pans clanging to scare the cats
"casting runes on the rooftops and alleys" (Jones, 1989)
or the mewling
starving lecher-wretches
of every newly industrialized city
to make the world sleepable
sufferable
PLEASE

In high school I was lucky if
I slept two hours in a night
On weekends I would crash fourteen hours
no moderation
An uninterrupted hour of
natural sleep
parenthetical: (sans medication)

Unaware at the time that alcohol abuse exacerbates insomnia (Morrison &

Storey, 1986)
      I drank to get drunk and pass out
Yes, drinking meant that there was a party going on
      amongst my alcoholic friends,
      or—more appropriately and usually—
      alone with my alcoholism
            "I can't tell one from another" (Byrne, 1982)
But, I drank hard liquor like it was
      work so hard I'd collapse from exhaustion
The drunken spider spins a clumsy web, (Cross, 2006)
      a joke-mistake-disaster-disappointment
      "or rather…
      this has been drawn to my attention,
      made serious and not just a joke" (Burroughs, 2003, p. 59)

June 30, 2006, after my friends went home
      I cried so hard I finished off that last bottle of scotch
          alone
I went dry
      alone
Induced vomiting before I passed out
      because I knew I was poisoned
      but, woke up lecher-wretching anyhow
          alone
Dry glue on the underside of the envelope flap

Agoraphobe
"As we stumble along
      'cross life's crowded dance floors,
          as we push and we shove
      we live and we learn." (Lambert & Morrison, 2006)
I didn't leave my apartment for a month
But, when I did
      I felt queasy walking around outside
      where the sky doesn't seem so limited
      like my nine- or ten-foot tall ceiling,
      where the sky feels

a hundred oceans wide
To alleviate intense panic,
    alcohol "withdrawal"
    covered in a slime
    of agoraphobia (Taylor, 2006, p. 952)

Enter quetiapine prescription
    tranq darts/
        "remote drug delivery systems...
    applications to common
    societal problems, such as control of stray dogs
    and nonlethal restraint of humans" (Bush, 1992, p. 159)/
        "'chemical pacification...'
            'brake fluid'" (Auerhahn & Leonard, 2000, p. 601)

Throughout my adulthood
    they have told me,
    "[You] will probably have to take medication
    for the rest of [your] life" (Karp, 2006, p. 21)
I've heard those words so many times
I am a consumer of prescriptions
"News about an outcome before it happens
    resonates with a person
    just as much as learning it at the time" (Kőszegi & Rabin, 2009, p.
    913)
Wrist underneath watchband,
    hospital band
"I love the passing of time" (Byrne, 1982)
Patient
Looking at the time, having it
Have you heard of the "psychiatric consumer/
    survivor/ex-patient (c/s/x) movement," (Harris, 2003, p. 52)
        the herds
            "subvert the diagnostic urge" (Price, 2009, p. 17)
        still
    out there
    outside

"And could it be that in this passivity I shall find my freedom?" (Linklater, 1991)

Kitaj opines about his Diaspora:
                "Free, Western, privileged,
                                [the laurel wreath]
                uninhibited, uncensored, permissive,
                                [no statute of limitations]
                elitist cloud-cuckoo lands" (2000, p. 40)
                                doctor's orders

I SAID, "Enter quetiapine prescription!"

If clouds could ingest Seroquel
                the sky would surely fall

Not long after the
                panic attack in my sleep,
                from drowning and suffocating
                                in my Seroquel-swollen sinuses
                a side effect of the new medication
                                I'd been given
                I'm a consumer of prescriptions
I was a stuttering zoetrope,
                hands and fingers quaking,
                extremities transformed
                into rickety needles
                on a network of flimsy seismographs
                eyes raced in ellipses,
                temporarily dysarthric,
                barely able to breathe, crawl, or talk
                                breathe, hhh…
                                        crawl, hhh… or
                                                talk, hhh…
                                echoing whale song
Panicked
The 9-1-1 operator and me,

competing against hyphenation,
and she,
calmly needing answers to questions,
and me,
thinking tenebrous thoughts:
            "This is fear of death;" (Nauman, 1985)
and the medics,
clocking my pulse over 180
Looking at the time, having it
One of the most terrifying moments of my life
            was a cakewalk for
            them

I felt so disabled by prescription
I'd been given
            inefficient use of cognitive faculties,
            I considered dropping out of college
A handful of credits needed
            to earn a degree
            so that I would pass
It would require the same amount of effort
            to complete the
            requisite forms
                  dittos, dittos, dittos
            to receive and consume disability benefits
"The diagnostic label may provide
            a sense of identity and resources...
                  unlikely to receive otherwise." (Howard, 2008, p. 190)
Lodged in the hive,
            a basement;
            remember the house metaphor:
                  "this excavation lay at an exceeding depth
                  below the surface of the earth" (Poe, 1998, p. 117)
Fifty pounds
            have something to do
            with being every day
            awake for only eight hours

in between
AM and PM doses –
    Snow White's somnolent apple –
and boxes of snacks,
    dittos, dittos, dittos
crumbs in my sweater,
enabling meals,
cheese, ice cream, and
to sit across the room from the TV:
    Mary Tyler Moore and Bob Newhart,
        hopped up
        on obsolete technology,
    the journalist and the psychologist,
    with color schemes and jingles and
        susurrous succor
    the alliterative couplet...
        drone in my ears
            in between hazes

It basically comes down to one question:
    "Has your mood been stabilized?"
I didn't understand
    etiological
    grammatical terminology well enough at the time
Would you topple over
    if I asked you in return:
    "How do you feel about my feelings
        about your feelings
            about me?" (Boyd, 2008, p. 369)
People who think they're being polite normally say, "How are you?"
    which is one of my least favorite questions
    because the answer is *always*,
    "Good!"
But, the question wasn't,
    "*What* are you?"
I'm lazy enough to just give the easy answer most of the time
I guess that makes me a bad apple

Forget the beehive metaphor,
            moral of the fairy tale,
            Eve's damned apple
                        Snow White's somnolent apple
                              Eris' bellicose apple
                                    Iduna's thanatic apple (Fontenrose,
                                    1983, p. 56)
            the sweetness of the honey I didn't even mention
"Not being something or not having certain features is not a scientific
definition for what
            an organism is" (Saey, 2009, p. 5)
Alright... Fair enough

I didn't consider myself a
            person
            with a disability
            until,
            wrist under watchband,
            I *learned* the phrase
            "person with a disability"
            when I started graduate school two years later,
                        when my prescriptions were changed two years later
"News about an outcome before it happens
            resonates with a person
            just as much as learning it at the time" (Kőszegi & Rabin, 2009, p.
            913)
I continuously doubt my ability to do anything

A child who barely knows anything
            about me,
            with complete, sincere, unbreakable
            confidence
            proclaimed that I will be
            a great teacher
"Being ordinary [is] the least important
            characteristic
            of a good teacher" (Murphy, Delli, & Edwards, 2004, p. 79)

I thanked her and smiled
>distantly, as if she were talking about
>someone else,
>unable to accept that she was giving me
>one of the highest honors a seven-year-old can give

Other students called me Dad,
>the highest honor seven-year-olds can give

And I'm the white student teacher,
>sitting at a low table in a tiny chair
>wearing a thrift store blazer that hadn't been dry
>cleaned

That was my third experience as a teacher

An undeliverable letter to my future students
Dry glue on the underside of the envelope flap
The day may never come
>that you will read this
>but, it's in my heart

Dear Students:
I have taken many of the prescriptions
>you've been given
I have faced many of the challenges you're facing
>out there
I know how difficult it is
Vivid
>beyond hatred and fear
Vivid
>beyond closed-door conversations
Vivid
You're the reason I'm here
I'll teach you the beehive metaphor
>so that you'll pass
>and figure out how
>to behave, to control the comb
But figure out how...
>how to figure them out!

You may feel discarded,
  unable to listen to
  them,
  like a bad apple
It would be "morally blameworthy"
  for me to "fail to do
  what [I] have sufficient reason to do." (Fischer, 2003, p. 249)
With complete, sincere, unbreakable
  confidence
  I want to be
  a great teacher
That's how normal days should be

References

Aiton, E. (1975). How Kepler discovered the elliptical orbit. *The Mathematical Gazette, 59*(410), 250–260.

Auerhahn, K. and Leonard, E. (2000). Docile bodies? Chemical restraints and the female inmate. *The Journal of Criminal Law and Criminology (1973-), 90*(2), 599–634.

Barnes, J. (Executive producer). (1974). *The letter people* [Television series]. St. Louis: KETC.

Benjamin, W. (2003). The work of art in the age of mechanical reproduction. In C. Harrison & P. Wood (Eds.), *Art in theory: 1900-2000* (pp. 520–527). Boston: Blackwell Publishers.

Bergal, I. (1985). Word and picture: Erasmus' 'Parabolae' in La Perrière's 'Morosophie.' *Bibliothèque d'Humanisme et Renaissance, 47*(1), 113–123.

Boyd, J. (2008). Have we found the Holy Grail? Theory of Mind as a unifying construct. *Journal of Religion and Health, 47*(3), 366–385.

Burroughs, A. (2003). *Dry.* New York: St. Martin's Press.

Byrne, D. (1982). This must be the place (naive melody). [Recorded by Talking Heads]. On *Speaking in tongues.* New York: Sire Records (1982).

Child, J. (2011). *Mastering the art of French cooking: 50th anniversary.* Bertholle, L. and S. Beck (Eds.). New York: Borzoi Books.

Coates, P. (2005). The strange stillness of the past: Toward an environmental history of sound and noise. *Environmental History, 10*(4), 636–665.

Connell, R. and Messerschmidt, J. (2005). Hegemonic masculinity: Rethinking the concept. *Gender and Society, 19*(6), 829–859.

Coopersmith, J. (2009). *Characteristics of public, private, and Bureau of Indian Education elementary and secondary school teachers in the United States: Results from the 2007-08 Schools and Staffing Survey (NCES 2009-324).* Washington, DC: National Center for Education Statistics, Institute of Education Sciences, U.S. Department of Education.

Copes, H., Hochstetler, A., and Williams, J. (2008). 'We weren't like no regular dope fiends:' Negotiating hustler and crackhead identities. *Social Problems, 55*(2), 254–270.

Coslow, S. (1939). (If you can't sing it) you'll have to swing it (Mr. Paganini) [Recorded by Ella Fitzgerald]. On *Four by four* [Album]. New York: PolyGram. (1999).

Crary, D. and Tang, T. (2011). Gay population in U.S. estimated at 4 Million, Gary Gates says. *The Huffington Post*. Retrieved from http://www.huffingtonpost.com/2011/04/07/gay-population-us-estimate_n_846348.html

Cross, V. (2006). The effects of alcohol on spiders: What happens to web construction after spiders consume alcohol? *The American Biology Teacher*, *68*(6), 347–352.

Crow, S. (2002). Weather channel. On *C'mon c'mon* [Album]. Santa Monica: A&M Records.

Cummings, E. (1970). Spring is like a perhaps hand. In H. Carruth (Ed.), *The voice that is great within us: American poetry of the twentieth century* (p. 175). New York: Bantam Books.

Curtin, F., Schulz, P., Healy, D., Gunnell, D., Saperia, J., Ashby, D., ...Thompson, M. (2005). Do selective serotonin reuptake inhibitors cause suicide? *British Medical Journal*, *330*(7500), 1148–1151.

Dexter, G. (1975). L'imagination poétique. *Bibliothèque d'Humanisme et Renaissance*, *37*(1), 49–62.

Eaton, W. (1985). American school penmanship: From craft to process. *American Journal of Education*, *93*(2), 252–267.

Fischer, J. (2003). 'Ought-implies-can', Causal determinism and moral responsibility. *Analysis*, *63*(3), 244–250.

Finder, M. (1955). Teaching English to slum-dwelling pupils. *The English Journal*, *44*(4), 199–204; 242.

Fontenrose, J. (1983). The building of the city walls: Troy and Asgard. *The Journal of American Folklore*, *96*(379), 53–63.

Gallo, V. (Director) (1998). *Buffalo '66* [Motion Picture]. USA: Universal Studios.

Gillen, G. (2002). *Mary Tyler Moore* [Sculpture]. Minneapolis.

Graham, R. (1986). *Joe Louis memorial monument* [Sculpture]. Detroit.

Hansen, M. (2004). Why media aesthetics? *Critical Inquiry*, *30*(2), 391-395.

Hardwig, J. (2009). Going to meet death: The art of dying in the early part of the twenty-first century. *The Hastings Center Report*, *39*(4), 37–45.

Harris, L. (2003). Protest at the APA: Women psychiatric survivors speak out. *Off Our Backs*, *33*(7/8), 52–53.

Howard, J. (2008). Negotiating an exit: Existential, interactional, and cultural obstacles to disorder disidentification. *Social Psychology Quarterly*, *71*(2), 177–192.

Howell, Y. (2010). The liberal gene: Sociobiology as emancipatory discourse in the late Soviet Union. *Slavic Review*, *69*(2), 356–376.

Jensen, E. (1994). Satie and the 'Gymnopédie.' *Music & Letters*, *75*(2), 236–240.

Jones, R. (1989). Satellites. On *Flying cowboys* [Album]. Santa Monica: Geffen.

Jordan, G. (2010). What does it mean to "consume" images? *American Art*, *24*(3), 18–21.

Karp, D. (2006). *Is it me or my meds? Living with antidepressants*. Cambridge, MA: Harvard University Press.

Kifner, J. (1970, May 5). 4 Kent State students killed by troops. *New York Times*, p. 1.

Kitaj, R. (2000). First Diasporist manifesto. In N. Mirzoeff (Ed.). *Diaspora and visual culture: Representing Africans and Jews* (pp. 34–41) New York: Routledge.

Kőszegi, B. and Rabin, M. (2009). Reference-dependent consumption plans. *The American Economic Review*, *99*(3), 909–936.

Langstroth, L. (1852). On the impregnation of the eggs of the queen bee. *Proceedings of the Academy of Natural Sciences of Philadelphia*, *6*, 49–50.

Lambert, L. and Morrison, G. (2006). As we stumble along. On *The Drowsy Chaperone* [Album]. New York: Sh-K-Boom Records.

Linklater, R. (1991). *Slacker* [Motion picture]. United States: Orion Classics.

Lucas, B., Schubert, E., and Halpern, A. (2010). Perception of emotion in sounded and imagined music. *Music Perception: An Interdisciplinary Journal*, *27*(5), 399–412.

de Mandeville, B. (1724). *The fable of the bees: Or private vices, publick benefits*. London: Shakespears Head Press.

Mann, A. (1999). Momentum. On *Magnolia: Music from the motion picture* [Album]. New York: Warner Brothers.

Maysles, A., Maysles, D., and Froemke, S. (Producers), Maysles, A., Maysles, D., Hovde, E., and Meyer, M. (Directors). (1975). *Grey gardens* [Motion picture]. United States: The Criterion Collection.

Messner, M. (2011). The privilege of teaching about privilege. *Sociological Perspectives*, *54*(1), 3–14

Morrison, J. & Storey, B. (1986). Adolescent insomnia. *The Clearing House*, *60*(3), 110–114.

Moser, S., Müller, T., Holzinger, A., Lütz, C., Jockusch, S., Turro, N., and Kräutler, B. (2009). Fluorescent chlorophyll catabolites in bananas light up blue halos of cell death. *Proceedings of the National Academy of Sciences of the United States of America*, *106*(37), 15538-15543.

Murphy, P., Delli, L., and Edwards, M. (2004). The good teacher and good teaching: Comparing beliefs of second-grade students, preservice teachers, and inservice teachers. *The Journal of Experimental Education*, *72*(2), 69–92.

Nauman, B. (1985). *Good boy, bad boy* [Video installation]. Chicago: Art Institute of Chicago.

O'Connor, E. and McCartney, K. (2007). Examining teacher-child relationships and achievement as part of an ecological model of development. *American Educational Research Journal*, *44*(2), 340-369.

Oursler, T. (2009). *Vampiric battle* [Video installation]. Pittsburgh: Mattress Factory.

de La Perrière, G. (1545). *Le théâtre des bons engins*. Paris: De l'imprimerie de Denys Ianot imprimeur & libraire.

Poe, E. (1998). *The fall of the house of Usher and other tales*. S. Marlowe (Ed.). New York: Signet Classics.

Pound, E. (1960). *ABC of reading*. New York: New Directions.

Powell, C. and Persico, J. (1996). *My American journey*. New York: Ballantine Books.

Premack, D., & Woodruff, G. (1978). Does the chimpanzee have a 'theory of mind'. *Behavioral and Brain Sciences*. *4*, 515–526.

Price, M. (2009). 'Her pronouns wax and wane:' Psychosocial disability, autobiography, and counter-diagnosis. *Journal of Literary & Cultural Disability Studies*, *3*(1), 11–33.

Pratt, S. (1998). Decentralized control of drone comb construction in honey bee colonies. *Behavioral Ecology and Sociobiology*, *42*(3), 193–205.

Riely, E. (2006). Benjamin Franklin and the American turkey. *Gastronomica: The Journal of Food and Culture*, *6*(4), 19–25.

Robert, M. and Powell, W. (1969). The Grimm brothers. *Yale French Studies*, *43*, 44–56.

Saey, T. (2009). Dissing a loaded label for some unicellular life: Prominent biologist calls 'prokaryote' outdated term. *Science News*, *175*(8), 5–6.

Saunders, A. (1986). Picta poesis: The relationship between figure and text in the sixteenth-century French emblem book. *Bibliothèque d'Humanisme et Renaissance*, *48*(3), 621–652.

Shearer, M. and Bermingham, S. (2008). The ethics of paediatric anti-depressant use: Erring on the side of caution. *Journal of Medical Ethics*, *34*(10), 710–714.

da Silva, F. (2004). The Madonna and the cuckoo: An exploration in European symbolic conceptions. *Comparative Studies in Society and History*, *46*(2), 273–299.

Sondheim, S. (1983). Everybody loves Louis. On *Sunday in the park with George* [Album]. New York: RCA (1984).

———(1986). Ever after. On *Into the woods* [Album]. New York: RCA Red Seal (1988).

Spitzer, L. (1945). Anglo-French etymologies. *Modern Language Notes*, *60*(8), 503–521.

Taylor, C. (2006). Panic disorder. *British Medical Journal*, *332*(7547), 951–955.

Temperton, R. (1982). Thriller [Recorded by Michael Jackson]. On *Thriller* [Album]. New York: Epic. (1984).

Thoreau, H. (1910). *Walden*. New York: Thomas Y. Crowell & Co.

Tullos, A. and Woolley, J. (2009). The development of children's ability to use evidence to infer reality status. *Child Development*, *80*(1), 101–114.

Varnedoe, K. (1994). Your kid could not do this, and other reflections on Cy Twombly. *MoMA*, *18*, 18–23.

Vaughn, M., Wexler, J., Beaver, K., Perron, B., Roberts, G., Fu, Q. (2011). Psychiatric correlates of behavioral indicators of school disengagement in the United States. *Psychiatric Quarterly*, *82*(3), 191–206.

Warhol, A. (2003). Interview with Gene Swenson. In C. Harrison & P. Wood (Eds.), *Art in theory: 1900-2000* (pp. 747–749). Boston: Blackwell Publishers.

Watkins, L. (1969). John S. Harbison: California's first modern beekeeper. *Agricultural History*, *43*(2), 239–248.

Whitmer, M. (2005). Using music to teach American history. *OAH Magazine of History*, *19*(4), 4–5.

Yoffe, E. (2009, Sep. 10). Dead letters. In *Slate Magazine: Human Guinea Pig*. Retrieved from http://www.slate.com/articles/life/human_guinea_pig/2009/09/dead_letters.single.html/

Chapter 4

Autistethnography

Elizabeth J. Grace

It is a surprise that in our society it is not more disabling to live your whole life unaware that folding the symbolic kissing cherry blossoms together just so creates a regular pentagonal dodecahedron. But I am glad people can live fulfilling lives that way, because does anybody wish ill to people who are without that inner visual ability to properly spin things? I had wanted to insert a picture here, for the love of you, the reader, who may be one of these people (who, according to all the statistical lore flying around, are now a large, but lessening, majority). But I cannot do that because of the typesetting costs. However, I can direct you to the URL of a magnificent rendering. Here is where you should direct your browser if you want to see this thing, the dodecahedron, that will, if you memorize it well enough to be able to spin it around in your head while changing its colors, enable you to loiter for ages with the greatest of ease, astonishing onlookers with your ability to do what they mistakenly believe is nothing whatsoever. Because you have chosen to read this book, you deserve to see this:

http://beachpackagingdesign.typepad.com/photos/uncategorized/2008/04
/30/dodecahedron.jpg

So I will tell you about my schooling, or some of it, in bits I can remember, highlights, things that stand out. Now I am an education researcher, and a teacher of other education researchers and teachers. Maybe the reader can make inferences.

I took IQ tests a lot. It was fun. I can't imagine it's a great idea to give those things to kids over and over so they can get better and better at them, but I didn't mind. Probably, the IQ test giver was being used as a highly educated babysitter. The classroom they took me out of most to do the IQ test a lot had this really excellent pencil sharpener with pitch-perfect twirling action. There has never been a better pencil sharpener in my 42 years of experience. The excellence of this pencil sharpener may have contributed to the: 1. large number of times I was able to go to the quiet room and participate in IQ tests, and 2. fact that I was given beautiful mechanical pencils at a relatively young age. Maybe I should ask my folks about 2.

One teacher sent me to the Principal's office all the time. This was supposed to be a Bad Thing, I was told, but the Principal, Mr. Moore, was really, really creative and kind. He showed me his microscope and let me look at things and taught me science. I think he must have started working out a science curriculum for me in anticipation of the fact that I would be being sent to him every day or so. He could snap, and the seagulls would come over the hill for us to feed bread (this was still OK in the seventies) and I was mesmerized. He wasn't just a great teacher to me, though; he was great to the whole school. He helped us clean up the playground and plant gardens and paint murals. He also helped us write songs. So then the PTA got Anita Bryant fever and decided he must be gay and he wasn't Principal the next year (learned this reason since then).

With the teacher that kept sending me to the Principal, you would think I wouldn't have friends, being the ghost of the classroom that nobody ever saw in there, but luckily I did, because of recess, which Mr. Moore made sure I got to attend every minute of, and especially because of Baseball, which is the best game. And now for the coolness of my parents. In those days, the local little league Baseball for kids was called South Powell Boys Baseball. I was a girl (now I am grown). My parents invoked the relatively new Title IX thing, which said by law girls had the same amount of rights to play sports or something like that, and pressed it (and I mean I think they really had to press it kind of tenaciously, because everyone was pretty much like, "What? It's Boys Baseball. We don't get what you're trying to say.") so that I could try out (we had try-outs back then and you could easily fail to get on a team). Meanwhile, my recess friends who played kickball with me (another great game, the same shape as Baseball) especially Wayd, Joey, Louie and Ronnie, and sometimes Jamye, all started spending a great deal of time and energy helping me get good enough at being a shortstop to definitely make a team. So I became the first girl ever in South Powell Boys Baseball League. I do not agree with the modern trend toward cutting down recess time. Here were great kids doing inclusion on so many levels, and being physically healthier in the meantime. Recess was where I learned the most, overall, in elementary school, and I am not being ironic or sarcastic, even though I do know how to be both of those, and know the difference.

The next year they sent me to the Library where we had a new Librarian who was Mrs. Gladstone who later became known as Bonnie or Beau, my mom's best friend, because she is awesome. She let me help her organize the books in Dewey Decimal and also sent me on expeditions to find poetry about things I loved, which I could then make my own anthology books of, and illustrate, even including my own attempts at poetry. I think my favorite part of this was the finding of things, though: treasure hunting for poems and stories and facts and pictures in all the wonderful books. Beau and Mr. Moore (along with my folks) helped me get set to become a scholar despite some of the intervening other things. The library was very beautiful, by the way. Also we had classes in there where all my other friends got to come in and make puppets and read and write and play together, so everyone else got to meet Mrs. Gladstone, too, and that is very good. Nobody may know exactly how many other things even besides this chapter have been and are being and will be written and made because people got to meet Mrs. Gladstone when they were little, but it's a lot.

When that district ran out of curricular resources, or something like that, my brother and I started riding the desegregation bus to the rich part of town by Reed College. This was a real thing. East of the Willamette, Portland, Oregon was shaped:

←N   African-Americans   Bluer-Collar Whites   Whiter-Collar Whites   S→

A very excellent part of this was the bus ride itself, in which girls were nice to me, which hadn't happened for a while, and never like this. They braided my hair all over my head even though it wasn't long, which felt great, and taught me songs and chants and clapping sequences. In addition to this, the bus ride was kind of long and at the end of it there were a lot of trees to go through, sending sunlight dapples through the windows on brighter days, and good metallic rain-sounds with the windshield wiper rhythms on rainy days. This friendship with the girls on the bus did not last for as long as I would have liked for it to every morning, namely all the way inside the school, because social forces I did not understand dictated that off the bus,

LaCinda and them couldn't see me, and I was meant to be friends with these other girls from the school neighborhood who had a "slam book." This is a real thing and I hear kids still do it, only digitally, and it is called something like a "burn page" now.

Let me take a moment to explain what slam books and burn pages are in the sanguine hope that not everyone already knows. It makes me happy to think of a world like that, where these things are not common knowledge, so I'm going to go with that theory. OK. So a slam book is a physical thing, a spiral notebook. On top of each page is someone's name, and the object of the exercise is that everyone else is supposed to write mean things about that person.The slam book comments were done anonymously. I understand now this sort of thing is also done on Facebook and is called a burn page, and if this is the case then I believe it would not even be anonymous. Someone puts up a page with a name like, "Elizabeth Grace is an Alien," and people chime in with their commentary. I am not sure whether it would be worse for the targets if it were anonymous or if the writers were named and identifiable. I came off relatively unscathed in the slam book; the best they could do was "aloof" and "kind of a weirdo," but people they knew better had very, very cruel pages. I could not possibly understand why people did this to one another when I had just come from a culture where your friends just tried to get you on the Baseball team and if they were mad at you they told you why and offered to rearrange your face and then you said maybe I'll rearrange yours instead and anyway I'm sorry because I didn't mean to tick you off it was by accident then they said OK fine then want to come to my house later and play catch? However:

If you ask the type of kids who organize slam books why they do it, and you are a kid, they get very angry and do not provide a real answer or stop doing it. If you are an adult, you may get a different kind of data, and luckily I have a doc student who is planning on working on this question, as we speak. But then we got going home and things were back to the magic rhythms of the bus. The long bus is different from the short bus. I wonder today if the bus rides were also pretty much the best parts of the school day for the other kids on there. They may well have been. It was excellent on there, and full of music.

The next year, still on the bus, we had a very wonderful teacher for a moment, who taught us Western Civ and How to Do Outlines, but something happened to make her leave and I'll not name her in case she doesn't wish to be Googled. But I always think good thoughts about her when thinking good thoughts about great teachers, and wonder what she did instead, and hope she got to be happy, because she was a seriously good and excellent person. Meanwhile, I found out you were not supposed to be friends with boys there, but I also found out the good news that we were going to go into Middle School the following year and my old schoolmates, who didn't have that stricture, would be in the same middle school as us.

But then: disaster. I went to middle school and learned the shocking truth: even my old friends had the newfound belief that girls were not supposed to be friends with boys. So I successfully asked to skip a grade, moving from seventh to eighth in the middle of the same year. I needed to get out of there in just the one year, being so confused and unhappy. Only the Librarian, Mrs. Marshall, cautioned that for someone who had a hard time socially, it might not be such a great idea developmentally to miss a year. At the time, I felt terribly betrayed. I had thought she was on my side, one of the few I could trust: the Librarian! Now I see that in fact she was on my side, thinking of my well-being. Mrs. Marshall, I'm sorry I stopped looking at you.

When I transferred to eighth grade mid-year, there were these three beautiful, glamorous girls that were the absolute queens of the middle school—from a third school that was neither of the ones I'd been to—and they randomly invited me to be their friend. I will never know why, but it was very flattering. They were also not kind to people and I asked them about it and they laughed and said I was such a funny little moron. It is not as if I didn't know this was insulting; I just craved friendship and did not know my way around it. I believed it was necessary to nod and smile at such things. This was a bit of a painful time. (Strangely, they did not dump me as a friend despite the fact that I continued to blithely piss them off with accidentally annoying questions, etc., while then they would tell me how hilarious it was that I was such a dumbass, but yet we would talk on the phone a lot. It was just our discourse. In high school I would later find that people will totally dump you for being weird, even if you are not particularly pissing them off with the weirdness.)

The "cutest boy" that everyone objectified and wanted to have as a "boyfriend" was actually a really nice guy named Darren and we found a way to be able to hang out by supposedly "going together" and ended up accidentally winning this big school dance contest. He let me have the

Loverboy LP that we won where you see a red leather clad butt with fingers crossed right there on that butt and we decided not to risk kissing because he had square braces and I had the round kind: tangle risk high. Super cool guy, very logical, and he was really good at tennis, like he could go pro someday, and also I never saw him be mean to anyone. In addition to that he had this long sleeve shirt that said Sex Wax written on it really big which was seriously cool because he was not Punk Rock or anything, or not that people could openly tell, when secretly he kind of was.

So actually pretty much I chose which high school to go to because Darren was going there. My parents may not know this. But he was the nicest to me out of any of the kids after the Baseball ended. Though that first high school place was difficult for me and I did manage to get myself kicked out, it did kind of change my life, because I met Jennifer there. Jennifer is my best friend. She is real and tells the truth. To be able to do that on the level that Jennifer does it is actually really kind of rare in the world. And plus she's hilarious about it, so bonus.

So in high school as I said the social scene became ten times more difficult and all I could think about was music and what was wrong in the world. I did get friends for a while but when they said things like, "You're too intense so we can't hang" I would try to say a cool, "OK," but would secretly be all shredded and I had a lot of trouble actually going in the door, making myself do it. This became worse when, the second year, I found they had coated the windows with something that made the view of the outside all browned and distorted and wrong. Jennifer randomly came up to me one day and proclaimed that she had been seeing me around and decided I was cool and we should be friends. I had been bracing to say the allegedly-cool, "OK," of course, but I must have said some kind of cheesy-grin "OK" instead because she surprised me by having such a friendly message. And also because she really does proclaim instead of just saying, which is a magnificent feature of Jennifer. You do not have to wonder to yourself what she said, because she announced it clearly with no subtext just like she meant it. Jennifer rocks. So then she said, did I want to go to Eurhythmics with her. Yes! We went, had a blast, hung around together a lot, and even went to each other's weddings in later years. Jennifer is among the greatest people in the world, and has a way of saying "bewilder" that is onomatopoeic. Ace. Remind me to get her to read this part.

Before the aforementioned truancy got me kicked out (I still think that kicking a kid out of school for having truancy issues is kind of silly... like paying bank robbers a lot of money... but OK...) I think I may have been somewhat difficult, so that is why I am very kind to teachers today, to pay it forward, karmically. It did not really occur to me that teachers were people trying hard, but more what I was thinking was that they were cogs in a rotten system. Like the 'honors' teacher who let me peel the brown stuff off the window so I could see outside, gaining my trust—he also (OK, correctly) assumed I was the one who did the permission slips so we could protest the nuclear weapons triggers being made at this place down the street and then turned us in after we were not in class when he failed to give us the OK to go to the protest. But we had asked him up front if we could engage in the civil disobedience he had us read about, and write positive essays on, and it just really looks like he was acting more like a cog in a rotten system than a man of honor right there, even with my older, wiser eyes of today—though I am more sympathetic, and I do know he is a person, so... An example of the things I did that I see might have been hard to deal with, now that I know teachers personally: in order to add drama and flair to a paper decrying the hypocrisy of schooling and what we are not taught, I went into graphic detail on some of the torture devices used in the Spanish Inquisition that basically bankrolled Ferdinand and Isabella's ability to sponsor Columbus as he "discovered America" using forcibly stolen "heretic" money. Nowadays, I can imagine that may have been a somewhat troubling read... And I also repeatedly freed the frogs, though that was never proven. (Oddly, nobody ever said, "Did you free the frogs?" or it would have been.)

When it started to be too difficult to enter the school after all of that, I would hang around at the riverfront a lot and watch the sun dappling on the water, sparkling on a sunny day or just lightly emphasizing the ripples if it were cloudier. That and the sounds—I love the sound there. There is another place further up called Forest Park where you can go, or you can wander for miles under the bridges that you walk by on the way. In those days there was amazing chalk art around there by the train station, but I don't know if it is still there. Walking around was good. Outside was good. Or there was a coffee house and a music store where they were kind to me and tried to keep me from running into danger I think. The coffee place let me hand-letter their menu boards and draw little pictures on the menus, and the music place let me play around on the instruments for ages. On very rainy days it was fun to randomly ride bus lines around. Sometimes I also hung around the big university. One fine day, Linus Pauling was speaking at that university, and I knew he was going to, so I had alerted some friends (when I became truant and political, I had gotten a lot of friends who didn't know me well. Jennifer explained to me later that I was now suddenly considered "super-cool" because I "obviously didn't give a shit") to skip with me and see him. "Dude, isn't that your Dad?" said a friend who knew me a bit more, the one who soon thought I was too intense. It was my Dad, sitting a few rows in front of us, to the left. But, like, shouldn't he have been at work? Years later he told me he was proud that if I was skipping school it was like that. He would be. When he came to this country he was accused of being an "anarchist leader." I am very, very proud to be the daughter of a man who was officially accused of being something that by definition makes no sense. I think it is really a good explanation for my essence. ;)

Upon my getting expelled, my parents got started getting me into this alternative school that was truly awesome. I think they were unhappy, chiefly because I had not told them what was going on with me, so they had been blindsided by the system announcing to them that I was finished. But I did not know how to explain it any better than "I can't go in there" and "there are no windows" at the time, so I did not try until it was too late. Today, my mother tells me she was heartbroken by how much of what I was and was not saying that she could actually understand and really feel, but do nothing about. So they pulled out all the stops again, like they did with Baseball, only this time they weren't assisted by a legal writ (because it was the eighties, so no categorical protections yet). They felt strongly that there was something wrong with letting me fall through the cracks and they still believed I had potential. Fortunately, this other school believed in their mission statement enough to be susceptible to my dad's no doubt precise (and intense) proclamations about it, despite having a long waiting list. I'm pretty sure by precise and intense I mean terribly guilt-trippy and tragic, because he wouldn't let my mother come with, in case it would traumatize her. Anyway, they got me in, after a drawn out process during which, to my delight, I was not in school at all. Heh.

But back to MLC, which was the name of the school. It was an alternative school based on Summerhill theories (my folks gave me that book at the time, probably so I could be somewhat theoretically predisposed not to think they were rotten-cogs; my parents are geniuses, by the way) and it was a public school, but very, very alternative. The other kids called it the

"Gifted Loser School." The teachers used their first names so that you both could tell and were forced to notice that they were people, and they made social contracts with you about what you were planning to do. They supported your ideas, helping you organize them and round them out so you could meet your academic goals. Whoa, dude—totally different culture. It started like this:

Gail, my new home-base (Baseball word: score one for them already) teacher there at MLC, which note, does not actually stand for Gifted Loser School, said, "How often do you think you can make it to school? Around eighty percent?" I think I probably said something like, "I'm really sorry about this, but I believe it's closer to the zero percent side; they sent you my files, right?" But I remember she looked at me with this crazy-earnest face going on that even I couldn't fail to interpret as crazy-earnest, and said: "I really think you can do better than that. I mean I have a feeling you really can. And I know you don't want to say you will, because then you really will, because of your integrity. And I bet this all can feel scary, all these changes." That was spooky. How did she know all that? That was no way in my files. So right then, and I remember this well, I had to look away from Gail's crazy-earnest psychic kindness and I looked around, and the windows were extremely large, with many smaller original glass refracting windowpanes in them—classic older school architecture, from a time when they needed many windows to make use of the ambient light—which by the way, Gail was doing, using no fluorescent overheads—and! Each window was covered in...no heinous vinyl crap of any sort or color! There were trees outside clearly visible and the grounds connected to a large park... I took a deep breath and told Gail something to the effect of my being willing to attempt eighty percent with the caveat that I did not have anywhere near her same faith in my abilities.

According to my mother, by the way, once I was enrolled in the school, despite the fact that it was difficult to get me in "because they had not yet met me" (yes, those are her words) they were absolutely delighted by everything about me, and really happy with their decision. As a research methodologist I have to point out that this is another viable lens or angle of vision that I have added in places in this account to triangulate my memories of the goings-on of days gone by: motherethnography. In motherethnography, for example, every person who was ever mean to the querent in any way was motivated by 1. Jealousy, 2. Frustration caused by hidden stalkerish unrequited affections, or most likely, 3. Both. This is because the children of the motherethnographer are the best people in the world in every way. However, my sons are the best babies in the world in every way despite the fact that I am not a motherethnographer but an autistethnographer in this instance. So, the portion of the foregoing explanation pertaining to the perfection of the practitioner's children in motherethnography is necessary, but not sufficient, to the exemplar conditions.

Anyway, I did end up going to school a lot because they organized it so a friend and I could work with the amazing Urban Studies professor from Portland State, Dr. Gerry Blake, may he rest in peace. He was so cool and supportive and real, and helped us research and create a small non-profit that was actually useful and needed in the area. The neighborhood the school was in had the highest concentration of senior citizens in Portland, many of whom lived in government-subsidized high-rises and also couldn't get out much so they ate cafeteria food and/or Meals-on-Wheels. Gerry (he told us to call him Gerry) helped Jill and me invent Project MAIN, which stood for Mobile Assistants in Nutrition. We, and a lot of our friends we were able to hire and train, shopped for the elders so they could have the fresh food they chose, or took them with us if they were able and just needed a hand. A very important facet of this was that we consistently each visited the same people so we got to know each other and build intergenerational bonds. We were based in the Neighborhood Center and Gerry made sure to tell me in front of all the social workers in the Center that the people I shopped for thought I had lovely manners, was a good listener, and brightened their day. This changed my life. I felt useful instead of hopeless and began to really want to be present, to see the logic in the idea that there could be some other reason for people to care whether I was there other than arbitrary totalitarian attendance-taking. I was also learning ways to respond to injustice other than roiling rage. This wasn't an immediate shift, but it was a great start. Because we had to write grants and budgets and do nutrition and we heard oral history… we got high school credit for this authentic project and I think that is legitimate and real. Last I heard the neighborhood center was keeping it up on a volunteer basis, a student project owing everything to the support of Gail and Gerry.

I have to say here, it was no special credit to me really that I was seen as a good listener. It was exciting to listen. These people I was shopping for were telling me first hand accounts of what the Great Depression, WWII and Beat eras were like, and could answer all sorts of questions about the history of Trains (because they were there! riding them!) without looking at me like the questions were dorky, and also knew details of what it was like when Flying was glamorous, and much, much more. So they deserve mass quantities of thanks, especially Juanita and Don. Thank you for helping to show me who I could be when I grew up.

I grew up. On the way I tried a lot of fun and interesting things like shoeshine and street florist and pub singer and barista before coming back to my track when another great teacher named Anne Rose, may she rest in peace, gave me a chance by hiring me into a non-profit adult special education job for which I was under-qualified academically and experientially, because she had a hunch that I was singularly willing to learn, and also she thought that my particular ability to relate to some of the people we were working with was a Good Thing. Her ability to: 1. notice that kind of detail despite my being on my best behavior for the job interview and 2. consider it a positive instead of a liability just really tells you a little bit about what kind of an amazing person Anne Rose was. As I worked through various agencies in that field and increasing levels of responsibility in which I was given a lot of professional training and taught how to do management and the like, Anne Rose pretty much watched over me as a friend and mentor and kept encouraging me to go to college, which I did not believe I would be able to accomplish because college was a type of school, and, well, you know. Think of the odds.

Finally I succumbed and went to college, the same college where I had seen Linus Pauling speak. While flailing around not even knowing how to sign up for courses, I managed to accidentally sign up for senior-level courses my very first term. Karen Carr of Ancient Greek History, and Byron Haines, may he rest in peace, of Philosophy, were patient about that, and walked me through how to be a successful college student instead of kicking me out of their classes. Byron and Don Moor convinced me to join the Philosophy major where I was very happy. This was when I decided I wanted to be a teacher, because other people wanted me to be in their study groups. College was excellent! It was not like school! Those two along with Larry Bowlden, another Philosophy professor, gave me the advice to get a minor in Acting, so I would be more comfortable being a professor in front of many people instead of just small groups. Theatre is another thing that changed my life. I will be writing more about this—watch for it. Theatre is powerful. They did everything they could to help me get into an excellent graduate school, including introducing me to the Dean of Arts and Sciences, Marvin Kaiser, and asking for his help. He also helped, especially by showing me how to be in advisory meetings and committees and fundraising parties, that sort of thing. Thanks to all of these great folks and their advice, I did get into an excellent graduate school.

I started with the intention of being a Philosophy professor but my heart wanted me to go back to working more directly in teaching and education as a profession while keeping philosophy as a beloved hobby, and the great Voula Tsouna noticed this and gave me that freedom for which I will always be grateful. George Singer, who is one of the finest people ever in special education, and seems always to be on the right-minded and kind-hearted side in any controversy, allowed me to switch majors at the doctoral level, which I gather is very unusual. Because of a project some friends and I were working on under his aegis, I had the opportunity to meet and work closely with the visionary Judith Green, and learned another thing that changed my life, and that is the ability to look at the world through the lens of ethnography, to see culture and social processes in a whole new way. During this period I also apprenticed with one of the most skilled, creative and effective teachers at any grade level anyone has ever met, and she taught me well to teach, and it was an absolute blast. Sabrina Tuyay, rest in peace, but not too much peace, because I think you'd rather raise a bit of a ruckus, and here's to you doing it your way!

Coupling the keenness of a well-trained interactional ethnographic gaze with the kind of ethical introspective imagination learned in theatre training, I have a great many tools for understanding now at my disposal. This autistethnography turned into a story of my greatest teachers, I think. Too right! So I will end my tale by repeating an early paragraph and telling you something else about it. Here is the paragraph I'm repeating:

> So I will tell you about my schooling, or some of it, in bits I can remember, highlights, things that stand out. Now I am an education researcher, and a teacher of other education researchers and teachers. Maybe the reader can make inferences.

I wonder what inferences the reader will make, but I want to add one more thing. Now that I have learned so much about how to learn, it is really true that I learn when I teach. I continue to have great teachers, and they are ironically called "pre-service teachers." I think this is an ironic name for them because they are already teaching me, and they are already teaching one another, and they are already teaching themselves and the children they come into contact with, amazing life lessons as well as academic lessons they do while enacting their curricular assignments. Especially as it pertains to the great things they teach me every day, speaking for my own self, since this is my opportunity to go on and on without being told to join On and On Anon: I would like to take this last sentence to energetically thank my "pre-service" teachers for their service.

Chapter 5

This Closet

Phil Smith

"We keep our true self (if there is such a thing) a secret and present to the world a plausible story." (Goodall, 2006, p. 189)

"There's no doubt about it, I was pretty crazy for a while there. I'm better now." (Varley, 1992, p. 471)

That's not true.
I mean, I was crazy.
But I'm not better now.
Different, maybe. But not better.
I'm still crazy (after all these—oh, never mind).
And I'm OK with that.
Lemme tell you about it.

*

This story is partly the story of a closet—
a real, not metaphoric, place to store clothing.
As I tell it, it is also the story of the metaphor
of my coming out of it
regarding parts of the story of my disability.
I tell only parts because the telling of the whole
is longer than this chapter will hold
and because a whole telling
involves writing the lives of others
that I believe I am bound to protect
(even though protecting some of them is not
what I want, what I need

given the ways that they've harmed me).
It is partial because I am partial—
not yet complete, not yet fully understood.

*

"I have discovered what I would have to call a soul, a part of myself I could never have imagined until one day, seven years ago, when hell came to pay me a surprise visit. It's a precious discovery. Almost every day I feel momentary flashes of hopelessness and wonder every time whether I am slipping. For a petrifying instant here and there, a lightning-quick flash, I want a car to run me over and I have to grit my teeth to stay on the sidewalk until the light turns green or I imagine how easily I might cut my wrists; or I taste hungrily the metal tip of a gun in my mouth; or I picture going to sleep and never waking up again. I hate those feelings, but I know that they have driven me to look deeper at life, to find and cling to reasons for living. I cannot find it in me to regret entirely the course my life has taken. Every day, I choose, sometimes gamely and sometimes against the moment's reason, to be alive. Is that not a rare joy?" (Solomon, 2001, p. 443)

*

This closet

> its in a beat-up old farmhouse, built about 1873, the
> barn long
>   since destroyed
>   (though I built a new one, then walked away from it)

doesn't have a door
hasn't since before I bought the place.
There's no light in the closet, either—
I put things in, or take things out, more by feel than by sight.
The floor is made of the same wide pine boards
with which the rest of the bedroom is floored.
I know this
because I'm sitting on it right now
cross-legged
in the dark.
Its always dark, always night
not just because I'm sitting in a closet without a light
but because night is mostly the time that I'm awake.

> Night is black.
> Black and bleak are different in two ways:

the letter e
and the letter c.
They are otherwise identical.
I'm sitting on the floor of this closet
in the dark
in the night
with my right ankle on top of my left thigh.
In my left hand is my pocket knife
the blade open.
I look at the knife –
though it is night and dark
there is a little light
from the moon coming in the window
on the other side of the bedroom
so I can see the knife –
I look at it, and, very carefully,
with as much precision as I can muster
I draw it across the skin on the side of my right ankle
just above the little knob of bone there.
The mark it makes is first a bit gray
and then reddens, and then leaks
the liquid I know will come.
The line on my skin is about an inch long.
I make one line.
And then another
parallel to it
about half an inch above.
That line reddens and leaks in the same way.
And then a third, above the other two.
It is a kind of I Ching hexagram
written in the blood of my body.
Perhaps if I knew its meaning
I could tell something of the future.
My future.
I look at the marks, watching them bleed.
I feel some small physical pain
but really, the sensation is   nothing.

Nothing at all.
Nothing
compared to the   deep and
                     abiding and
                     terrible blackness of soul and heart
that engulfs my entire body
that has blossomed like some   internal
                               unseen
                               viral monster
come to eat up and suck out all meaning and
                                 life and
                                 sensation except: darkness.
Blackness.
Bleakness.
Indescribable terror and horrible, horrible soul-pain.

*

I'm crazy.
More specifically, I'm batty. Deranged. Gone around the bend.
Berserk. Loonie. Dotty. Mental. Lunatic.
Cracked up. Insane. Psycho.
Bonkers. Fallen off the deep end. Raving. Daft.
Loco. Demented. Touched.
Nuts. Disturbed. Loopy.
Lost his marbles. Screwy. Unhinged.
Whacked.
Completely and totally bugjob.
Mad, so the saying goes, as a hatter.

*

The first time I went to jail
because of this pain
I sat in the back of a police cruiser
handcuffs wrapped too-tightly around my wrists
holding my arms behind me against the backseat
on an otherwise wonderful, blue and sunny, mid-summer day.
The car raced across half the width of the state

in just a few short minutes.
The officer listened to country music,
talked on his cell phone, and
ignored the police radio.
They looked in all the holes of my body
took away my belt, my shoelaces.
In a holding cell, I sat on a stainless steel bench
watching a black man sleep
on another bench on the far wall.
After six hours, someone brought cash for bail
and I left.
The black man continued to sleep.

*

You can look me and my silly little symptoms up in the DSM *IV (TR)*.
That's the *Diagnostic and Statistical Manual of Mental Disorders Fourth Edition (Text Revision)* to you, sport.
My symptoms make up a diagnosis, a label, a thing to be called.
The thing has a number:
296.3.
Major Depression Recurrent.
Recurrent means it happens over and over.
Here's what it says:

"A. Five (or more) of the following symptoms have been present during the same 2-week period and represent a change from previous functioning; at least one of the symptoms is either (1) depressed mood or (2) loss of interest or pleasure...
(1) depressed mood most of the day, nearly every day, as indicated by either subjective report (e.g., feels sad or empty) or observation made by others (e.g., appears tearful)...
(2) markedly diminished interest or pleasure in all, or almost all, activities most of the day, nearly every day (as indicated by either subjective account or observation made by others)
(3) significant weight loss when not dieting or weight gain (e.g., a change of more than 5% of body weight in a month), or decrease or increase in appetite nearly every day.
(4) insomnia or hypersomnia nearly every day
(5) psychomotor agitation or retardation nearly every day (observable by others, not merely subjective feelings of restlessness or being slowed down)
(6) fatigue or loss of energy nearly every day

(7) feelings of worthlessness or excessive or inappropriate guilt (which may be delusional) nearly every day (not merely self-reproach or guilt about being sick)

(8) diminished ability to think or concentrate, or indecisiveness, nearly every day (either by subjective account or as observed by others)

(9) recurrent thoughts of death (not just fear of dying), recurrent suicidal ideation without a specific plan, or a suicide attempt or a specific plan for committing suicide...

C. The symptoms cause clinically significant distress or impairment in social, occupational, or other important areas of functioning...

Recurrent

A. Presence of two or more Major Depressive Episodes.

Note: To be considered separate episodes, there must be an interval of at least 2 consecutive months in which criteria are not met for a Major Depressive Episode..."

*

I was eighteen the first time I tried to kill myself.

I took some pills.

Looking back on it, I didn't put everything I had into it.

Kind of half-hearted.

I remember talking on the telephone in my parent's bedroom.

I felt quiet, calm. Relaxed.

I remember thinking to myself: Finally. It's done.

I can take THAT off the list of things I need to do.

*

I shopped for a therapist.

I didn't know what a good one looked like.

But I knew it when they weren't good.

One psychologist diagnosed me with this.

Another claimed I had that.

This therapist said I should do these.

That therapist said I should do those.

I finally met one who made sense to me

(although the psychiatrist I went to

said she made no sense at all).

A social worker, we met in her living room

every week for a year

she in one corner, me in another.

A big soft red easy chair

with a floor lamp and low shelf of books nearby.
After months of talking
I asked her what I should do.
She said, "You already know what to do."
She was right
and I knew it—knew it before I asked the question—
knew it before she answered it—
though I didn't want to admit it
didn't want to do it
was afraid to—terrified that if I did
there would be nothing else.
Afraid to admit the mistake I had made two years before.
When finally there was no choice—
me kneeling on the wide pine floor boards of the long, narrow kitchen,
sobbing—
when there were no other options—
I did what had to be done, should have never needed to be done.
Later, when she asked me, "Why did you do it?"
I asked her back, "What other choice did I have?"

*

Is the label who I am?
Is that my identity?
Are the things they call symptoms—
are those the meaning of my life?
If they aren't, where do I draw the line
(like the knife, on the skin
above my ankle)
between who I think I am as a person
and the words they use to describe me
(the words that make me not a person
but a thing, an object, an it)?
Is the thing that they make me be
by the words they use to describe me—
is that the true me?
Is the me that I think I am—
is that just another symptom

another manifestation of my sickness, my disease?

*

My psychiatrist's office is on the second floor
of an old and handsome Victorian house
on upper Main Street. Pale yellow, with white trim.
Inside are wood floors, varnished wood trim, high ceilings.
There is no waiting room
just chairs and a table at one end of the hall
near a window that looks out over the street.
I never know if I'm supposed to wait there before going into his office.
I always do.
He always comes out and calls me in.
He doesn't have a secretary.
He calls me in and asks me about the drugs he has prescribed.
That's what psychiatrists do, now, is prescribe drugs.
He has thick white hair, and glasses, is clean-shaven.
He is calm and quiet while he asks me about the drugs.
The first time, he gave me free samples
like the grocer who used to give me candy
when my mother and I went shopping.
He asks me about the drugs and then it starts.
The therapy. The part where he uses words to make me—
better.
He shouts at me.
Really, shouting.
He yells.
He's enraged.
Very, very angry.
At me.
His face is red. His eyes, glaring. His mouth is pinched. He sweats.
He puts his face close to mine and screams at me.
Startled, I pull my head back.
Can people in other offices in the building hear this?
I remember thinking:
is this what therapy with psychiatrists is supposed to be like?

*

Le Guin (1991) talks about being afraid "to lie down and fall black" (p. 69).
And that to think about the black makes it come.
The thing I remember most about the bad times
is the darkness.
It was everywhere, in everything.
It is everywhere, in everything.
Waiting. To come out. To take over, engulf.
Not a fog, or miasma.
Instead, it is a taking away of lumination.
Its not just that there was—is—no light; it was—is—a literal, physical
presence.
An object you could pick up. A metaphor.
Everything that occurred, happened at night. There was no day.
In the bad times,
even when there is day, there is only the darkness.

*

The second time I went to jail
I rode in a van, handcuffs attached to a leather belt around my waist.
They took me in front of my daughter
who cried out when they said
why they had come.
The cell was four feet by six feet
three walls concrete, one wall bars
that opened up to face another concrete wall.
Along one side was a metal bed, a foam mattress covered with plastic.
At one end was a toilet: a hole in the concrete floor
with a roll of paper next to it.
I lay on the bed all night
listening to someone yelling,
another vomiting.
Breakfast was two pieces of toast soggy with butter
and a single cup of bad coffee.
Mid-morning, a man (I had known him in another life)
came and asked me some questions, and went away.

*

The darkness came when I was 14, one night.
An animal arrived—not my fault.
I remember circling the house
walking in the grass, over and over
head up towards the stars, looking south
facing Blackman's Hill
and then north, towards Tanner's Pond
howling, silently.
No sound.

*

Gravity sucks.
It pulls my body down
relentlessly, ruthlessly, mercilessly.
Gravity is made entirely of extraordinary sadness
and its job is to ensure that I do not get up
do not ever rise.
It is an invisible force that grabs my neck
and pushes my body down to the ground.
It makes me sleep for 14 hours, 16 hours
at a time.
It makes me give up eating.
It makes me give up thinking.
It makes me give up feeling.
Gravity wants me laid out,
spread-eagled, pinned down.
It lets me up to put on a little show
of what it means to be a person
a few moments every day
for the women, for the children
for the neighbors and the bosses and the colleagues
so that I (and so that they)
can pretend that everything is alright
can pretend that everything will be OK.
And then the show is over.
Making breakfast or doing laundry

or going shopping or
simply
smiling.
The show is over and I can go
back to doing what gravity wants.

                    *

The darkness came next
the time when I lived in a barn.
And then again
when I lived in the log cabin.
No one knew. I kept it hidden.
It seemed important to keep it hidden.
Even from myself.
Really, I didn't know it was there
until much later—many years later
and only realized it, looking back
seeing it again with fresh eyes
recognizing the signs.
Yes. I see it now. Yes.

                    *

I went back to the psychiatrist.
Really, you ask? Why would you do such a thing?
I decided that I didn't want to take the drugs anymore.
It wasn't just that they weren't doing any good.
It was also because they were doing active harm.
Causing other, um, symptoms. And I knew
that if I tried to get off of them
on my own
without a plan to slowly get off of them
doing that would make it all worse.
So I went to him, and asked him to help me get off of them.
He looked at me.
He got up, said, "I'll be back," and left.
I waited. He was gone
a long time. I didn't know why. I don't know now.

He finally came back, sat down. Didn't look at me.
"You shouldn't stop taking them," he said. "You shouldn't come
back, anymore, either. I can't help you. There's nothing I can do for you."
I waited.
Silence. He didn't say anything more. Shuffled and wrote on some papers.
I got up and walked out.

> (I went to my general practitioner, and asked for help to
> set up a plan to get me off the drugs. He looked in some books,
> wrote some prescriptions, told me how long to stay on what drugs,
> at what strength, how to slowly reduce the amounts, told me
> to call him if I had any problems. It worked. I haven't taken
> them for 9 years.)

*

I worked once for a state bureaucracy
in a couple of different roles
out of a couple of different offices in a state complex.
The complex consisted of a set of large brick buildings
built around the turn of the twentieth century
the state hospital for people said to have psychiatric disabilities.
The buildings were connected with each other
by a fairly complex system of underground tunnels
so it was possible to travel throughout the complex
without going above ground.
Off of several of these tunnels were a set of locked rooms
which at the time I worked there were used for storage.

One of the offices I worked out of
was on the third floor of the building.
The office suite was one wing of that floor
and consisted of two long hallways
at right angles to each other.
The hallways intersected at a large room
(then used as a collective work room)
off of which was a sun porch
enclosed on three sides with large windows.
The porch was used, when I worked there, as a meeting space.

My own office was about 6 feet wide
and ten feet long.
It had a single window at one end.
At the other end was a metal door
with a six-inch by six-inch window in it.
The walls were concrete block.

As I worked there
I began to realize
that it was likely that the space I called an office
 was the living space for someone
 possibly for many years
when it was part of the mental hospital.
 This person would have spent most days
on the sun porch, or the large room
 which was probably what was then called a day room.

I came to understand
 that the side rooms off of the tunnels connecting the buildings
were places where particularly violent
so-called patients
lived.
They would have been completely out of sight
of most visitors to the complex.

At one corner of the complex
was the last remaining portion of what was
even when I worked there
the State Mental Hospital.
It was completely surrounded by high fences
topped with razor wire.
There was only one door
through which someone could enter the facility.
It was publicly described as a place
for people alleged to have committed crimes
to undergo so-called forensic psychiatric evaluations

and that these evaluations typically required people
to live there for no more than 30 days or so.
I came to understand, however
that there were a number of people living in the facility
who had been living there for many decades
and about whom it was said by long-term politicos
in the state bureaucracy
that they would never leave the facility alive.

As I worked in the complex
I began to realize that in another time
the space that I used as an office
might have been my home.
Given the story that I've told here
in some ways its a kind of miracle
that I managed to stay outside the razor-wired walls
of the so-called hospital.

*

How much of this is real
I wonder?
How much have I made up?
How much is fiction, how much is fact?
How much have I kept hidden to protect myself?
How much have I kept hidden from myself?
How much can I tell, and still be safe?
Who can I tell, and still be safe?

*

I have spoken as if it was all in the past tense.
As if it was something that was already done, finished.
Complete.
Over with.
That, of course, is not true.
It is always here, always becoming, always present.
It never goes away.
It doesn't know how.

And I wouldn't know what to do without it.
I don't know what to do without it.

References

Goodall, H. (2006). *A need to know: The clandestine history of a CIA family.* Walnut Creek, CA: Left Coast Press.

Le Guin, U. (1991). *Searoad: Chronicles of Klatsand.* New York: Harper Collins Publishers.

Solomon, A. (2001). *The noonday demon: An atlas of depression.* New York: Scribner.

Varley, J. (1992). *Steel beach.* New York: G.P. Putnam's Sons.

Section 3

Living Alongside Disability—
Stories From Family Members

Chapter 6

I Am Not of This World, and Yet I Am in It: A Daughter's/ Disability-Studies-in-Education Alien's Log of a Journey Through Hell

Alicia A. Broderick

I am having issues with figure/ground. There is only profound alienation the likes of which I have never before experienced—and I had previously considered myself intimately familiar with alienation. I am the black sheep, the leftist, atheist daughter who somehow was spawned of this conservative, Catholic family. I am the outlier, the outsider, the prodigal, the alien. It is my role within the family, and it is familiar, if not yet welcome or comfortable, to me. I am not myself here; within this cultural geographic space I exist only as the caricature they believe me to be. Which is to say that I do not exist. I read the paper, see the billboards, watch the television, find it surreal, dislocated, ethereal, imaginary. I am surrounded by Fox News, country music, casual racism and homophobia, and more references to god and guns every day than I would ordinarily encounter in a week or a month. I am not of this world, and yet I am in it, invisible, alienated, nonexistent. The ICU adds an additional layer of alienation to this experience. I am already alien outside the hospital doors; that alienation exponentially increases inside them. Reality is shifting, elusive, unstable. And hostile to my very existence.

You see, I am a disability studies scholar. A what? That doesn't exist here. It causes me to see, hear, experience most of what happens to me with an additional layer of horror that most of the people around me are oblivious to, do not perceive, cannot imagine. It makes me—here, now—confused, crazy, paranoid, unreasonable. Dangerous. I find myself compulsively reflecting upon my own identification with two different fictional characters—and I am torn as to which is the stronger identity. The first is that character in *The Stepford Wives*—the last person to realize that everyone and everything around her had already been appropriated, assimilated, consumed, and reconstituted as, quite literally, alien. I feel the need to hide my identity, "pass" as a member of this world, lest they come for me. There is a sense of predation—I must hide my difference, my identity; I will be hunted down soon enough as it is. The other character is Ophelia. She is raging within me, and I must consciously, purposefully, with deliberative and Herculean effort squelch her, keep her at bay, silence her. I have always found Ophelia's character to be something of a caricature—self-indulgent, a hyperbolic dramatic affectation that never quite worked for me. I considered her one of the weaker characters in the canon. I was wrong. She has become terrifyingly real to me—she is not insane, disconnected from reality. She is the only character that is honest, real, authentic, connected to the cruel reality that she is living. That I am living. Embracing my "inner Ophelia" is tempting—it offers a way out of the alienation, a way of being present, honest, true, real. A means of existing. Yet I am torn—to embrace my own existence is simultaneously to be regarded, and therefore discounted, by everyone else as crazy, insane, damaged, ill. Dramatically there is nothing to be done with such a character but to kill her off. Which is not a narrative resolution I am open to embracing—yet. But to embrace the Stepford narrative of maintaining sanity in the face of insanity, self in the face of alienation, existence in the face of predation is also to lie, hide, mislead, misrepresent, pretend—not only to others but also to myself. It is a classic existential figure/ground quandary—what is the relationship of self to reality? How to balance the tension between existence and alienation? Am I crazy? Do I exist? Do I still want to?

*

I am on a different planet. In a different universe. My relationships with space and with time have been radically altered. I am in the cardiac intensive care unit. Time here passes so differently. I have been here only 4 days (and nights), but I feel as though it has been months since I left my other life. My ordinary life. My life on the outside. My world has simultaneously, radically, both expanded and shrunk. I have lived lifetimes in some hours as they've passed, with the worst minutes and hours stretching into their own horrible eternities. Those moments still exist, because I still inhabit them, irrevocably etched as they are into my brain. They are, in this sense, interminable. My world has also diminished spatially—there is only what happens within these walls; nothing outside is relevant, or meaningful, or real. The world outside has ceased to exist, except for incomprehensible glimpses I continue to be assaulted with from time to time. I go to the cafeteria twice a day, for coffee, cream of wheat, an apple. When I leave the building, I see people laughing, hear them talking about trivial things, see them engaged in meaningless activity, and I stare uncomprehendingly at them. How can they possibly think that what they're doing or talking about matters? Is important? Is even real? I find them alien, incomprehensible. I also hate them. I listen to several of the doctors chatting at the desk. They spend 10 minutes talking loudly and nonsensically about what brand of snowblower is best, where it is on sale. They are animated and laughing, and discuss the topic in prolonged, inane, meaningless detail. One of them finally leaves this ridiculous conversation, comes to the door, spends 60 seconds with me, gives me the standard script—that things are more or less the same—then smiles patronizingly, "god blesses me, and says that he will talk with me again tomorrow. He leaves. I hate him. I know it is unfair of me. I do not care.

I send insensitive text messages to those I love most: "Surgery. Heart attack. ICU. Congestive heart failure. Ventilator. Kidney failure. Dialysis. I am in hell. I think I am dying. Please do not call." "You look so exhausted," people say. "I'm fine," I say. "I'm going to die," I think to myself. People seem disturbed by me. I watch their brows knit with worry and apprehension as they look at me. "Are you getting enough sleep?" they ask. I assure them that I am. I do not tell them that my sleep is riddled with nightmares. It offers me no respite, no escape, no rest. "Have you had enough to eat?" they ask. "I eat something every day," I assure them. I do not tell them that my weight is dropping like a stone. Nor do I care. They think that I'm tired, hungry. I catch a glimpse of my own face in the bathroom mirror, and I understand why they recoil—it is not the dark circles under my eyes; it is not the puffy redness from the perpetual tears that run down my cheeks. I look into my own eyes and I see that they are vacant. There is an absence there that is difficult to describe, and apparently difficult for others to witness. The surgeon is more blunt than most: "My god, you look like hell," he says. "As I should," I say. "Where do you think I am?" To my husband, who is worried about me driving in this state he interprets as exhaustion, I say, "This is *not* lack of sleep." To myself I admit, "This is despair."

I am not given to magical thinking. I have never been superstitious, give no credence to horoscopes or karma or fate or deities. Nevertheless, I find that I cannot leave this place for longer than the couple of hours twice a day that I must leave to go home to care for my mother. I have slept on a bench in the hallway for the past 6 nights now. I believe that if I leave, he will die, and I do not want him to die alone. I know that this is irrational, but I don't care. The last time I left ("go home, get some sleep, everything's fine here"), I received a call early the next morning on my cell phone from the surgeon. I have come to live in mortal fear of the phone ringing when I am away from the hospital. "Your dad has had a massive heart attack. We have moved him to the cardiac ICU. How soon can you get here?" I call my 89-year-old grandmother, beg her to come and take care of my mom—get her up, dress her, feed her breakfast, give her her medicine. And I drive like a bat out of hell back to the hospital.

Dad tried to send me home again that first night in the ICU. He got agitated, kept taking his oxygen mask off to tell me to go home, causing alarms to go off every time he did so because his blood oxygen levels dropped to dangerously low levels. I left at midnight, telling him I was going to go to sleep. He quieted down, left his mask alone, went to sleep. I left the ward and wandered around the hallways for a couple of hours. I finally lay down on a bench in the hallway, just outside the ICU, at 2:30, exhausted. A woman came and lay a blanket over me at some point. I did not see who she was, but I was grateful to her for her kindness. They woke me at 4:30, saying I should come. "He's not able to get enough oxygen to survive; he needs to be put on a ventilator." I can't yet write about that hour. But I can say that he was not alone. And this is why I do not go home at night. My sleeping on the bench has become akin to carrying an umbrella on a cloudy day to ward off the rain. It is my talisman. And he is still alive.

My family knows very little of what has gone on here in the ICU. I cannot begin to tell them about these experiences. There is not time in the day. I have not a single ounce of energy to waste in explaining. Retelling leaves me with two options—reliving these experiences, which I simply cannot bear to do, or becoming desensitized to them, which I also cannot bear to do. I say very little. These experiences do not exist for the rest of my family, unless I make them exist by telling them. It seems kinder not to drag them into this reality, any more than they already have to be. I have slept on a bench in a hallway for the past 4 nights. Two people died in the ICU last night. I watched a woman collapse in the hallway, her body wracked with sobs, her family flocking around her. I quickly realized that she is on yet another planet from me, though she is only halfway down the hall—we are each here on our own isolated planets. There is nothing I can do to ease her pain. I lie back down on my bench and close my eyes. I spare a tear for her, but I reserve my sobs for my father. I am grateful it was not him tonight.

I go home at 11:00 each morning to get my mother out of bed. I gather the supplies I need, then paste a smile on my face as I enter her room with a "good morning" and begin the morning routine of changing, bathing, and dressing my mom, before getting her out of her bed for breakfast. Sometimes she remembers where I have been, and asks me how my dad is doing today. But only about half the time. The other half, she asks me where he is, why he isn't getting her up himself, why he hasn't come home from the office yet for lunch. One morning she was furious with him, telling me that he hadn't been home all night and that she was betting that he'd been out drinking with the guys, that there'd be hell to pay when he got home. "Remember, Mom? Dad's not here because he's in the hospital. Remember? He had the surgery? Because of all the bleeding he was having? They did surgery to stop the internal bleeding." "Oh, yeah," she says. "I forgot. So when are you bringing him home? Surgery should only take a week or so—is he coming home today?" "No, Mom, he's not. Remember? He had a heart attack after the surgery? He's in the intensive care unit. He's really sick, Mom. He can't come home today. They're giving him a lot of medicine and a lot of treatments right now to help him get stronger. I can't bring him home today." I'm trying, Mommy. I'm trying as hard as I can. Fast forward 10 hours. I have dressed her, fed her, given her her morning medications, set her up in her chair (with my husband's or brother's help—I can no longer lift her safely on my own) with her favorite country music video channel on. My grandmother or sister-in-law or husband have kept her company, made her dinner and fed her. It is time to put her back in bed. I walk in the door from another long day spent in the ICU. "Did you bring your dad home?" she asks. "No, Mom. I didn't. Not today. I'm sorry." "Why not?" she asks. I swallow the sobs until after she's in bed. Then, exhausted, I drive back to the hospital, where my father's hell awaits me. Again. Still. I'm sorry, Mommy. I'm trying so hard.

I think back to the horror of the first night. My dad had gone in to surgery early that afternoon. I sat in the waiting room all afternoon. My brother stopped in after work and sat with me for an hour or so, waiting for the surgeon to come. At long last he came, with cautiously optimistic news. He believes that he found and successfully removed the source of the bleeding in his bowel. Only time will tell if there were another source that he may have missed. He's just now waking up, and is experiencing some post-operative "discomfort." I can go up and see him in a few minutes if I want. It is late; my brother has to leave. He has children to feed, bathe. Homework of his own to do and homework of theirs to supervise. I tell him to go ahead and go. I will tell Dad he was there. Nothing could have prepared me for what I witnessed that night.

My dad is screaming, moaning, crying, begging. He has an 8-inch incision in his abdomen, plus several more inside, where portions of his bowel were resected and sewn back together. "Oh, god, oh, god, oh, god, oh, god—my belly! My belly! Oh, god, it hurts—oh, god, my belly!" He seems barely aware that I am there. He is aware of nothing but the acuity of his own pain—it is an all-consuming reality. The presence of pain diminishes—and even eradicates—the very existence of everything else. Where there is intense pain, there is nothing else. I am crying, begging the nurses to give him some more morphine. I am told condescendingly by an LPN that he is in discomfort, he is not in pain, because he has been given morphine. "How the fuck can you look at him and tell me that he is not in pain?" I scream at her.

There are 4 or 5 bodies bustling around the room, busying themselves with the bureaucratic tasks of a newly admitted patient. They are moving his limbs, adjusting his gown and his sheets, attaching electrodes to his body for a whole variety of monitoring devices to be hooked up. With every single touch, he grimaces, cries out, begs for them to stop. They are having difficulty with the leads for one of their machines—the battery in the device seems to have failed; it is not reading as it should. I watch as they try battery pack after battery pack, casually dropping each new pack and its attached bundle of wires on my father's abdomen. They also drop rolls of adhesive tape and scissors on his abdomen, as if it were an instrument table, as they blithely go about the business of performing their bureaucratic tasks, oblivious to his cries, his screams, his entreaties to please help him. They seem not only insensitive to, but somehow actually unaware of, his pain. Perhaps it is a coping mechanism; the only way that people can do this job, day in and day out. If they don't acknowledge it, it doesn't exist. Nevertheless, I find their oblivion violent, obscene. I hate them.

I cannot take this any longer. "Stop!" I cry, literally, tears coursing down my cheeks. "You're hurting him! His belly was just sliced open—can you give me one single, fucking reason why you need to keep dropping all of this crap directly on his incision as if it were a table? If you need a table, I'll go and find you a fucking table—just stop hurting him!" The RN looks annoyed with me, but apologizes and wordlessly moves her supplies from his abdomen to the mattress. There is still a bundle of 8-10 wires taped together lying directly over his incision. I wait. It stays there. I pick up the bundle and gently move it to his chest. He still flinches at the touch. "Please don't touch me!" he begs. The LPN grabs the bundle from me, and repositions it, considerably less gently than I had done. He flinches and cries out as she does so. "It's light as a feather, Dearie," she says to me, dripping with condescension. "He can't even feel it." She is completely unaware of the irony of her words, as she has utterly failed to note all deeply disturbing evidence to the contrary. I want nothing more in the world than to scratch her eyes out of her fucking head. I am exerting extraordinary amounts of effort and self-control in not physically assaulting her, and I watch in horror with fists clenched as she continues to assault my dad. After admonishing me, she has the audacity to turn to my dad, to speak loudly and condescendingly into his ear, "You're just fine, Dear! You've had plenty of morphine—it doesn't hurt that bad. You're just upsetting yourself and your daughter and you need to settle down!" My dad has the momentary presence of mind to spit out a stream of expletives at her. It is the first moment of relief I have experienced. He's still there.

I ask that he be given more painkilling medication. I am told that they have given him all that they can give him and that any more would require a new physician's order. They seem to expect that this will be the end of the story. "Fine," I say. "Get the order. How long will that take?" The request is submitted. I am told that it will take 15 minutes for the order to come in before they can put him on a morphine drip with a switch that he can control. They then tell him that they have to roll him over to do a skin check of his back side. "No!" he screams. "Don't roll me over! Please! Don't touch me!

Don't touch me!" "We have to do our initial skin check, then we need to roll you over every two hours so you don't get bedsores—you don't want to get bedsores, do you?" the monster asks with condescension. "I'm not going to get a goddamn bedsore in the next 6 hours—just let me be for 6 hours, just 6 hours, please, please, please, don't touch me!" he begs. This time the torturer is an RN. "Do I have to go and get the pictures?" she asks. "Do you want to see what a bedsore looks like? Do you want to see what will happen to you if you don't let us roll you over?" I explode again. I tell her that he's been single-handedly taking care of my bedridden (yes, I said "bedridden"—I was pissed) mother for over 20 years and he knows a thing or two about skin care and that she's never once in 20 years developed a bedsore under his care (though she did develop one during a week spent in a hospital). I tell her that he's making an exceptionally well-informed decision and that he doesn't need to be coerced by her going to get the pictures. Besides, I say, even if he had consented to the check (which he had not), was there some logical or rational reason why she would be attempting to immediately move a patient who was clearly in considerable pain, rather than waiting the 10 minutes or so until the patient could be made more comfortable with the supplementary morphine order that was expected momentarily? Other than needing to fill in a bureaucratic box on her bureaucratic form and get to the next room in order to get her fucking rounds done 15 minutes earlier?

She changes tactics. She expresses her concern over how difficult this must be for me. It's so difficult for family members to see someone that they love in pain, particularly if you've not spent much time around sick or injured people before. She flags down a colleague of hers, and asks him to get me a cup of coffee. To play good cop to her bad cop. He is the only male RN on shift (perhaps she thought that would help), and I am gently led away to the coffee machine in the family waiting area. He is kind, and gives me tissues and coffee, and asks me if I want to talk about it. I am aware that I am being manipulated, but find it difficult to say so without sounding like a paranoid, and possibly delusional, person. I cannot even hold the coffee; my hand is shaking so badly that it spills out of the cup and onto the floor. "I'm going back," I say, turning to run, and I hear my father's screams from the hall as I near the room. The door opens as I approach, and the troupe of torturers leaves. A conspiratorial look of gratitude passes from the one who sent me away to the one who took me. I ask her if she'll be back after the morphine arrives, to see if he feels able to do the skin check at that time.

"No, never mind," she says. "We don't need to do it." I know that it was done during the three minutes I was whisked away—against his will, without his consent, and with his feckless daughter having naively been an instrument of his own torture. This was my first major failure of many horrible tests yet to come. And I failed them all.

I have here accounted for less than a half an hour of the first night after his surgery. It was fully five hours that night before his pain had diminished to a point where he was able to stop flinching, moaning, crying, begging for relief. I cannot bear to recount it all. I helplessly moistened his lips, wiped his brow, fed him slivers of ice, bore witness. There was nothing else I could do. My brothers, relatives seem to think that I am excessively suspicious of the medical staff. They find my critiques ungenerous, and point to all the reasons why I should be grateful to them—for all they've done for him but for which he would literally not have been alive. All of which is true. Yet my father is at their mercy, completely and utterly. His life is quite literally in their hands, a circumstance that exponentially increases the egregiousness of each small transgression. I am trying to conceptualize what has happened to me in bearing this witness as change, evolution, possibly even growth. But I cannot. I have experienced only violence, assault, trauma, and damage. I have been brought to my knees. And there I remain.

My crisis is, in part, epistemological. There is no certainty in the ICU, no clarity, no simplicity. Yet I am assaulted daily with epistemological reductionism, with people readily acknowledging that they don't know the answers to my questions, yet justifying decisions with a certainty presumed to be legitimated by the oft-cited numbers, levels, and tests. My father is on a ventilator. He has been on it for a week. During most of that week he has been sedated, for his own comfort. His breathing, his heart function have steadily improved during that time. The doctor says he will likely try extubating him today, so the sedation is removed, and my father finds himself conscious, uncomfortable, terrified, with a tube sticking down his throat, and his arms bound to his sides in restraint. His heart rate and respiratory rate immediately shoot up, his eyes dart back and forth, he struggles to free his arms. He looks terrified to me. I try to explain (because they do not) what is happening. They feel it is necessary for him to be conscious for some hours while on the ventilator before they will remove the tube. They frame it as if it were a privilege that he must somehow earn. The doctor comes in, looks at the numbers on the monitor, says to my father (loudly, condescendingly), "Slow your breathing down. Slow your breathing down! I'm not going to take the tube out until you slow your breathing down." And there will be no dessert until you've finished your vegetables, either. He stays for 30 seconds or so, looks exasperated, shakes his head at me, and leaves, saying, "It's got to be at 20, or we can't do it today." He refers to the number on the monitor that records his respiration rate. Except that's not actually what it does.

I try to calm my dad down—most of the speed of his breathing seems obviously, to me, to be related to his visible anxiety over the predicament in which he finds himself. His hands are twitching, his brow is sweating and deeply furrowed; I can see the terror in his eyes as he looks at me—"Oh, god, what have I done?" The surgery was risky and he took a gamble, bet everything he had on it, and appeared now to be losing. As the anxiety subsides a little, the numbers go down, but they go back up as he begins coughing from the discomfort of the tube in his throat. His mouth is dry, his lips and tongue cracked; I can't imagine how dry and uncomfortable and painful his throat and esophagus must be, and they have a plastic tube rubbing against them making it worse. He coughs uncontrollably. Each time he coughs, there are 6 or 8 or 10 quick little exhalations of air from the cough, and he coughs a couple of times each minute. The machine records each of these coughing exhalations as a breath, and the machine now says that his rate of respiration is 48-50 breaths per minute, sometimes higher. The doctor comes back in, glances quickly at the monitor, shakes his head and says (to me, not him, because a person who is incapable of speaking must also be incapable of being spoken to, apparently), "He's in respiratory distress—there's no way we're extubating him today. His respiratory rate needs to be at 20 or 22 before I'll consider it." He leaves without speaking to my dad. I tell my dad not to worry, to keep trying to take nice deep, slow breaths, and I'll talk with the doctor. I know that numbers are the only thing he understands, so I need to produce some.

Every time a doctor or nurse enters the room, the rate of his breathing rises; he is clearly anxious about what they are going to do to him, what is going to happen to him, will he have any control over it (the answers to which are "we don't know," "we don't know," and "no"). When he is calm, settled, when they have left him alone for a few minutes of peace, I quietly sit with a pencil and watch the clock on the wall. My hands are out of his line of sight; he does not know what I am doing. I am recording his breaths, and disregarding his coughs in the calculations. I do this for 20 minutes. Every single minute that I record, he takes somewhere between 19 and 22 breaths a minute. I go to find the doctor, tell him I need to speak with him in the room.

Surprisingly, he comes. I show him my numbers, explain to him that the number on the monitor (which still reads a "respiratory rate" in the 40s) is not giving him the information he seems to think it's giving him. He patronizingly explains to me how the machine calculates and records every single exhalation of breath, thus the number represents his respiratory rate. I point out to him that the assumption underlying the mechanism of the machine and his interpretation of the numbers is that an exhalation of air represents an exhalation of an inhaled breath; in this case, it does not. Because of the discomfort caused by the tube, my father is coughing uncontrollably several times a minute, thus inflating the "respiratory rate" by anything between 18-30 "breaths" a minute. I explained to him that I had calculated his patient's *actual* respiratory rate for 20 minutes by actually watching his patient breathe and documenting his breaths. I show him my scrap of paper. I tell him that if he can spare more than the 7 seconds he devotes to looking at the machine to actually look at his human patient and exercise his powers of clinical observation, he can decide for himself if he concurs with my observations or if he wants to believe the machine. Shockingly, he takes out his stethoscope and presses it to my father's chest, silently watching as his chest rises and falls. My dad coughs a couple of times. After about a minute and a half, the doctor looks up at me with a hint of a smile on his face. "You know, he's actually doing pretty good," he says. "His breaths are strong, there's very little fluid, the pace is good—it's just the coughing that's inflating the numbers." You don't say. Jackass. "I'd like to take him off," he says, taking the stethoscope out of his ears and putting it back around his neck. "What do you think?" What do I think? Really? You're actually asking a family member to participate in decision-making about my father's care? It's about fucking well time, I think to myself. "Yes, please," I say, a tear running down my cheek.

My crisis is not merely an epistemological one; it is ontological. He went from "being in respiratory distress" to "doing pretty well" with some involuntary coughing in a matter of minutes, solely because The Doctor discursively constituted him as such. It did not matter that my father was the same person during that time, experiencing the same inhalations and exhalations of breath. He was not "in pain," he was merely "in discomfort,"

because he had been given some morphine and The Nurse had declared it to
be so. Ergo, it was so. His reality is not fully constituted by his own
experience; to a considerable extent, it is constituted by the discourse of the
professionals around him.

And the professionals do not agree on the reality that he is living. There
are a dozen or more physicians involved in my dad's care—surgeons,
cardiologists, kidney specialists, an oncologist, "intensivists"—each of these
roles is occupied by one of 3 or 4 different people, depending upon the day
and their various practices' rotation schedules. Of course there will be
differences of opinion—sometimes striking—sometimes between people in
different roles; other times, between different partners playing ostensibly the
same role. But in this case, there emerged from the chaotic mix a yin and a
yang, a good and an evil, a savior and a nemesis. Anyone who has taken
Psych. 101 would probably tell you that I was "splitting," overly identifying
with one and overly demonizing the other, and they may be right. But this is
my experience, not theirs.

Some very dear family friends come to the hospital to visit. He is
unconscious—sleeping or sedated, it is difficult to say. "How is he?" they
ask me. "What do the doctors say?" "That depends on whom you choose to
believe," I say. The surgeon had been in that morning, telling me that he was
having a difficult time of it, and that the odds were certainly against him, but
that he still strongly believed that there was a realistic chance that my dad
would pull through, and that he would be able to go home eventually,
although he'd never again be able to take care of my mother. "This is up to
him," he said to me. "Don't you dare let him see you sitting here crying at
his bedside—you swallow those tears and look him straight in the eye and
tell him that he's doing well and that he's going home, he's just got to hang
in there and fight." And he gave me his word that he would tell me the
minute his opinion changed, if it did. He is my savior—not because he tells
me that my father might live, but because he knows my dad, understands
about my mom, knows who I am and who my brothers are, and he speaks to
us with complete candor and honesty. He does not condescend, he does not
have a bag of useless platitudes that he drags out for what seems like the
appropriate occasion. He speaks to me as though I am capable of
understanding what is happening and deserve to have all relevant
information, not as though I ought not to worry my pretty little head about
such complex details (as others do). And then there is The Other One.

The One That I Loathe. The one who still, after being in the ICU with my dad for two weeks, does not know that I am his daughter (does not know that he even has a daughter; this, despite the fact that I took the trouble to introduce myself to him after a week, since he never felt it necessary to introduce himself to me). I have never yet seen him set foot in my dad's room (and I am here 18-20 hours a day). He spends his days sitting in front of the computer at the desk—looking at charts, numbers, test results. Making decisions, writing orders, all based upon the information in the chart. Never looking at the patient, never talking to the patient, never talking to the patient's family. He is not treating people, nor even patients—he is treating bodies, collections of organ systems. Perhaps it is a necessary coping mechanism. I don't care. He is inhuman to me, because my father is inhuman to him.

After my dad came off the ventilator, I went to him, told him I had questions I'd like to discuss. He looked annoyed, impatient, yet put on his best (though still abysmal) bedside manner and asked me what my concerns were. My dad had been off the ventilator for 5 days, and still he was not speaking. He could reliably nod or shake his head for a yes or no, but the only words he spoke were "home" (over and over), and the occasional expletive when we told him he couldn't go home yet. "Were you even aware of any of this?" I ask him. "Have you even noticed? I don't see how you could have—it's not the kind of information that is transmitted through a wireless signal to your computer terminal, so I'm guessing that you have no idea what his cognition or language or neural status may be like." He admitted that no, he had not noticed the things I was pointing out, nor did he particularly care. At the moment, he cared about his heart, and his lungs, and his liver, and his kidney function. He told me that 9 out of 10 people whose bodies experienced what his had would already be dead by now (implication that he ought to be, too), and that if he were still alive in a month, he'd be happy to sit and talk with me about these issues, but it was premature to even concern ourselves with his higher brain functions since he was unlikely to survive. "I could drop another $1300 on him and do an MRI, and then I'd be able to tell you for certain if he's had a stroke or not, which is a possibility, but it wouldn't change anything—would that make you happy?"

Ableist though the metaphor may be, I now understand the term "blind rage," for I lost my vision to the rage that swept over me like a wave, engulfing me and leaving nothing in my sight but his cold eyes, floating in a sea of static, mocking me in my pain. Would that make me happy? Really? Drop *another* $1300 on him? So he had already cost too much money, and all for a life that was, in his opinion, not worth the investment that had already been made in it? Nine out of ten people had the good sense to just die and get it over with....and here was my dad, hanging on and fighting like hell and costing money and inconveniencing this beast with his daughter's concerns about trivial matters like neurology and personhood. Dripping with venomous, unrestrained hatred, I sarcastically thanked him for his compassion and stalked away, unable to see through my rage and my tears. I find out later, from the surgeon, that during this entire confrontation, he did not even know to whom he was speaking.

These are the two physicians I vacillate between most often on a day to day basis. The one wrings tiny seeds of hope out of the sea of despair that I am swimming in. It is only his hope that keeps me from jumping off the top of the nearest tall building. The other one mocks that hope with contempt and disdain, dousing it with buckets of utilitarian ethics and the cold calculus of a cost-benefit analysis that decrees my father's life not worth the effort and expense already taken to sustain it. So when they ask, "How is he doing? What do the doctors say?" I am momentarily speechless. They are playing ping-pong with my brain, except that it is racquetball and they are hitting my brain back and forth with considerable force and obscenity and violence. The most maddening part of this is that I suspect that the horrible, evil, inhuman one who calls himself a physician is correct, and that my father ultimately will not survive. When this suspicion of mine is finally borne out, I am tempted to go to him, say, "Well, you were right—does that make *you* happy?" I do not. I may be on my knees, but I will not stoop as low as him.

A nurse is absentmindedly making conversation with me. Some of them do that. Others respect my silent presence, and say nothing. This one is blathering on about how this (my father's present condition) is what he fears the most. "Diabetes and heart disease—that's a lethal combination," he says. "Heart attack, stroke—then you end up like this for who knows how long before you die, and you're probably going to die in the end anyway." Charming conversationalist. He goes on. "The only other thing worse than this would be MS. God, that's a horrible illness—just devastates the body and the brain. Yep, I think that's probably the worst thing in the world. I'd rather just die than go through that." I let it sit for a moment, then say, "My mother has MS." He tries first to sympathize, how horrible it must be, then finally turns to see my face. He backpedals, noticing finally that I am staring at him with cold contempt. I say no more. So neither of my parents' lives are worth living to him. I cannot argue that this is not horrifying, that my mother's life is not difficult. But you'd rather be dead? Fine by me. One less ableist bigot on the planet.

I find that I am implicitly expected over and over again to respect ableist bigotry as a "value" that someone holds and to accept a relativistic discourse on the matter—there are no right answers and no wrong answers, here, only what your dad would have wanted. A relative (who shares many of my dad's conservative political and religious beliefs) tells me that I need to respect his values for what they were, and that she knows that he valued independence so highly that he would rather die than be physically disabled. She is probably right, though I loathe the values myself. And yet I know that my dad shared that deeply ingrained devaluing of disabled existence as an existence not worth living. He cared for my mother faithfully for over 20 years, but he experienced her disability as burdensome and pitiful, and he no more wanted to live a life of dependence upon others than he wanted to compel someone else to be "burdened" by his care.

The necessary reach of disability studies goes far beyond education, far beyond cultural analysis and critique. I tried, over and over, and somewhat in vain, throughout this abysmal experience, to imagine what it might have been like if so many of the interactions and subtexts and so much of the explicit discourse had not been quite so deeply and un-self-consciously steeped in ableist bigotry. No one that I interacted with recognized this bigotry for the reality that I experienced it to be; almost all would have been shocked and deeply offended at the mere suggestion that they were bigoted in their thinking or assumptions. What might the world be like if everyone (or, hell, anyone) had experienced an education informed by critical disability studies frameworks? I am not of this world, and yet I am in it. If I must be constituted as an alien by the dominant culture, fine, so be it.

Let the alien insurrection begin.

Chapter 7

Listening: A Star Is Born!

Bernadette Macartney

Our first child Maggie Rose was born at home in a southerly storm. The wind howling outside the night she was born matched the intensity of what was going on inside our house—I had a sore throat for three days! Maggie's dad, Tony, and I had been living together for eight years before Maggie was born. We had lived this time in our small community by the sea. Our village had one of everything. One harbour, one mountain, one shop, church, early childhood education centre, school, library, community hall, rugby club, even a local bar... What we had in abundance were hills, beaches, friends, sheep, and horses!

Tony and I wrote a song for Maggie after she was born. We wanted to welcome her to our family and to promise a place where she could grow strong within our community. She had no disability labels when she was born—they came later. Tony and I invited our family, friends, and community to help welcome and celebrate our newborn Maggie. They gathered with us at home. We planted Maggie's placenta back into the earth under a Kowhai tree that blossoms yellow in the spring. We all sang the song Tony and I had written for her:

Maggie's Song
Underneath this little Kowhai tree
Growing strong by the sea
Welcome Maggie to your big family
Growing strong by the sea

Kei raro i te Kowhai nei
E tipu e rea kei te moana e

Naumai ki to whanaunui
Maggie Rose kia kaha e
Kia kaha e, kia kaha e!

   People brought gifts and wishes for Maggie and her life. We've kept
them in a special box for Maggie to open on her 21st birthday. We sat
together in our lounge and shared our dreams and wishes. Tony and I wished
for Maggie: *To grow up strong, feel good about yourself and have things in
your life that you feel passionate about...* It was a beautiful day for Maggie
and our whanau (extended family and community).

*

Maggie 5 months old, baby book:
"Maggie has been getting the giggles! She loves animal sounds and
impersonations, blowing raspberries, being read to, listening to music, hot
baths, fires, light playing through the trees and Tony playing his guitar. Her
cousin Jessie has taught her to kiss! She is so lovely and we can't imagine
life without her beautiful little presence..." (Mum)

*

One day some friends from the city came to visit our home. Maggie was
about 7 months old. We had all been early childhood teachers, and lecturers
in the University teacher education programme in the city. One of my friends
rang me later that day. She said she was worried about the slowness of
Maggie's development and what she wasn't able to do yet. I felt sick as she
spoke to me about taking her to see a pediatrician. I talked to Tony when he
got home and we decided to have Maggie 'assessed'. This was our first
introduction to medical views of disability as parents.

*

Maggie 8 months old, paediatrician's letter:
"Thank-you for referring Maggie who is delayed with her development and of
short stature as well...Maggie was a floppy baby and she was also jaundiced,
she was slow to suck and establish breast feeding which did not really get
going until she was 3—4 weeks old. After that weight gains have been steady
and have taken off recently with a marked increase in weight so that now

Maggie is quite obese. This is accentuated by her short limbs and short length. She needs further investigations..."

*

After Tony, Maggie and I left the paediatrician's office, we went to a favourite place in the country to stay for a few days and gather ourselves. The first morning that Tony and I woke, we went to see Maggie in her cot. She was awake and happy to see us. She was still Maggie, and we were still her doting mum and dad. She had not changed overnight and neither had we. This was an epiphany for Tony and I. It felt like what *had* changed was the rest of the world and how Maggie was now perceived and treated and might be in the future. For a few months we had tests and procedures at the hospital. We stopped these when we realised that Maggie wasn't unwell. Through the years our view of Maggie is regularly interrupted and resisted by teachers, therapists, and schools viewing her through deficit eyes. For us, there is so much to like and to love about Maggie. Everyone misses out when people are disrespected.

*

Maggie 2.5–6 yrs old, playcentre

Maggie and I attended our local early childhood centre three mornings a week from when she was two and a half. Her centre was a not-for-profit, parent co-operative. A paid and qualified teacher led groups of parents to develop the curriculum and work alongside the children at each session. I was the lead-teacher at the centre from when Maggie was three years old. My friend Mary was paid by an early intervention service to be Maggie's 'education support worker' at the centre. It felt easy working with Mary because she was also a teacher, friend, and parent at the centre. We shared our teaching and parenting roles inside and outside of the centre. Mary's three children all attended the centre alongside Maggie too. Maggie had an early intervention teacher and speech language therapist who visited the centre once a fortnight. Mary and I suggested that they came only if we needed them—their fortnightly visits interrupted Maggie's play and learning and our work in the centre. The end of that conversation was when they said that we wouldn't get funding for Mary if they couldn't come once a fortnight and that visiting was in their job description.

*

Maggie 4–5 yrs old, stories of learning and participation from Maggie's playcentre:

"First day back at Playcentre after the holidays today. Maggie said, "Can I help you make the playdough?" before we left home this morning! She enjoys tipping cups of flour and salt into the bowl as well as mixing it up. Jacob, Sarah, and one of the parents always make the dough too. We're learning the recipe off by heart! Maggie got into making prints in the dough with her chin, saying, "Maggie made a chin print!" laughing and giggling and then doing it again. The children are all into making prints in the dough at the moment—mainly hand and foot ones! Elliot made dough 'scones' and Maggie liked the sugar on top (flour)…" (Mum)

*

Elliot, Maggie, and I went outside, we walked over to the shingle pit, which is a favourite of Maggie's at the moment. Maggie enjoyed making a bell tower (we had just got back from a trip to Europe and there were a lot of bells over there!), sprinkling the stones and, of course, eating them. She asked to play Goldilocks and the three bears before morning tea, but we had left our run too late. Next time… (Mary)

*

Mary read 'Goldilocks' with Isaac and Maggie. Maggie likes holding the Duplo Goldilocks and following the story. She put Goldilocks in the places during the story (e.g. the big bed, the middle sized bed etc.). Isaac helped make the Duplo stairs for Goldilocks to climb up and down… (Mary)

*

We've been working on a production of Goldilocks and the Three Bears. Today we listened to the story on a tape Maggie brought from home—she had a Big smile when the story began and at the end she said "Thanks for doing Goldilocks and The Three Bears!"… (Mary)

*

Jasmine and Sasha were dressing up and Maggie and Mary walked over. Mary put a purple cape with gold trim on Maggie. Maggie looked in the mirror and said, "Goldilocks!" She stood looking at herself in the mirror and I asked her if she'd like to paint her face—she nodded yes. She nodded yes to being Goldilocks too. Later Maggie was searching through the dress-ups. She found the bear face t-shirts we have been sewing at the centre. Families bring old shirts in from home. The children are right into using and/or watching the sewing machine. She reached her arms up high for the Goldilocks puppet above her on the shelf and said, "Hello myself!"... (Mum)

*

Maggie 4 yrs old, Early Intervention teacher and speech language therapist recommendations for next fortnight:
(1)   Sequence play—dramatic play e.g. bathing dolls etc. using words like First, Then, Next, Last
(2a)   Activities at the kai (food) and collage tables. This will encourage interaction with one other child. Being at the tables means the children are at the same height therefore Maggie is equal
(2b)   Maggie initiating change of activity—clear the activity away and wait for Maggie to choose a new one...

*

Maggie 4 yrs, Mum's journal:
Maggie loves using her imagination and book world to express herself, make sense of the world and connect with her experiences and reality. She's into literature, music, playing with words and sounds. At the moment she's passionate about fairy tales, plays, books, music and drama concerts and performances, jazz music, especially Charlie Parker, poetry and rhyme, sand, sea and water... We have decided to wait until she's six to start school, it's going well at her centre, it feels better to keep her where she feels comfortable and is learning lots...

*

Starting school!
We're feeling really nervous about Maggie starting at our local school. At least she will know most of the children in her class. Almost all of the kids went to our local early childhood centre. Some of their little brothers and sisters are still there, including Sally, Maggie's little sister, and myself. We connect with centre families out and about in the community and at home all of the time. We have invited the new entrant classroom teacher, and school principal to a MAP (Making Action Plans, a person-centered planning strategy) meeting to help them get to know Maggie and share our dreams for her. We hope that having her school teacher and the principal there might help us all feel more

confident and prepared for her start at school. Their participation is very important to us in planning for Maggie's transition and her learning and sense of belonging there. We want to be involved with what happens for her there.

Maggie Rose, her friends and their parents, our extended family, Maggie's Education Support Workers, centre teachers, the early intervention people, school teacher, and principal were all there at the MAP meeting. We had the meeting at the centre because that's where we feel most comfortable. We also want the school to develop a closer relationship with the centre. So far they ring us annually to find out who's starting at school the next year and that's it.

Tony and I felt really positive about the MAP process. We ended up having two meetings to complete the MAP. It's heartening to know that so many people care about Maggie and know her really well—the joys of living in a small community! We liked the discussion and what we came up with, I just hope it works. The teacher seemed nervous and defensive when it came to being invited to explain what happens in her class. They looked like they were sitting in a dentist's chair, rather than our cosy old couch. I think the teacher found us making suggestions about what she could do for Maggie in her class really difficult. It seemed like the teacher and principal couldn't wait to get out of there. Hopefully they will relax and be more open once Maggie starts and they get to know her more.

*

Some of Maggie's Map
A PLAN FOR MAGGIE ROSE—to make the dreams happen and avoid the nightmares!
+ Important that Maggie does what her class is doing (topic work, assembly, library. Music etc...)
+ Other children have access to any different activities and resources that are introduced for Maggie
EARLY GOALS
+ Easing into the day together
+ Forming meaningful relationships at school
STORY WRITING
+ Keeping it varied, interesting and relevant
STRATEGIES
+ Children and adults scribing for Maggie while she dictates her story
+ Maggie recording her stories on a tape

+ Bringing familiar photos, books, objects, tapes from home to write about and retell
+ Sequencing activities in the classroom
+ Making her own books
+ Magnetic board stories, pictures and sight words
+ A back-up choosing box

*

Maggie loves swimming!
One of the things Maggie is really looking forward to about starting school is getting to go swimming in the school pool during the weekdays—she is a complete fish! Me and Tony have to take turns with her in the sea, 'cause we get cold and she wants to stay in. We've got a school pool key and have been swimming there heaps over the summer holidays; it's a great way to catch up with local kids and families and familiarise ourselves with the school grounds. It is so lovely there—sheep grazing in the paddocks through the classroom windows, the playground and playing fields stretching out to the harbour and hills.

*

I was talking with Isaac (a friend in Maggie's class) after school today. It's two weeks since the summer school term began:
Hey Isaac. Did you go swimming today?
Yeah, we did...
Have you been swimming much since you got back to school? It's just Maggie keeps coming home with dry togs, but the weather's been nice...
Maggie doesn't go swimming, she's not allowed...
Why?
I don't know...
Next morning I approached one of Maggie's teacher aides:
Hi June, is Maggie going swimming with her class? It's just, her togs are coming home dry.
Uum, yes, I mean no, she isn't swimming.
Why not?
(looking embarrassed) You'd better talk to Mrs Clyde (Maggie's classroom teacher).
I approached Mrs Clyde:

Hi, June says that Maggie's not going swimming at school. How come?

Mrs Clyde: Oh yes. Mrs Urwin (school Principal) was going to talk to you about that. It would be best if you can talk with her about it, I'm not really sure of the full situation.

I approached Mrs Urwin:

Oh yes, we are worried about Maggie having an accident in the pool. She could wee or poo in the pool. It's not fair on the other children. To miss out on swimming if there is an accident in the pool.

But she wears swimming diapers to address that issue when she's swimming in the sea or a pool.

Yes, but accidents can still happen.

But babies and toddlers swim in the school swimming pool on the weekends and after school. They're allowed to swim in the pool and they wear swimming diapers, what's the difference?

I need to take it to the next School Board meeting. We'll discuss it there and I'll get back to you.

When is the meeting?

In two weeks.

But Maggie has already missed out on two weeks swimming.

It's not something I'm able to make a decision on. It's a School Board matter.

In the meantime, I want Maggie to be able to swim in the pool, it's too long for her to wait. I wish you had told me it was going to be a problem last year before the new school year began. I told you then that she loved swimming and you said that was great and you told her she'd go swimming a lot in the summer term.

Did I? Yes, well, she'll be at school a long time, so it's not really that big a wait given how long she'll be here for (smiling). I'm not able to give permission, I need to wait for the School Board to discuss it.

I want you to make sure Maggie is helped to get changed for swimming and that she's allowed to paddle her feet sitting on the side of the pool every time the class goes swimming.

That should be alright.

I rang Maggie's 'Lead Co-ordinator' at the special education service. I told her what was happening and asked her to help me get the school to let Maggie go swimming.

Let's wait until after the Board meeting and see how you go. It may get resolved at that stage and you won't need me to intervene.

*

Notice sent home to parents and displayed in swimming pool area:
"Change of school swimming pool rules, effective immediately. In the interests of hygiene and safety, infants and toddlers wearing swimming diapers are not permitted to swim in the school pool at any time." Principal—Elaine Urwin

*

School Board meeting
Swimming issue discussed. Jean Caldwell (school parent and Board member responsible for Health & Safety) to investigate City Council-run-pool policy and protocols for incontinent swimmers and report back in one month to the next Board meeting...

*

Swimming on the weekend
Today we went swimming at the school pool. Maggie was very excited to be going in. She slid herself along on the soles of her feet and said, "I'm sliding like a penguin!" She held the side rail, kicked out her feet and said, "I'm blowing bubbles!" She bounced up and down on her feet and shouted, "I'm jumping like a kangaroo!" Josh, from Maggie's class was there, he said Maggie was doing what they do in their swimming sessions at school. Sandy, Josh's mum, was there with her toddler who was in the pool too. We talked about the new rule regarding babies and toddlers not being allowed in the pool. She told me that everyone was ignoring it because it was ridiculous.
*

School Board meeting one month later
Jean reported back: Public pools require incontinent children and adults to wear swimming diapers. Sometimes they leak though and if poo leaks out, the pool has to be closed to the public and re-filtered. It takes 3 days to filter our school pool. I think it's too big a risk to let children in diapers use the pool. If the pool is contaminated, all of the children will miss out on 3 days of swimming. We can't have that, its not fair on the majority of children.

Christine: But it may not even happen. Isn't it fairer that we take the risk and maybe the pool has to be closed for a few days once or twice, than Maggie misses out on swimming altogether? It's part of the curriculum. She is a student at our school and swimming is part of the curriculum for everybody isn't it?

Board decision:

That incontinent pupils be allowed to participate with their class in regular school pool swimming lessons on the expectation that they wear swimming diapers.

*

Tony is on the School Board (poor him!). He came home from the meeting and told me that Maggie is now allowed to go swimming with her class. We are annoyed that it's taken two months of her missing out for them to confirm what was already common bloody sense! Summers almost over!

The Kowhai blossoms are carpeting the ground. It feels like it's been an unnecessary waste of Maggie's and our time. It's taken so much of my energy! Not a very good start to the school year for Maggie or our family.

The next day after the Board meeting, I packed Maggie's togs in her school bag and told her that today she was allowed in the pool with her class. It was a lovely, sunny day. After school, when I checked Maggie's bag, I saw that her togs were dry. I rang her mate Isaac and he said they had been swimming but Maggie was just paddling at the side of the pool. Next day I asked Maggie's teacher aide why Maggie hadn't been swimming. She said:

You had better talk with the Principal about that.

So I went to see the principal.

Oh yes, June (teacher aide) doesn't feel comfortable getting into her togs and being the only adult in the changing shed with Maggie and the other girls. Going swimming isn't in her job description so we can't really expect her to do it if she doesn't feel comfortable.

Can't she get changed somewhere else by herself and then change Maggie say in the bathroom?

We hadn't thought of that. It's not just the getting changed anyway, June doesn't want to go in the pool.

I wish someone had told me about this issue ages ago. We could have sorted this out, now Maggie still isn't swimming even though she's supposed to be allowed to.

Well we can't make the teacher aides get into the pool if they don't want to.

We have to work something out. What about if I arrange for a friend to change and get into the pool with Maggie?

That might be okay. Come back to me when you have someone in mind and we'll see what we can do...

I wish you had talked with me about this earlier. Summer will be over soon. We told Maggie all holidays that she'd be able to go swimming at school. You told me last year swimming would be great for her. These things need to thought about in advance and planned for so Maggie doesn't miss out.

I didn't know swimming would be a problem for the teacher aide until the beginning of the year.

That was two months ago, Mrs Urwin.

*

Help!

I rang Maggie's 'Lead Co-ordinator' at the special education service again. I asked her to help me to sort out the school's issues so that Maggie could be supported and included in swimming. She said:

Children are excluded from swimming for all sorts of reasons, not just disability. It's not that unusual you know. I hear that she is enjoying paddling her feet and watching the other children, so it's not like she is unhappy or having a bad time. The Ministry can't really tell schools what to do. Unfortunately it's the school's decision what they do. Hopefully it should work out if you find a friend to go swimming with her. Let me know if there's anything else you need, I'm only a phone call away...

*

I wrote a 10-page letter (!) to the special education regional manager complaining about being given the cold shoulder by his staff member. I asked how schools are made accountable when they exclude children from participating on the grounds of disability, and where we could go to find support and advice when things weren't going well for Maggie at school, and the school wasn't being responsive. I asked who supports and guides schools, principals, and teachers to develop an inclusive culture and practices in line with Government policies and the curriculum.

The special education manager wrote back to me. He agreed that there was a problem with disabled children being excluded at school. He arranged for myself and a few families from other schools to come to a lunchtime meeting at the Ministry of Education offices to discuss issues about our children being excluded at school. I went to the meeting and we had a good, open discussion. The other families were facing similar problems and situations with their disabled children at school. Towards the end I said:

So it's clear we have a problem with schools not meeting their full obligations to include our children. What can the Ministry of Education do to address this? It's a breach of what they are legally required and ethically obligated to do. The schools need to know what is expected and required of them. Our school didn't even know about the Special Education Policy Guidelines. They need to be made accountable for their actions. They obviously need support and professional development too, to help them become more inclusive. Where can we go when we have a problem? Who is going to help families?

Manager: I really empathise with the issues and concerns you have raised here today. Thank you for taking the time and energy to share these issues with us. I would be being dishonest if I didn't say that we are very well aware of some schools not stepping up to the challenges of being fully inclusive. However, schools are self managing units. We can help make them more inclusive by listening and gently making recommendations when we are aware of specific problems, but unfortunately we can't tell schools what to do because, as I said, they are self-managing. At the end of the day, how each School Board and Principal interpret their responsibilities is up to them. Some issues you have raised represent quite grey areas. If a school refused to enroll a child because of the child's special needs, we might have something to say about that. But many of the issues we have discussed today are much more complex and open to interpretation and differing opinions. We will help you all we can within the parameters that have been set..."

*

Eventually I arranged for a friend to take Maggie swimming with her class but there weren't many opportunities for swimming left because it was now autumn. The Kowhai flowers had gone for another year.

*

Easing into the day

After Maggie had been at school a few months, the Special Needs Co-ordinator (SNC) from school rang me at home. She said that Mrs Clyde (classroom teacher) was concerned about Maggie losing interest and becoming disengaged during the teacher-led whole group time at the beginning of each day. The SNC asked one of Maggie's teacher aides, Karena, to take Maggie Rose out of class at the beginning of each day to work in another room with her on her "fine motor skills." The teacher aide suggested to the special needs co-ordinator that she talk with me about that first. This teacher aide had worked with Maggie and our family at Maggie's early childhood centre. She knew I wouldn't be supportive of Maggie being taken out of class to do things by herself. The special needs co-ordinator said:

Hi Bernadette, Sandy here. Mat times aren't going very well lately.

Hi Sandy. Oh really? In what way?

Maggie Rose is losing concentration *very* early on. She becomes disruptive to the class. We think it would be better for her to be doing some things with her teacher aide in the Resource Room.

Oh? The resource room, is that the room next to the classroom?

Yes. There's a table and two chairs down the end and enough room to be working on her special learning needs. We were thinking scissor and fine motor skills and things like that. Cutting things out and pasting them. I think it will be good one-on-one time. At the moment she's distracting the other children.

I'm not really happy about Maggie being taken out, especially at the beginning of the day. I noticed the children getting wriggly and finding it hard to sit still at morning mat-time when I was visiting with Maggie. I think Maggie probably isn't the only child who finds it hard to sit and listen for that long. I'm wondering about Mrs Clyde changing what she does and maybe making that time more interactive and a bit shorter? Perhaps you could talk with her and look at how that time is structured and maybe change it to suit the children better? I'd be happy to come if that would be helpful.

Yes, well, Karena thought you might not want Maggie taken out of class. I don't think that's appropriate or necessary for Mrs Caldwell to be expected to change her programme. It's working well for most children.

Maybe for some, but it is a long time to sit still and listen isn't it? Some of the kids, particularly the boys, seem to struggle with it too. I'm not happy about Maggie being withdrawn, especially as it's the beginning of the day. I don't like the message that taking her out would give to her and her peers. They've always stayed together, since Playcentre. She can work on her "fine motor skills" alongside her peers in class. The teacher needs to consider how to adapt it so that it works for everyone, including Maggie.

We'll probably leave it as it is then. Goodbye.

*

Maggie loves literature!

Maggie is so into her books at the moment! She's been reciting whole poems and pieces of prose from her books. She's got a really good memory! When we're reading together and I leave a space for her to fill in the words and sentences in a story, she always knows the text! I've noticed

that she often links what's happening in her lived world to something from her "book world." The other day we were getting out of the car and there was a dog barking somewhere. I didn't really notice the barking until Maggie said, "Can I hear a dog barking in the distance?" which is a quote from one of her favourite books. The way she makes sense of the world is so fascinating! Her familiarity with text and literature should set her up well for getting into reading.

*

A speech language therapist "tested" Maggie (6 yrs old) when she visited her at school. She took Maggie out of her class and asked her questions about a series of pictures. As a result of the "test" she wrote a report to the classroom teacher saying that she had:

"...determined that Maggie-Rose (6 yrs old) is at the pre-literacy, pre-numeracy level... Therefore the current recommended speech and language therapy targets for Maggie-Rose consist of:

1. **To match a 2-part pattern**
2. **To continue a 2-part pattern**

3.   **To identify the days of the week; and to identify what day it is today, what day it was yesterday, what day comes after and what day comes before.**

4.   **To match single words to pictures"**

*

School news: 'Going to the rugby!'
I went to see the Hurricanes and the Crusaders (New Zealand rugby teams). I went with Chris. The Crusaders came in on horses. They played rugby. I said: "It's only a game of rugby!" There were heaps of people. They were very noisy and I blocked my ears. It was like a tornado. "Ha! Ha! Ha!" I laughed. Dad bought me a Crusader's sword and I slept with it in my bed! Charlie Parker laughed! The Crusaders won the game. Crusaders wear red and black. Hurricanes wear yellow and black.

*

Maggie dictated a letter to our friend Charlotte at home after school today. I didn't realise how much of the script for the school concert performance she knows. Amazing!
Dear Charlotte,
Buzz Lightyear's going to come to my birthday! They've got cream pies on the end of their sticks! Roger played a funny song at grandpop's 80th birthday party!

I'm listening to Nga Pihi, and I'm singing. The vines bleed upon Papa (the land), staining her red. Ochre red, earthen red, red the sacred colour. Ranginui joined Papatuanuku in darkness. And out of the infinite night came thought. Te mahara—thought. And from thought came hau ora breath of life. From darkness, from thought, came Haumumu. And from the hundredth to the thousandth night they lay.

"We've had enough of this! Shall we slay our parents? Shall we kill our parents?" they asked. And from the hundredth to the thousandth night they pondered. "Yes! We will kill them! It is better so!" For ages they deliberated. Then spoke Tane Mahuta: "No! Not so! Let us separate them, not kill them!" They all agreed, all but one. All but Tawhirimatea, and all that dwell in the sea. Boing!
Lots of love, from Maggie

*

IEP meeting at school

I'm feeling pretty panicky about this meeting. I hate IEPs. There's a million other people in the room and they've all got their opinions about Maggie. It feels like no one really listens to us. I don't think they get where we're coming from, which is weird because we've talked to them about it enough times. I don't think they want to know. They just think we're "difficult parents."

I don't like the special needs co-ordinator. I can't even tell if she likes or cares about Maggie from what she says and how she talks to her. I don't really know what's happening for Maggie at school. Her teacher, Miss Lewis, sends a notice home each term about what they're going to focus on. But it's really general and completely topic-based. It doesn't mean a lot to me. I think she must use a template to write it on and take the text straight out of the curriculum document or somewhere.

*

I talked at the IEP meeting about what Maggie's interests are at the moment:
Maggie is really into the plays and scripts in the School Journals she's bringing home at the moment. I think she likes scripts partly because they provide her with a sort of framework and some predictability for interacting with her peers, its sort of like scripted communication. Like its safer or something. She's been writing plays at home with us too. She also loves to perform and to be part of a group activity. I reckon working with play scripts has the potential to support Maggie's peers to include her. Perhaps we could incorporate a focus on plays into reading and writing and maybe even work on some small performances around a topic of interest or something this term? Is that possible, Miss Lewis?
Hmmm, interesting. The literacy programme has been planned for this term. Maybe we can look at plays next term. This term, we are learning about how stories are structured. In particular, stories have a beginning, a middle and an end.

*

Maggie loves performances!

We went to a Buskers Festival performance at the beach last night. It was the Blackstreet Boyz from Los Angeles. Their names are Alfred and Seymour. Maggie said:

Their dancing was funny and they told some jokes. Mummy laughed, I laughed, everybody laughed! From Alfred's heart came jokes. From Alfred's hand came laughter.

*

A couple of days before the school concert Maggie's teacher and teacher aide seemed to get worried about Maggie not saying her lines when it comes time to perform. They thought the whole thing might be "too much" for her. They asked Maggie if she wanted to have a speaking part in the play, and she didn't say anything.

So they gave someone else Maggie's part. Maggie sat at the side and played a drum instead.

Chapter 8

Help Wanted

Casey Harhold

"When the going gets tough, the tough get going." As much as I hated this phrase growing up, embracing it has helped just as much. Strength. The women in my family have always proven their strength. When something in this world knocked us down, that was our motto. Get up and get going.

There always seems to be someone in every family who unites the rest. A rock. My grandmother was the rock in our family. The person we loved, cared for, looked to for advice, and sought comfort from. As time ticks away, nothing stays the same. Strength is chipped away, with the passage of time and the inevitability of life changes. The world has a funny way of testing our strength as we move along.

*

The afternoon was cloudy, a light mist in the air. The sun was trying to peek out of the clouds, finding its way through the kitchen window where my mother, sister and I sat. It was Sunday, an afternoon spent thinking about and remembering the past. Talking. Sometimes laughing; sometimes crying. Talking about the one woman in our lives that we missed the most: Grandma. The woman who had impacted our lives in so many different ways. The woman who sat with us, so many times, at this very same table. Her chair is piled high with mail and paper, as if holding a place for her.

I remember how she used to sit in that chair and listen to us talk. Now and then, she would chime in, sometimes unexpectedly, always with something positive, something enlightening. I would do anything to have her here with us again. I guess the memories will have to do.

*

Memory is an extraordinary thing. I often wonder: is there one distinct moment when our consciousness begins? We talk about how memory fades as people age, but what about the beginning? Do those earliest of memories shape our experiences? Do they guide us in our decisions, in the pathway of life? Does our memory pave the way for who we are and how we perceive things?

I try to think: can I remember events before the ones of that day? I can't. My mind always takes me back to that one day.

My dad had already left for work. My older sister and brother were well into their school day. I was not old enough for school; Mom was a stay-at home mother. My grandfather and grandmother lived with us, all in the same house.

It was a day for spring cleaning. Grandma, Grandpa, and Mom were all working on cleaning chores, both inside and out. It was a beautiful Michigan day, not a cloud in sight, the sun shining brightly, still a little chill in the air. The earth was beginning to bud again, and the grass was growing back strong.

Grandma started on the kitchen. Grandpa and Mom headed outside to work on the lawn. I was placed outside in my red wagon, on top of a cozy fleece blanket. I was focused on playing with my Minnie Mouse dolls, getting lost in an interior fantasy world of my own creation.

But then, I looked up. I remember the feeling: my world of fun and fantasy came to a screeching halt. In its place: panic. A sudden, painful fear; an abrupt intrusion of reality. People talk about being stricken with panic; I think that's the right word. It was a feeling I would come to know well as I grew older. Yet the feeling of it, that very first time, is when I remember it best, most poignantly.

The buzzing of the lawn mower stopped suddenly. My grandfather ran past me, yelling for Mom, so loudly. My mother sprinted, knowing the routine, knowing what she was running to. Knowing what she needed to do. Mom ran past me by, then turned and scooped me up, racing to the house. She had to get to her mother, to be a mother, for both her and me.

Panic. Grandma face down on the living room floor. "Call 911!" Grandpa yelled to my mom. "Taffy, call 911, I am going to start CPR." Grandpa pumped and compressed her chest, put every ounce of his body and strength into saving hers. Mom started the breaths.

The ambulance arrived within moments; the paramedics came into the house in a rush. "Grandma! Grandma! Wake up!" I yelled, crying. The stretcher went by me out the door. I saw that the flawless white skin of her face had a bluish tint as it went past.

Up to that point, I don't think I had ever felt any kind of fear in my body. My first real experience with it, and it looked me right in the face. One moment, innocently pretending to be Minnie Mouse. The next, within mere seconds: sickness, life, and almost death. I looked up, held up my hands for Mom, Grandpa, someone, to pick me up. Their faces were filled with exhaustion and worry.

*

The funny thing about memory is, it comes and it goes. I don't remember much else about that day, or what happened in the days following. Grandma was going to be okay; Grandpa had broken her ribs doing CPR. I don't know if I remember it from that day, or if I was told about it later. I know that a few days later, a man from the newspaper came to the house to interview Mom for a feature article: "Saving Mom's Life: A Daughter Gives the Gift of Life for Mother's Day." He took a picture of my mom holding me.

*

As all the panic and attention subsided, my mom and grandpa sorted out what had happened. My mother had come in the house to grab another layer of clothing. She noticed Grandma staring out the living room window. "Mom? Mom. Mom, are you okay?" Silence. Not a blink of an eye as a response was given. "I'm going to get help."

She left her, and ran outside to get Grandpa. By the time they returned, Grandma had collapsed, falling to the floor, her lips starting to turn blue. She had had a seizure from the medication she had been taking for depression. Though I didn't know it then, this was not the first time she had been rushed to the hospital, but it was the first time I remembered.

*

As my mother, sister, and I sat that day in the kitchen, the air was still for a moment. We felt love, hurt, contentment, sadness, and pride. Amazement, that we were all interlinked by the blood that runs through our veins. By the family of which we are so proud. By the support given to us and by us. We had all been through a lot because of Grandma's depression, something that has haunted us, brought us closer, and taught us about life. A lesson about what is important in this world, having others to love and depend on. Something we wanted others to understand, yet about which we were still unsure ourselves. A light danced across my mom's caramel eyes, and then they filled up.

"She was so strong," my mom began, trying to brush away any negativity she may have felt. "Did you ever hear her whimper? Complain? Any time? She always just wanted me to help her. I used to look her in the eyes and say yes, tell me. I have the rest of my life to sit here and have you tell me what it is that makes you feel the way you do. She would respond with "you don't know, you just don't know." Silence fell over the table, as we all stared at the table, thinking.

My sister went on, "Do you think she was even capable of explaining it to you? Maybe she didn't have an answer. When you have—I don't know—bad thoughts, maybe she just couldn't find the words."

Mom interrupted. "She just wanted help. She never wanted to complain about anything. She fought it a lot on her own, never wanted to bother the family with it. I used to sleep sometimes in fear she would leave to check herself into the hospital. She just wanted to be OK in her thoughts. She was always the first to help another. She believed in people, the goodness that people are capable of. She believed that each person had something to be proud of. Even if someone else didn't think they did, she would try to foster that in the person and have it shine through."

*

Grandma was often described as a light, a radiant beam that people noticed when she entered a room. There was something about her that made others want to be in her presence. Her beauty and features were compared to Marilyn Monroe by people who knew her, but my grandma had a modesty about her that always shone through. Supporting others and making them feel worthy was a strength of hers. I sometimes wonder if this is where my passion for the inclusion of all in schools came from.

She always found the good in people. She believed in that. A person known to be troubled—Grandma would have taken them under her wing, to advocate for them. As I think of this trait of hers, I wonder how she could do this so well for others, yet feel so badly about herself in her own mind?

My sister asked Mom, with curiosity in her eyes, "What about your graduation day, Mom?" The question caught her off guard; I could see the memory returning to her, like a waterfall. She turned and said, "I had to go visit her on graduation day. Hmph. Eloise Hospital. I got a brand new 10-speed bike that day, though—powder blue." We all laughed, relieving some of the sadness of the memory.

"That's so you, Mom. Turning the memory of a bad situation into a good one. You are so good at that," I said.

My mom smiled and continued. "Eloise is on Michigan Avenue. There was a rock in front of it. It was in the shape of a flower; well, really, a flower basket. I think it's still there, and as much as that basket should bring hope, I really disliked it. We took a walk over to it that day. Grandpa, Grandma, my brother Greg, and I. I was in my cap and gown, right after commencement. Grandma couldn't come, she was in the hospital for the depression. She did make it to yours, though," turning again to my sister. "She made it there in 1999, but her legs were killing her. Too much medication. The pain was eating away at her, so we walked her out early."

"Her depression was odd," Mom said." She loved and wanted to help others so much, but it was always what bothered her the most. She often let people bother her. She had her ups and downs. She was always organized and knew what she was doing, but she then would have a bout of bad thoughts."

Looking at the two of us, Mom went on: "That surgery she had was the start of it all. I was 18 months old when she had it. I guess I was crying and crying. My grandmother—your great-grandma—she got home and heard me crying, so she knew something was wrong with my mother. It was not like her to leave me alone. Your grandmother was 23 at the time. After the surgery, he was in and out of consciousness. At first, they were going to lock her up in to a psych ward, as if she was out of her mind. She was so afraid. Afraid to be alone, or afraid something would happen in life or to her loved ones. She was scared and we could not figure out of what."

*

At the age of 23, Grandma had been married to my grandfather for 5 years, and had given birth to my mother. My grandfather and grandmother's love was like something out of a storybook. They described it as love at first sight. The love and respect between the two of them was an astounding foundation for creating a family. But her world changed, because of something she could not control. Something that shaped the path her life. And she couldn't see it coming.

As I sat that day in the kitchen, I thought about the story as my grandfather told it to me, from his point of view. The story about a day, he felt, that changed their lives forever. A day that had an impact on everyone in the family, even if we hadn't been born yet. As much as I hated bringing it up to him, the history of that day needed to be told by someone who had lived it. I remembered his words.

*

"We have to go all the way back to when I got out of the army," Grandpa said. "Grandma and I, we used to go to the show all the time, and she would fall asleep, all the time, right in the middle. I noticed, as time passed, that she could never stay up late. She would always fall asleep.

"One day, I was working with my brother, Sidney. We used to be hired to do dry wall jobs in people's homes. It was a Friday and it was raining. We had no material and so we had to postpone our job for the day. I stayed home. In the morning, I went to wake your grandmother up and she could not get up. I sat her up and she fell back down. She was in a coma-like state.

"Your great-grandmother, your grandma's mom, was living with us then. I called her right away. We could not get grandma up. She would not wake up. It was scary. We called a doctor, who was a good friend of ours, who would come to the house. House calls were becoming rare, but he still came over. The doctor came in and he tried to revive her. He couldn't either. He called the ambulance right away. He wanted her in the hospital and to have her at Eloise. One side of the hospital was a typical hospital and the other was for mentally ill people.

"So then the ambulance took her out there. I followed her. They put grandma in the mental side. They thought there was something possibly mentally wrong with her, since she was not waking up. They did not know yet. As Grandpa told me this, I remember wondering how such a decision was made. What would constitute as a mental or physical need for medical care? I envisioned people who were sick, and how quickly they were categorized as having a psychiatric disability, or a physical illness. Grandpa continued.

"I argued with them," he said. "'I do not want my wife in here, I want my wife across the street in the regular hospital.' You know what a mental ward looks like? You know? People are all lethargic and are given nothing. The bareness of the rooms are enough to irk your soul. The nurse said, 'Listen, leave her here. You go home and come back in the morning. We'll attend to her.' They talked me into it, honey.

"The next morning, I came back into the psychiatric part of the hospital. The nurses told me that she was not on that side of the hospital anymore and that her attending physician had decided to transfer her across the street to the medical ward. The doctor was an intern from the University of Michigan. He had examined her and thought that there was something physically wrong with her, not mentally, so she was transferred. When we went across the street, we met the doctor, he seemed to be a real nice man. He said, 'I think we know what is wrong. But we have to do an exploratory surgery.'

Grandpa paused for a moment, and cleared his throat. I could almost see the flood of memories rushing through his head, as if he could see himself standing in front of the doctor and the image of my grandmother in the hospital bed.

My grandfather went on. "When I got there, your grandmother was sitting up in bed. They would give her orange juice and she would be okay for a while. Once the juice was taken away, she would relapse."

My grandfather became silent. He started to speak: "She—." He stopped. He cleared his throat again and went on. "She was begging me, 'Please, please, honey.'" He stopped again.

"Grandpa?" I said.

"Wait a minute. I wish I wasn't so emotional. I just can't help it when it comes to her." He continued on, his eyes filling up. "She was begging me, as she lay there. 'Please tell them not to do that anymore.' She wanted me to have them stop making her go in and out of consciousness.

Finally, the doctor came in and talked with me more about how to proceed with the surgery. He said he didn't believe she was diabetic, that something else was causing her to black out. I signed the paper for the doctors to proceed. I thought this was going to save her life.

A man named Dr. Gloss was the surgeon. I remember that. We waited about 8–9 hours until they brought her out and she went into recovery. I slept there, waiting for her to wake up. They found a tumor, as big as dime, in the tail end of her pancreas. The doctors believed that the tumor was causing an issue with her insulin and glucose. Ever since that day, your grandmother did better. She was not falling asleep."

He paused a moment—he was thinking so much, sifting through his memories, deciding where to continue and what to tell me. He went on, "It was a strain on her, honey, but it was a success. They had a file about 3 inches thick of paper. This was a rare case at the time. Your grandmother was a success. We brought her home as soon as we could."

I knew that when my grandfather said, "It was a success," that it was nothing of the sort. Of course, it was a success to have the tumor removed. The things that continued to happen to my grandmother were nothing of a success. She continued to struggle with her thoughts. Her body experienced so many side effects from the constant change of medications.

My grandfather continued to explain what life was like after the surgery. "A few months later, I began to notice that she was showing symptoms of being depressed, or so the doctors said. Just thinking of what she went through, it may have stemmed from that. Something was going on, off, and on in her mind. She went to a lot of hospitals for it and received a lot of treatment. They said she was bi-polar, but I think it was from all that she had experienced. That was the beginning of her problems. She went for a long period of being well." As my grandfather said that, I knew that's what he wanted to be true. That everything was okay. But after a moment, he spoke about what really happened: "Well, off and on things went bad and then she would be well again."

*

Eloise Hospital was a well-known hospital throughout the twentieth century and into the 1980s. It was popular for people in Southeastern Michigan, located as it was in Westland, a suburb of Detroit. Eloise was most well-known as a psychiatric hospital. Its shadow remains today. Today, most of the buildings have been torn down, and the property sold. There are still ruins of a few buildings standing, where it is rumored to be haunted by the "crazy" patients who inhabited it and died there. Young people occasionally sneak onto the property hoping to see a "crazy ghost."

Hearing about that makes me angry. The people who went there were real people, with real families, stories, and lives. They were not "crazy" or "handicapped" or abnormal. They were folks like my grandmother, looking for help and support.

As someone employed as a special educator, and working on my masters and continuing education in the area of disabilities education, I see everyday ways in which our society reacts to people who are "different." Overlooked, they only rarely are given the opportunity to be part of regular schools, or typical communities. Instead, they are labeled and pushed away to be "with their own kind." Growing up, I often stayed at my grandparents to help take care of Grandma. As she got older, she became more ill. In high school, I missed sporting events or other activities, because I spent time looking after her. Instead, my time was spent studying and being a caretaker. When I went to college, I scheduled my classes around the times my grandfather needed the most help. For as long as I can remember, I was worried about leaving her, scared that she would die with no one there.

Through it all, she was my rock. She struggled, but she put up a fight. She was strong. Stronger than most people could dream of being.

So in high school, and on into college, I would sleep next to her at night. I slept to the sound of her breathing: inhale, exhale, inhale, exhale. Sometimes I just kept my hand on her, to feel the rise and fall of her breath. Once, a loud noise made me jump; I looked to her side of the bed. Not there. "Grandma!" She had fallen off the bed, and lay on the floor, on her side, unable to get up herself. In a panic, I thought she might have broken a hip.

I looked at her. "Are you alright?" She smiled, then grimaced. "I'm fine, just cannot believe I would fall out of the bed like this." I laughed, relieved. "Let's get you up." She hated when she was a bother. She wanted to just stay there for the rest of the night, so I wouldn't have to trouble to pick her up by myself.

"Yeah, right," I said. "I would never leave you lying on the ground like this." Struggling, I hooked my arms under her armpits, and finally got her back into bed.

About a week before she passed away, I again woke beside her because of a noise she made. She was agitated, trying to speak. She was twitching, making horrific noises, her eyes glazed over. "Grandpa, get up!" I screamed in a panic. I turned the light on, and cupped her head so she would not hit it on the headboard of the bed. "Call 911 Grandpa, hurry!"

I kept talking to her, told her she was okay and to stay with us, that help was on the way and that I was there for her. Finally, the ambulance people arrived and rushed her once again to the hospital. I was exhausted. It turned out to be a seizure; she made it through, and we were able to bring her back home—but only for 5 more days.

It was just before Thanksgiving. We noticed that Grandma was eating less and drinking less—with the medications she was on, she was always drinking water. Her mouth was beginning to move in odd ways—her tongue would push up to the top of her mouth and back down again. She scratched the bottom part of her scalp, and described this itch as painful. My mom, sister, and I spent the whole Saturday at my grandparent's house. We relaxed, cooked, and watched TV, enjoying some time before the holiday busyness. As the evening approached, my mom and sister headed home, and I went to the movies with some friends. The movie was going to be done late—I had not decided yet if I would return to my grandparent's house or if I would go home that night.

I remember sitting at the movies, trying to decide what my plans were. I knew my grandfather always cleaned on Sunday mornings, so he did not need me right away in the morning. However, the recent seizure had me worried. Finally, after midnight, I decided to go to my grandparents. As I walked in the front door, I heard the soft Christmas music playing that my mom had left on. I went into Grandpa's bedroom, but he wasn't there. When I reached the other bedroom, I saw that they were both there, side by side, sleeping soundly, with his arm around her. I couldn't remember the last time Grandpa had slept in the same bed as Grandma. I went home and went to bed.

The next morning, my grandfather helped her get up and take her shower: "Good morning lady, how are you?" She smiled back at him, "I'm good, honey"—and dropped to the floor. Grandpa ran to the phone, to call the paramedics. They finally arrived, revived her again, and took her to hospital.

*

My mom, sister, and I sat in the kitchen, talking about that day. "I remember waking up to the phone ringing, and hearing grandpa's voice on the other end," Mom said. "I just knew the moment I answered that we had lost her."

The three of us sat in silence. My sister and I looked at each other; we knew what had happened when we heard my mother cry out.

Just like my grandmother, my mom had been a rock. I guess that's the circle of life. As one person moves on, the next one fills their shoes. Or maybe my mom had been the rock the whole time. Someone for my grandmother to talk to, and be there, when she couldn't help herself. Someone to help take care of the family and myself. As we all need in this world, I guess. Acceptance. Acceptance and love, no matter how different they are. And though the world is slowly moving towards increased inclusion for those who may never have experienced it, it's just not fast enough. Not for me; not for Grandma. That's why, perhaps, the women in my family say to each other, when the going get's tough, the tough get going. In order to persevere.

Chapter 9

Picture This: Snapshots of My (A)typical Family

David J. Connor

Focus

When asked to identify a person with a disability who has influenced my understanding of disability, I am hard pressed to pin this on one individual. Instead, I think of many family members, a cast of characters who have managed their "differences" over time, integrating them into their own daily life and the lives of others in our family. In this chapter I share my own perceptions of this ensemble cast and I posit that readers will likely have a similar experience when reflecting upon their own extended families.

In the modern classic documentary *Including Samuel* (Habib, 2008), Douglas Biklen, Dean of the School of Education at Syracuse University, ponders the question "Is there any place within this society where inclusion exists 'full blown'?" He concludes, "The answer is yes. It exists within a lot of families." His response is plain and simple, so much so that we forget how much families include their children with disabilities by necessity, and in doing so, become creative, flexible, accommodating people in general, while learning about particular bodily and psychological differences. In brief, disabilities or differences are usually normalized within families. It therefore follows, though it is not usually recognized, that families who have members with a disability can serve as examples to our larger society—illuminating ways in which everyone can be included. In particular, the education system has much to learn from how families view children with disabilities and integrate them into all aspects of daily life.

The cast of characters in my family (actual names are changed) with disabilities include: my uncle Frank, who never fully recovered from a "nervous breakdown," and was unable to return to work; my cousin Allan, who has dyslexia, and has worked hard in "unskilled" jobs supporting adults with various disabilities; my cousin Janet, born without a thyroid gland, and used as a case study for student doctors; another cousin, Peter, cognitively impaired, who stammers, finding it difficult to speak at all. In addition, several years ago, Jonathan, my brother's nephew by marriage, was born with Cornelia de Lange Syndrome, a rare genetic condition. Recently, against doctors' counsel, Pamela, a cousin's wife, prepared to deliver a child who was predicted to die soon after birth; and my mother, who has lived with chronic varicose veins, influencing how she walks and sits. Although these provide a range of instances in which disability is manifest, they are only a sample. That there could be so many others is testimony of disability being everywhere, in all families, without exception.

My Own Snapshot

As a career educator who is interested in disabilities, I have met many graduate students who have entered the field of special education because a person in their family had a disability—often a sibling or a parent. While this is often assumed to be the same for me, it is not the case. That said, of all of the influences I am subject to, including multiple framings of disability circulating within medical, psychological, scientific, historical, cultural, and social discourses that, in turn, influence professional and institutional discourses—including education—I always revert to my family's understandings of disability. They have grounded me and guided me throughout my career with "home grown" notions of inclusion, fairness, support, respect, and interdependence.

On a personal level, as a gay man, I believe I have been profoundly influenced from a young age by realizing the injustices of being told what being gay was supposed to mean. In coming out—in addition to the predictable pejoratives—I was informed I would live a lonely life, heard numerous times "what a waste," and "what a shame." In other words, my status was diminished in the eyes of others as the "majority" group positioned me as inferior, even pitiable. Finding few or no role models in a culture saturated with misinformation made me even more determined to challenge demeaning and stereotypical images so I could live a life of dignity. I learned the inner strength needed by minority people who are positioned as inferior by those in the majority group who conversely cast themselves as superior.

Being gay, I experienced feeling different, which influenced coming to know the world differently than straight relatives and friends. Like other minorities, I experienced a Duboisian-like (1903) double consciousness needed to navigate a world configured for the majority of others, while simultaneously staying true to myself. This epistemological awareness, specific to my positionality of negotiating a majority world as a minority person, made me curious about other ways of knowing, especially groups who had also been historically stereotyped, marginalized, and misunderstood, and how they challenged barriers that maintained their diminished status. I soon became interested in how all people respond to various forms of "difference"—be it race, ethnicity, gender, sexual orientation, and so on–groups placed at, or outside of, the margins.

I wondered, who draws those margins? When are they drawn? Why? How do they serve to empower some citizens by disempowering others? How do they enable some people by disabling others? What can be done to counter forces that seek enforcement of these symbolic lines? Such questions have always remained close to me, influencing how I operate in the world. In my mid-20s, when entering into the teaching profession as a special educator, I become increasingly aware of people with disabilities as a minority group that experienced institutional segregation and cultural stigmatization.

In this chapter, twenty-five years after starting work within education, I contemplate the interconnected questions of: *What have I come to learn as the lives of family members with disabilities have been played out alongside, and interacted with, my own? What have they taught me? In what ways has this impacted me as an educator?* In contemplating these questions I am guided by the work of several autoethnographers and other researchers who have helped shape this method (Clandinin and Connelly, 2000; Crawford, 1996; Ellis, 1997; 2009; Ladson-Billings; 1995; Lincoln and Denzin, 2000; Richardson, 2000). Although each family member has their own short narrative, I recognize that my story has emerged woven together with theirs, as I consider what is understood by their differences all grouped beneath the amorphous label of disability.

Notes on Arranging the Data

In keeping with the conceit of pictures, I write about family members in "portraits," selected images designed to provide a quick representation of how I view each character. This chapter is influenced by the pioneering work of Lawrence-Lightfoot and Davis (1997) in research using portraiture. It is similar in that "...we create opportunities for dialogue, we pursue the silences, and in the process, we face ethical dilemmas and great moral responsibility" (p. 11). However, in contrast with their work, I forgo in-depth, layered, and lengthy portrayals in favor of short, sharp snapshots. In brief, the image created becomes analogous to a portrait as a photograph rather than a painting.

In some ways, it might be useful to envision a mantelpiece, sideboard, piano top, shelf, or any other furniture surface that is used to display framed photographs. Each frame contains a snapshot of an individual family member. Each snapshot can stand alone, telling a story about the person depicted. Yet, taken together, these images cohere from a disparate collection of individuals into a family, united by blood, kinship, history, and culture.

As a reader, you are invited to view each portrait, created one at a time. I employ a non-linear method, used by Ellis (2009), who often forgoes linearity in favor a holistic rendering of a compelling and coherent tale. In arranging the snapshots of family members within this chapter, I echo these sentiments when telling part of my own story's connection to disability, allowing readers to feel some of what I have felt.

Granny and Her Mother

My grandmother was born in July, 1917. Now ninety-four years of age, she lives in a nursing home. Having Alzheimer's disease, she goes "in and out" of the present, often collapsing the people who visit her into others she has known. As well as being her son, my father becomes her father, her husband, her brothers. My sisters become each other. Occasionally, she enters the present moment, with a fleeting recognition of my brother and I. She holds our hands and calls us "daft buggers," a common phrase in our regional culture.

I steel myself before visits to Granny every summer, the only time I return to my birthplace, a typical small town in Northern England. She has lived longer than anticipated, biding her remaining time with others near the end of their lives. They sit together in armchairs, held hostage to the blaring television that fills the room. I only visit with another family member; going alone is too hard. Being with my brother or father helps me concentrate, focus on the task at hand. I find myself repeating silently: *I can get through this, I can get through this.* But it takes everything I have to maintain my composure. Even then, I can feel hairline fractures begin to crack the façade I've erected, and fear it may implode at any time. In desperation, I bite down on my lip or chew my cheek hard. The self-inflicted pain provides a jolt, serving to snap me back into position, stifling the groundswell of a sob. *I must remain in control.* She gently squeezes my hand and smiles.

On the never-played-anymore piano in my apartment sits this gray-framed photograph of my Granny and her mother. Granny is twelve, the last of many children. Her mother looks about fifty, "big-boned" (as they say back home), with a smiling face. The date on the back reads April 1930, and my pre-teen grandmother rests her head on her mother's shoulder, staring into the camera with open eyes. Framed by fashionably bobbed hair, Granny's youthful face stares at me across time. It is one of my favorite photographs.

I hold many good memories of my grandmother. Some of them include her telling about other family members, people I never met because of time, circumstance, location. Now, in the home, she asks for her mother, a woman I only know through Granny's memories. From years ago, I recall her saying, "She was crippled," a turn of phrase that now seems harsh to the ears. Granny would continue, "My Mam could only use one arm... but she used it," continuing, "She would slap all of us if we were bad," ending in laughter that flooded the room, engulfing all present. I witness this burst of love, realizing its source is her mother. When I pressed for details about what Granny termed "the bad arm," I found out that, as a young woman, my great-grandmother went to bed one night with two functional arms and woke up with one. "She never let it stop her from doing anything," Granny shared, "Including raising children." In a quiet voice, she'd say, "I helped her comb her hair," adding softly, as if the act of recollection had momentarily transported Granny to stand behind her mother with a brush in hand, "She had beautiful long hair," with the hint of a smile. "I loved to comb it."

Over the years, various snippets and tidbits came together about Granny's mother: "She was very proud," "She wouldn't let anyone do anything for her," "She worked hard," "She had all those children," "She had a hard life." Granny would almost always end with, "She was a lovely person," and Granda would nod his head in agreement. So, in my mind's eye I hold a composite picture of a strong, loving, hard-working woman, a "cripple" who loved her daughter, with whom she shared her knowledge of life. And although I never knew her, I know she is part of me.

Uncle Frank

My mother's brother, Uncle Frank, is dying of cancer. He has just turned seventy, outliving the initial prognosis by over two years. During that period, the whole family has mobilized to spend time with him and provide emotional support for what was, at first, the unthinkable, which has now transformed into the inevitable.

Frank is the oldest of five siblings and the first to enter into the middle-class profession of education. Becoming a teacher was a "big thing" in a working-class family, a white-collar job without the grease of the shipyards or the coal dust from the mines permanently lodged beneath his fingernails. The family was proud of his accomplishments. Yet the script of a successful career changed overnight when Frank had a "nervous breakdown" in his mid-40s, from which he never fully recovered. With his confidence shattered, and an emotional state permanently impacted by medication, what came to be seen as Frank's "mental illness" prevented his return to teaching.

Frank also developed an obsession with his father, my grandfather. For Frank he was an incommunicative "common laborer," a wife abuser, a selfish tyrant who drank heavily and showed little affection to his children. Every time Frank spoke, he criticized his father relentlessly. Frank's siblings, after allowing this for a while, would forbid him to continue. Anyone, anywhere, anytime would become the recipient of his discontent. Fiercely Catholic, Frank volunteered for various charitable organizations, administering Holy Communion to local parishioners who were unable to attend mass. Not long ago, in recognition of his community services, Frank was awarded a medal by the regional cardinal for service to the church. He was as happy as if it were the Nobel Prize.

Over the past twenty-five years I have watched his wife, their five children, and his siblings strive to support him at every turn. He has always lived at home, surrounded by a large family, three of whom are teachers (all of whom are married to teachers), a testimony to his influence. Recently, he discovered facts about his father. When my grandfather was born, his mother was in her forties and his father was in his sixties. My grandfather therefore was a child when his father died, and, in my uncle's revised, more empathetic understanding, "never stood a chance," without paternal guidance. A photograph of his father, publicly reviled for over two decades, now graces Frank's bedside table. He is, I feel, making peace with his demons before death arrives.

Whenever I hear the term "mentally ill," my mind defaults to Uncle Frank and his stable position as husband, father, grandfather, brother, uncle. The same term is used to describe the most common disability portrayed in films, characters who are usually seen as psychotic, emotionally unstable, often with criminal tendencies, dangerous to themselves and others (Safran, 1998). He no more resembles these images than the multitude of mentally ill characters throughout classic literature, from *Jane Eyre*'s (Brontë, 1847) madwoman in the attic to the heavily medicated ensemble in *One Flew Over the Cuckoo's Nest* (Kesey, 1962). Yet the term, so deeply stigmatized in our society, is rarely used by our family, save for rare instances when we find his behavior odd, unacceptable, selfish. "We forget his mental illness," I have heard myself say to family members, in an attempt to better understand how he maneuvers the world.

Uncle Daniel

My mother's youngest brother, Uncle Daniel, has variously been described (in endearing ways) as "restless," "unable to stay still," "always wanting to be on the move," "no sooner settled than he wants to go," "unpredictable," "hyperactive," "erratic," and so on. As far as I can remember, he has always been this way. He will visit another family member's home, and as soon as the tea has been freshly made, will remember he has to go somewhere else, do something else, or meet someone else. At the same time, we know Uncle Daniel to be kind, funny, and generous—a man who spoiled all the children in our family. Indeed, his frenetic, fast-paced personality was what endeared him to us as children. We all liked to be with him.

Since becoming an educator I have wondered when and how the above descriptors are applied to children. By contemporary accounts, Uncle Daniel would likely be labeled as having attention deficit hyperactivity disorder (ADHD). First a miner, then an electrician in the shipbuilding yards, he has always worked in jobs that allowed bodily movement whenever needed. The whole family are used to Uncle Daniel's high energy, accept his habit of pacing around wherever he is, and expect sudden arrivals or departures. Throughout his life we have just shrugged and said, "That's the way he is."

Cousin Allan

My cousin Allan is dyslexic and, despite this being an area of professional interest to me, we have never had a full conversation about it. I am not entirely sure why, but suspect that I adhere to some deep-rooted and arguably repressive cultural practices of not talking openly of such things lest they make another person feel badly about themselves. Younger than me by fourteen years, I recall his mother sharing samples of his school work, noticing how Allan's writing was composed of tiny, well-spaced letters strung together in undulating sentences across the page. School reports consistently praised his creativity and unique ideas, while calling attention to his struggles with formalized academic processes of literacy and numeracy. In the long run, standardized school examinations proved difficult and after leaving school, Allan's job opportunities were somewhat limited because of this.

Now in his mid-30s, Allan has had a successful career as a caregiver for what could be generally described as vulnerable adults. Beginning with working in residences for the elderly, he now oversees a community-based household of four adults with cognitive impairments. Like most care service jobs, the hours are long and the pay is low, but Allan genuinely likes working and the people he helps. A gentle man, possessing great empathy for others, he always roots for the underdog.

Cousin Peter

As a child, when playing with Uncle Frank's children, I noticed how my cousin Peter looked at me. His gaze seemed different. It stayed longer, lingering long enough to make me feel a little uncomfortable. Peter did not follow our rules of children's games. As years passed, it became noticeable that he was different. In today's disability terminology, he is likely to be described as cognitively impaired. Back then, Peter would have been considered "retarded," although I have never heard any one family member use this word in relation to him. Instead, Peter was described as "slow." He also has a speech impediment in the form of a significant stutter that makes having a conversation difficult for him.

Early in his educational experience Peter was transferred to a school for children with disabilities, where he remained until completing his education. He has always lived with his parents, and is close to all four siblings. In terms of employment, Peter holds a job collecting shopping carts from the car park of a large supermarket. Because of distance, I rarely see him, yet when I do he is always happy to see me and asks about life in America ("Do they have chips there?"). Like many from our Anglo-Irish heritage, he enjoys a good drink.

Cousin Janet

I recall my Nana, mother's mother, relating how my cousin Janet was exhibited to a group of young doctors in training who were then asked, "What is wrong with her?" None of their answers were successful. She was, in fact, a rarity: born without a thyroid gland. The initial fear about her condition was based on how it would impact the growth of all of her body systems. However, medication was available to help regulate growth, and Janet grew up under watchful eyes that sought to make her life as close to normal as possible. As it turns out, it has been.

Recently turning thirty, Janet lives with her parents, Uncle Frank and his wife Aunt Jean, and her previously described brother Peter. She works as a ticket taker in a cinema, proudly drives her own car, and vacations with her siblings and their families. At the same time, I wonder to what degree Janet's gender and status as the "baby of the family," has inhibited the possibility of greater independence.

My Brother's Nephew, Jonathan

My sister in law's sister gave birth to a child, Jonathan, with a rare condition known as Cornelia deLange Syndrome. As soon as he was born I began to look at information found on the internet, and realized how off-putting the descriptions were. Instead of seeing little Jonathan as a baby, he began to be replaced by an abstraction in the form of a tangled list of symptoms that painted a depressing picture. It was then I realized how for many people, wanting to know more disability-related information likely leads down a path to fear and pessimism rather than understanding and optimism.

When I visit my brother's house, he and his wife often have Jonathan over to visit. My nephew plays with his cousin, and notes how he communicates through sound and movement. Oftentimes, Jonathan takes my brother's hand and pulls him to the object he wants. "He must feel so frustrated knowing what he wants," remarks my brother, adding, "...being unable to express it." Jonathan is very small in stature, has a thick eyebrow that crosses over his nose, noticeably long eyelashes, a short nose and a downturned mouth. He is always on the move and frequently makes unusual sounds. When we all go shopping, I notice how people look at Jonathan's distinct body with curiosity. He is, after all, 1 in 20,000.

Baby Duncan

My cousin Malcolm and his wife Pamela were expecting their third child when they discovered it was a boy who would be born with a rare disorder. The name of it escapes me, but it signified a high likelihood of the baby to die in utero or be born only to live for a matter of days. Going against the advice of doctors to abort, Pamela, a devout Catholic, chose to carry her baby to full term so that nature—or God's will—would take it's course. I cannot imagine how she navigated the pregnancy knowing such inevitable odds, but she managed to do so with great dignity, respecting the life that grew within her. She and Malcolm informed their children about their new brother who would not be able to stay with them for long.

The baby was born and christened Duncan. He lived for a little more than a week. A funeral service was held to celebrate his short life. At the time I was in England for a six-day visit to attend my sister's wedding, but could not bring myself to attend the service where my cousins would bury their child, and, for my Uncle Frank, his grandson.

My Mother

I was born when my mother was seventeen years old. She often would tell me the story of being young and afraid as the doctors came toward her with medical scissors in their hands, cutting her flesh to let me out, all nine pounds and fourteen ounces. Growing up, I knew she was youthful and pretty in comparison to my friends' mothers, but suffered significant problems with her legs. She had developed varicose veins at an unusually young age, a condition that progressively became worse as she continued in her occupation of hairdressing. My mother's legs often became purple, swollen, tender—causing her to wince when they were accidentally brushed or knocked.

The first operation was not particularly successful. Had she been more experienced, less trusting, and perhaps from a different class background, she would have had a better surgeon. It was only after the surgery that she came to know the doctor's nickname of "The Butcher." The operation, she claimed, did nothing to ease her pain, and possibly exacerbated the condition.

Years passed by and while she spoke of the chronic ache in her legs, we heard without listening. Her legs, "netted with veins," as she described them, became part of the everydayness of our lives—and her three sons paid little attention. From an early age we saw her wrap crinkly cream-colored bandages around her legs, stretching from ankle to knee. As time passed, she had a second operation, and eventually a third. Each time the recovery process was long and painful. One time, as she tried to walk after her final operation, a stitch popped open and a stream of blood spurted onto the nearby hospital wall.

Over time, she has come to wear thick support hose to the knee. Pairs of them dangle from the washing line like beige bunting. My mother stopped complaining about her legs years ago stating matter-of-factly, "At the end of the day, no one really wants to hear it." Since their birth, both of her twelve-year-old grandchildren have been raised to understand that the first thing she must do in the morning is one hour of leg exercises to improve the blood flow in her legs. These exercises can take many forms. Most involve lying on her back and raising her legs in a variety of ways, from resembling a human pair of shearing scissors to pedaling a bike upside down.

In brief, my mother cannot stand still for more than a very short period of time, needing to walk in order to reinvigorate blood circulation. However, she cannot walk too far as this makes her legs throb in pain. One flight of stairs is manageable, but several are intolerable. While sitting at home, my mother raises her legs above pelvis level at any opportunity. When eating in a restaurant she carries a short stool to be placed under a table. Usually she calls ahead to ask if there's enough space as she "needs to keep her legs up," humorously aware of how suggestive this sounds. Oftentimes, if space is tight, my mother sits opposite my stepdad, her feet appearing in his lap. The pain felt both during and after long-haul flights means she can no longer visit me in New York. Traveling on two-hour flights within Europe (while paying for extra legroom) is all she can do. Standing in lines is not possible. Airports, supermarkets, concerts, public toilets...all prove to be potentially problematic situations. On a good day, her legs sometimes "play up" unexpectedly, requiring her to change plans, and maybe stay home. "You just get on with it," I've heard her say many times.

Portraits: Looking Back

In returning to the autoethnographical questions posed earlier in the chapter— *What have I come to learn as the lives of family members have been played out alongside, and interacted with, my own? What have they taught me? In what ways has this impacted me as an educator?*— I am struck by the following notion. As a researcher, what I write is in relation to myself; my interests, my beliefs, my desire to influence societal change. As a research participant, the content of what I write is in relation to others; my context exists, in part, because of their existence. While this arguably can be "true" for any research, autoethnography explicitly acknowledges this occurrence.

I consider my family members primarily as that: family members. Yet, in this instance, they are also the source of my data. In addition, through their own positionality, they contribute to constructing my position in the world— as son, brother, cousin, nephew, and so on. Within our shared histories, a nexus of relationships exists as the site of ongoing interactions that I perceive as a source of knowledge about, among many other things, disability. By linking my personal connections and experiences with the larger cultural phenomenon of disability I have informed, and continue to inform, my professional work within teacher education.

In contemplating the everyday "ordinary" lives of family members, larger questions are raised, such as: What is an ordinary family? What is considered a typical family? What is an ordinary human being? What is considered an extraordinary human being? Who gets to decide? I am also struck by ways in which families mediate differences among themselves. In mine, differences are acknowledged and accepted. Disability is not stressed, but seen as an integral part of a person. It is not a tragedy, just an ordinary part of life. In other words, disability is normal. While I have many family members with disabilities, I do not think we are the exception; I see that most families do. Within all of our families exist members with disabilities who are neither "overcomers" nor "supercrips," but rather ordinary people who negotiate the everydayness of life. In analyzing the portraits of family members, I am able to answer, at least in part, the larger question posed.

In some respects, it could be argued that to a degree we all live autoethnographic lives. By this I mean we constantly connect personal experiences to the culture(s) we inhabit, thinking about what things of interest and importance *mean* to us. We cannot live otherwise—as there is no culture-free context and no life without meaning. As an educator, I am constantly thinking about ways to connect with, and engage, an audience— whether it is as a teacher or a writer. Part of engaging others means striving to create connections with an audience, usually quickly—lest they "tune out." When teaching, I have calculatedly shared information about all family members mentioned in this chapter as a way to stimulate aspiring or actual teachers to reflect upon how their understandings of disability and/or "difference" were shaped, and continue to be shaped, by their families. Unpacking both oppressive and progressive interpretations and practices lead to substantive conversations about why we think the way we do, and how this influences our interactions with others—including the way we teach.

In particular, I have found the narratives of my family members useful when teaching classes about inclusive education. Their everyday experiences normalize disability, while simultaneously revealing the realities of limitations placed upon them as they move through their lives. I continue to learn about disability both through my personal observations and by vicariously coming to know their experiences, whether it is: my mother having to convince the local authority to renew her "Disabled" parking permit when they changed their criteria for eligibility; my Uncle Frank's obsession with his parents; cousin Janet's slow but steady move to increased independence; Granny's physical fortitude despite being frail, and how she is positioned in the "Old People's Home."

In terms of education, I am mindful of Lisa Delpit's calling attention to how teachers (including special educators) who teach "Other People's Children" (1995) yet should always reflect upon the question: Would I want this for my own child? More often than not, the answer is "no." A guiding principle of education, implicit in Delpit's work is: Teach others as you'd like your own family members to be taught. Physical, cognitive, emotional, and sensory disabilities are often viewed by teachers as liabilities, reasons why children don't "fit" into classrooms, serving as justification for segregated environments. However, conversely, acknowledging and valuing diversity as a natural occurrence helps teachers become more confident and comfortable educating students with disabilities in their classrooms. Teachers often have to unlearn the disability stereotypes and the fear these ignite before they can see the child according to their name, and not defined by their Individualized Education Program (IEP).

In terms of writing and providing service to the academic community, I feel my family helps me reflect upon, and keep grounded in, working toward a more equal and just society. As an academic, I primarily work within the discipline of Disability Studies in Education (DSE). This discipline guides most of my scholarly work—and is compatible with other areas of social justice. In my role as a reviewer of manuscripts for academic journals, I feel compelled to share my thoughts, insights, feelings, and suggestions when disability is primarily portrayed as a flaw (still prevalent in traditional special education publications), something to be remedied and ideally, cured. A central tenet of DSE is to work with, or be closely informed by people with disabilities.

In this text, as with others, I have tried to share who I am, what is important to me, and why—an outright rejection of a positivist research paradigm in favor of a fully acknowledged, personal context (Connor, 2004; Connor, 2008). Being male, white, an immigrant in the US from the UK, of working-class origin, and gay, are identities that contribute to how I conceptualize and execute all aspects of my research. In this particular chapter I am aware of being able-bodied while writing about disability, and how that may be problematic for some readers. At the same time, I am cognizant of a degree of empathy that comes from being a sexual minority, while acknowledging that markers of identity are not automatically analogous or interchangeable. I do not assume to understand another person or group's reality based on my own—yet I do self-identify as an ally to people with disabilities. I also know that the status of ally can only be verified by people with disabilities and their family members as we work together in various ways, including: improving teacher education, developing curricula, co-teaching, carrying out research, and participating in disability related projects.

During my life I have witnessed the *management* of disability by individual family members, as well as how the collective family at large negotiates it. Disability is not primarily cast as a misfortune, but rather, a fact of life. Differences among humans exist, and life always moves on. Each situation has yielded much to consider in day-to-day terms: my mother carries specialized foot-stools wherever she sits and, unable to stand in one place, consciously avoids all lines; my Uncle Frank's "demons" are understood and accepted, although not always tolerated; Allan's difficulties are sometimes alluded to, but people are sensitive toward discussing dyslexia explicitly as he has always survived in a working-class community, maintaining a job and paying his rent; cousins Peter and Janet look after each other, both employed, and accepting of being 30-somethings both living with, and helping, their parents; my brother and sister-in-law host Jonathan for weekends, and he plays with his cousin; Pamela's pregnancy was not feted in the way other family pregnancies were yet everyone was respectful and supportive of her decision.

Through describing a family's response to disability, I am able to reflect upon how my relatives influenced, and continue to influence, my own thinking in relation to my profession of educating students with disabilities. Through their response to individual differences, they have demonstrated the principle of inclusion. They have also helped raise the question for me about the absurdities of grouping so many human conditions under the umbrella term of "disability." Regardless, each person within the family has accepted and understands differences known as "disabilities"; members are given support in accordance to who needs it; and, above all, there is always a conscious effort made never to leave anyone out. While disability is accepted and understood, it is not always necessarily foregrounded. Instead, it is seen as part of, but not the defining aspect of an individual—unlike how it is viewed in education systems.

Conclusion

In originally contemplating how I might make a contribution to the theme of this book, I immediately thought of my family as a whole. Even though I live far away in a different continent, I consider them close. Both disabled and non-disabled members enter my mind every day and influence my thoughts in personal and professional situations. In sum, they provide the context of my thinking and guide me in my desire to question parameters that are imposed upon others within education and society at large: What is (a)typical? What is (ab)normal? In ways might we look at things differently in order to include other people in all aspects of life? It is this unashamed ideal in which I am interested. I view my folks as neither more nor less (dys)functional than any other family, neither more nor less (im)perfect. In observing how they live their lives, I continue to learn from them all.

Post-Script: Exposure

This chapter has been the most personal writing by far within my academic career. It was originally undertaken in the summer of 2011, and revised during the following summer. In the interim, both my Granny and Uncle Frank died within a day of each other last September. I decided to leave the text as "then," rather than "now," feeling I conveyed what I want(ed) to share. Grief takes many forms. To date, I have chosen not to fly home for funerals. I did write the eulogy for my grandmother that my brother read at the small service, emphasizing her extraordinariness found within the ordinariness of her life. I also heard about the large service for Uncle Frank at which so many spoke so highly of him.

Their passing surprised me in that no matter how much the inevitability of death is expected, it still comes as a painful shock that overcomes our entire being. Everything stops in that moment when we hear the news about death forcing us, ironically, to feel the intensity of life as it floods our consciousness, uprooting and sweeping away all that we try to make solid, safe, secure. And when the feeling subsides, even though we recover what was temporarily lost and regain what we consider "ourself," unexpected emotions return to wash over us, rendering us powerless.

Writing about my family, and how they impact who I am as a person and a professional educator, is a humbling experience. There is a feeling of exposure, vulnerability—for both myself, and those lives I have chosen to share. Have I portrayed myself, my thoughts, fairly, accurately? Have I done justice, in some small way, to the lived experiences of my family members? I have, to some extent, shared my interpretation of their lives, and how they remain in my consciousness, influencing who I am, what I believe, and how I teach about disability as natural human difference.

I turned fifty years old this year. Although an admitted cliché to some extent, nonetheless this event—coupled with the loss of family members— triggered greater reflection on how I have spent my life to date, what I have learned so far, and ways in which I can contribute to society through teacher education. In sum, this chapter serves as a short contemplation on the relationship between the personal and professional, how we can recognize and use these realms of experiences as educators, and the potential of what can be learned from one another both within families and within classrooms. Throughout life, in a variety of ways, my family has taught me that *disability is not seen as the exception, but the rule*, and this has served to keep me grounded in my chosen field.

References

Brontë, C. (1847/1987). *Jane Eyre*. London: Penguin Classics.

Clandinin, D. J., & Connelly, M. F. (2000). *Narrative inquiry: Experience and story in qualitative research*. San Francisco, CA: Jossey-Bass.

Crawford, L. (1996). Personal ethnography. *Communication monographs, 63*, 158–170.

Connor, D. J. (2004). Infusing disability studies into "mainstream" educational thought: One person's story. *Review of Disability Studies, 1*(1), 100–119.

——— (2008). *Urban narratives: Portraits-in-progress—life at the intersections of learning disability, race, and social class*. New York: Peter Lang.

Delpit, L. (1995). *Other people's children: Cultural conflict in the classroom*. New York: New Press.

DuBois, W. E. B. (1903). *The souls of Black folk*. New York: Bantam.

Ellis, C. (1997). Evocative autoethnography: Writing emotionally about our lives. In W. G. Tierney & Y. S. Lincoln (Eds.), *Representation and the text* (pp. 115–139). Albany: State University of New York Press.

——— (2009). *Revision: Autoethnographic reflections on life and work*. Walnut Creek, CA: Left Coast Press.

Habib, D. (2008). (Producer). *Including Samuel*. [DVD]. Available from http://www.includingsamuel.com/home.aspx

Kesey, K. (1962). *One flew over the cuckoo's nest*. New York: Signet.

Ladson-Billings, G. (1995). Toward a theory of culturally relevant pedagogy. *American Educational Research Journal, 32* (3), 465–491.

Lawrence-Lightfoot, S. & Hoffman, David, J. (1997). *The art and science of portraiture*. San Francisco: Jossey-Bass.

Lincoln, Y. S., & Denzin, N. K. (2000). The seventh movement: Out of the past. In N. K. Denzin & Y. S. Lincoln (Eds.), *Handbook of qualitative research* (pp. 1047–1065). Thousand Oaks, CA: Sage.

Richardson, L. (2000). Writing: A method of inquiry. In N. K. Denzin & Y. S. Lincoln (Eds.), *Handbook of Qualitative Research* (1st ed., pp. 923-948). Thousand Oaks, CA: Sage.

Safran, S. P. (1998). The first century of disability portrayal in film: An analysis of the literature. *Journal of Special Education, 31*(4), 467–479.

Chapter 10

An Open Letter to Wyatt

Erin McCloskey

Dear Wyatt,

You have always been a mover and a shaker. You set the pace for me as my first-born, and you were always just *doing*, without a care in a world about who was watching or what they were thinking. You lined up toy cars, or numbered, with a marker, everything you could get your hands on. I remember cleaning out the fridge one day when you were just a tot and placing all of the bottles and jars on the kitchen table so I could wipe down the shelves. You came in the kitchen, and with eyes as wide as saucers, asked if you could get the permanent marker and number all of the jars. All of those jars and bottles and containers, just ripe for numbering. You love order and you love repetitive motions—your body like a metronome, keeping track of your inner rhythm. I can't remember the first time someone asked me why you rock or bounce or jump, but I came to realize that it's almost worse when they don't ask the questions, but just look at you, and then look to me for an explanation. Waiting for me to explain, to tell them, "Oh, he has autism," so they'll be more comfortable, as if categorizing you and labeling you makes it easier for them to understand who you are and what you do, so that they can go about their business.

You used to bounce in your high chair; and now you bounce back and forth on the couch, or stand in front of me, one foot in front of the other, rocking back and forth to ask me for a snack or if you can ask me a question (which you know, by the way, drives me crazy!).

I remember going to pick you up from day care. I would see your face peering out of the small rectangular window in the door, watching me walk toward you down the long corridor leading to your room. I could see you jump, jump, jump. I would open the door to your classroom and find all of the children were jumping, following your lead. Up and down, up and down, all smiling from ear to ear. There is no greater joy for me than to see your own joy, and I loved how your happiness made all the kids in the class happy, too.

When you got older it wasn't fine anymore to be so jumpy and so rocky. Jumping high in the air as an expression of delight became a symptom, a sign, a marker for the word that is the opposite of fine. A lot of the time, kids wouldn't notice, but if they did, they'd ask you why you were rocking back and forth. You would reply, "It's just my hobby." That seemed to explain it to them. Occasionally, you would tell me a story about the playground and wanting to play with certain kids, and they not letting you, but what second grader hasn't had that experience? You would report these brushoffs in a nonchalant way, saying that it was okay, because you could go on the swings and just watch while swinging.

I remember you wanted to play soccer so badly. The attraction, of course, was that you got to wear a number on the back of your shirt, which you thought was just super cool. Soccer isn't an easy sport for someone who wants everyone to get along. When you played defense, an offensive member would charge down the field, right at you, and you would smile, let them pass, and then chase them with this joyful skip. During games, the parents would yell at kids (one particularly loud parent would yell, "ATTACK!"), and the yelling was just too loud for you. You would put your fingers in your ears and rock away. At practice one day, a mom mentioned that her son had sensory integration issues and she wondered, from observing you, whether you did too. I said, "If you ask Wyatt, he'll just tell you that rocking like that is his hobby, but yes, he does seem sensitive to loud sounds." Another parent, also sitting nearby and hearing us, began to discuss her son who she described as having ADHD.

I was so conflicted about this conversation. On one hand, it was sort of nice to have a group of women who understood the experience of having a child whom others deemed "different" (unlike the soccer coach, who not so quietly pulled me aside to ask me what was the matter with you, and asked me if I wanted to tell him anything), but I was so leery, and still am, of people categorizing you. Didn't those women know that by saying those things out loud, the people who heard them, myself included, would start to alter expectations of their children? I'm still unsure whether it's better to say nothing, or to try to offer up an innocuous explanation that might appease those who prod.

Me

I remember thinking that disability and special education were things that were so tangible. I could hold onto them, just as I could wrap my hands around a textbook that could easily explain who was and who wasn't disabled and so "entitled" to receive special education services. For me, disability and special education were woven together and depended on each other—one didn't exist without the other. A person with a disability depended on special education to fix or remediate or accommodate what their bodies or brains couldn't do. In graduate school I took classes that certified me as a special education teacher. Up until my first job, I don't think I ever really thought about disability or special education, but I learned a lot through the lack, the absence, of conversations—my arm was pulled or my words were shushed. Some things were okay to talk about and to look at, and some weren't. My family was not a talking family, but we were very polite. Yes, very polite.

You see, my undergraduate degree was in fine arts, and although I majored in sculpture, I considered myself a painter. My mom (your grandmother, who you never did get to meet) urged me to take classes in art education, and I received a credential to teach art. My first job was to do just that, in a New York City school that "served" students who were classified as SIE, VII, and VIII—special codes that schools in New York used to describe students who had "severe" needs in some way or another. In fact, the school I worked at, and many others in the city like it, had students enrolled that the school system decided were so different that the school could not possibly be a part of the local district, but rather were a part of District 75, "the only separate superintendency in the United States for students with moderate and severe disabilities" (Connor, 2010, p. 158).

I had virtually no experience as a teacher (minus my student teaching placement, in which I taught art to children who were long-term patients at Kings County Hospital in Brooklyn). I walked through the doors of that elementary school and found out that I would push a cart from classroom to classroom with my supplies. While "art on a cart" was not what I had envisioned, I was happy to be given the opportunity to teach.

On my first day, I discovered that I was expected to restrain children who were deemed by myself or others to be out of control, by holding their arms behind their backs while lowering them to the floor. After they were on the floor, I was to sit on them so that they would not be a threat to themselves or to others. When we felt that they were not longer a threat, I was to get off of them and continue on, with my lesson or down the hall. Sometimes, while I taught, another teacher would sit on a child at the back of the classroom. It was so commonplace that everyone, students and teachers alike, just went on with their business. The administrators rarely came out of their offices. During that year I met children who had experiences that were unimaginable—I had a sense of confusion and chaos every day I walked into the building. I drank too much, I couldn't get enough sleep, I felt completely inadequate. I only lasted there one year.

I moved to another school, trying my hand at a high school in Brooklyn, where I taught self-contained special education English classes part of the day, and in a resource room for the other part of the day. I was so surprised to get this job, because I had no experience at the high school level, and I didn't have a special education teaching credential. I enrolled in graduate school at night and on the weekends, and took classes that would certify me as a special education teacher while I taught at the high school during the day. I hoped that I could figure out special education, with all of its acronyms and policies, and that my graduate training would prepare me to handle the job.

In school, I learned how to apply task analysis to skills I wanted my students to learn, and how to create a behavior management chart. I learned how to administer tests so as not to compromise the way that they were standardized, and how to write reports that would be used to classify children as having a disability. In one class, I worked with an 8 year-old student who came to the college for tutoring. Princess, who I was told was learning disabled, needed help with reading and writing. I had to test her on our very first meeting. I remember looking into her eyes and seeing such fear—she looked so ashamed. I wanted to throw the test out the window and put her at ease, but I didn't. I don't remember a thing about what the tests showed; what I do remember was that she loved Whitney Houston and wanted to be singer when she grew up.

When people asked me what I did and I told them that I was a special education teacher, they said things like, "Wow, you must be so patient." I didn't really understand this reaction, because I wasn't really always so patient (as you, Wyatt, are very much aware). But these reactions from people became layered—they created a shiny lacquer on my special education teacher image. By definition, because I was a special education teacher, I was therefore compassionate and caring and patient, without ever having to prove that it was actually true. This was so different from when I went out into the world and called myself a painter.

As the years unfolded, I became more confident in my role as a special education teacher. I noticed in my experiences working in many different settings—from a residential treatment center for adolescents to several different public elementary schools—what helped students learn and what didn't. During the day, I spoke with parents about how I would help remediate their child's weakness in a particular area, as though that process was somehow different from teaching.

In graduate school, I learned a new language about how it all happened, and then went to work and applied it. I believed in the idea of special education so completely that I gave no thought to what this language was doing, the power that those words held. When it came time in my graduate program to choose a concentration (I could pick between learning disabilities or emotional disturbances), it seemed like a logical question to ask—I had come to believe that everyone could be categorized. I chose learning disabilities, and after another six or so years teaching, I went back to school to get a doctoral degree in reading, again taking classes at night and teaching during the day.

I made the decision to go back to school again to focus on reading, because the one class I had taken about literacy learning while getting my special education certificate, the class I tutored Princess in, was completely inadequate. In it, I spent a lot of time learning about the structure of special education, but only a little time learning about how to help kids actually learn to read. You see, the idea was that the kids had learning disabilities and so it was them, not me, that stood in the way of their progression in reading. My professors in the reading program pushed me to explore what I meant when I, almost without thinking, described a student as disabled, or remedial, or gifted.

In many ways, the work I did in this reading program was more about unlearning than learning. It changed my teaching, in a huge way, and it made it hard to be a part of the special education machine. I still tested children, and I still contributed the standardized scores to support their labels, but I also taught them to read, and really believed that they could learn and that I could teach them. I had been taught in my graduate special education program that reading curricula designed for learning disabled children could move them ahead. There were decodable books and lists of words and worksheets and Orton Gillingham. Although the kids did not particularly like this instruction (heck, who likes to take their medicine?), I could make them do it and they would get better. I could have them read lists of words and see what percentage they got right and correlate that with a grade level. I could create an IEP with goals like, "Sue will read 100 high-frequency words with 80% accuracy over a two-week period as measured by the special education teacher."

Everything felt out of whack—for me, for general education teachers—when I discovered that I could engage my students in the same meaningful activities that their peers down the hall in general education were doing, and at the same time develop their reading ability alongside their love of reading. When I started to "push in" to general education classrooms, I saw how 'my' students were made different by their labels. They had to get up and leave class right in the middle of a lesson because a therapist had come by to pick them up; or they were called on to read aloud, as though reading had to be some kind of public performance.

I noticed, as my doctoral professors pointed out, that learning was often thought of as "fixed" and that the language used to describe learning was powerful—that language was action (Johnston, 2012). I began to read about how students with learning disabilities could be made. Children were who they were; we made them disabled by creating that category for them.

My relationship with my students and their families changed. I began to talk to my student's parents about what their children *could* do rather than what they couldn't. I made peace in some ways with my role as a special education teacher, but there were always situations where I bumped up against the deficit model of special education. With each bump, I lost a little bit more of my passion to be a cog in the special education machine. Why couldn't I just work with kids who needed extra help in literacy? Why did they have to be labeled?

I began to realize that it was the label, and the expectations that went along with it, that made me feel, almost constantly, uneasy, made my work so much harder. Constantly, I had to show kids that they could do it. Some had come to believe that they were so innately disabled that there was no way they could improve their reading (McCloskey, 2012). I witnessed the lowered expectations, the other children's reactions to students with special education services, the school psychologists' interpretations of children's drawings that seemed to define and confine them, and the endless reification that disability was innate and fixed and all inside the child.

I left teaching in the public schools when you were two years old. If my literacy degree was the first opportunity to redefine my beliefs about special education and disability, you were the second.

You

Once, I asked a friend what she thought of you sitting on the couch and bouncing back and forth. What I wanted to hear was, "Looks like fun!" What she said was, "Well, it's a little quirky, don't you think?" For some reason, that moment really stuck with me. I think it's because it was the first time that I asked someone else what *they* thought, and it felt like a betrayal to you. I wish I could say right here and now that I knew then that I would just accept how wonderfully quirky you were, how wonderfully quirky we all were, and that I stopped asking other people what they thought of you. I wish I could, but I can't.

Instead, I looked for reasons and cures. I drove you to doctors who tested you. Some said don't worry. Others said start worrying, but they always talked or wrote about you in ways that were all too familiar to me. A psychological evaluation done when you were just three and half years old said that you "...do not seek out interactions with other children. He does not seem to have the same interests as other children. While they enjoy playing with cars or other toys, Wyatt is more interested in numbers and letters to the point of being fixated on them." Another said that you would qualify for the label of autistic, then at the next meeting wondered out loud if you might have ADHD. Sometimes your pencil grasp was poor, your eye contact was limited, and your play was parallel. Other times, you were described as inquisitive and really great with numbers.

Going to school was so exciting for you. You looked forward to riding the bus and being a big boy. For me, it was scary, because I knew what lay in wait. Normal was lurking around every corner; how could I prepare you for that? Really, how could I prepare *myself* for that?

I wanted you to be with a teacher about whom I'd heard wonderful stories; she taught in an "integrated" setting. For me, this was a bonus. Instead, you were placed in a "straight" kindergarten classroom. When I asked the principal if there was any way you could change classrooms, he said no. The teacher I wanted you with met you during the summer at the kindergarten orientation program, and she knew that you belonged with her. So she told me to write a letter saying that we were in the process of testing for a special education classification. And while it was true we were seeing a developmental pediatrician who would have formally tested you if I wanted, it wasn't one hundred percent true.

Remember when you were confused about how Martin Luther King Jr. could be placed in jail for being a hero, and we talked about how sometimes you have to do what's right even though it might technically be wrong? That's exactly how this felt. I knew it was wrong to say I was doing something that I wasn't, but I also knew that this was the best classroom for you. You were granted entry to the "integrated" classroom, but on the flip side, they wanted you labeled as autistic. After you were in the class for a month or so, we had a meeting about it. I said no. They looked at me with *those* eyes, those "she's in denial" eyes, those "how could she deny him special education services" eyes, those "she's got a long road ahead of her" eyes. They told me that they would allow you to have speech and language services anyway, but I didn't really want that for you. I didn't want it because I didn't want you to think that you needed fixing. The thing was that you did want it. You liked going with the speech therapist, because you played games and had fun, and so I relented.

Us

Since you started school, I have lived with an experience that I try to describe to my students. I ask the college students in my *Introduction to Special Education* class to think about what it means—*really* means—to a parent to hear the words disability and special education applied to their child. "What are the first words that come to your mind," I ask them? And more importantly, "Why these words and not others?"

Twice a week I teach my students—young people who will someday be teachers—about special education. We spend two and a half hours a week talking about disability, school and society's response to disability, and the experiences that people have had in special education. Many of these students disclose—sometimes publically, sometimes privately—that they have disabilities, that their mothers or fathers have disabilities, that their brothers or sisters or friends have disabilities. Although many people who take this class have or know of someone with a disability, when I ask them to raise their hands on the first day of class if they have any experiences talking about disability in school, only one or two hands go up. Sometimes no hands go up.

This is the one class that students are mandated to take in order to receive a teaching credential in the state of New York. Many of the people in this class will end up sitting at special education meetings and making decisions about what kids can and cannot do. I see myself at their age looking for answers, having never really thought about the questions. Wyatt, you make the questions important, and here's why.

I walked into your second grade classroom, having been asked to meet with your teacher. She had sent home a note saying, "These past two weeks he has exhibited some behavioral challenges." The note went on to say that the special education teacher who joins your "integrated" classroom for half of the day has noticed "peaks and valleys in his emotions." Of course I would meet with them, but I knew what lay in wait. Normal still lurked in the shadows, and now the spotlight was being adjusted.

Just like the year before, I walked into the school to have this conversation. Before I knew it, the small, kidney-shaped table was filled with bodies, some that I knew, and some that I didn't. Your teacher, the special education teacher, the speech and language therapist, and the school counselor all took their places. I think about Mehan (1996), who notes that disability is constructed through the language of testing, and that the mother's voice—the nontechnical voice—too often gets little validation. The thing is, because of my training and experience, I can play the game. I can be technical and invoke research. I know how to refute, invalidate, and contradict the medical model of disability that I am sure will rear its ugly head. But I heard your dad's voice, and I tried to keep my promise to him, not to play the role of the expert.

Don't get me wrong, these were lovely people, and they cared deeply for you. But we—our whole family—were about to get constructed. I'd promised your dad that I would listen more, talk less. I reminded myself to really hear what they had to say, that their words came from a deeply caring place. Remain calm and listen, I thought to myself.

And then it began. The room swirled with words like "stimming" and "flapping" and "rocking" and "jumping" and "students with his profile" and "lack of eye contact" and "body doesn't face the speaker." I tried to really hear them, but a tornado of rocks spun in my stomach. At one point, I noticed that I was hunched over, and I lurched my body upright. The speech and language therapist looked at testing done a year ago and predicted problems: "Third grade has a lot of writing, could be trouble. State testing, could be trouble."

Everyone around the table agreed that the third grade "integrated" class was the right fit for you. I agreed! "I would love for both of my children to be in integrated classrooms," I said. "In fact, I believe in inclusion, and agree with you that this is best for Wyatt, and, really, the best for everyone." I was so happy, because this is what I wanted for you.

But wait, they said, he can't be in this classroom without a diagnosis. It wouldn't be fair, they said; why him and not some other non-classified child? Why don't you have him classified so he can be in this class, they asked, this class that we all think is the best fit for him? Why don't you?

Well, it would be easy to classify you as autistic. Your pediatrician already said so. So why don't I?

What kind of mother am I?

And here Wyatt, I can't fully explain it, but something happened, and all of the separate parts of my life came together—the mother, the special education teacher, the college professor, the student, the ally, the woman who is constantly asking questions. Not only did I feel the responsibility to advocate for you, but I felt the responsibility to talk about disability and special education outside of the college classroom in which I teach, in real-life, in that moment, right then. I had never had this conversation when I was a special education teacher with parents or even the other teachers with whom I worked. I thought philosophy and theory were important, but somehow separate from practice. I thought that people would say that I was speaking from the ivory tower with no foothold in reality. It was you that gave me the legitimacy to start this conversation.

I decided not to react to the implied taunt of "bad mother," but to present another definition, one with which I was sure they could all relate. I mean, didn't I, too, have a tidy hold on special education? Wasn't it these kinds of conversation that helped me broaden my understanding of what I thought I knew about special education and disability? So I began to talk, about exclusion, graduation rates, expectations, and deficit perspectives of autism. I replaced the swirling words based in deficit with new ones like "loves to do math" and "Ari Ne'eman" and "an amazing need for fairness." I asked them questions, big questions. The one I am most proud of is, "Do you want to change who Wyatt is?"

The special education teacher looked at me and said, "I always wondered why you wouldn't classify him. You know, what you're saying makes a lot of sense." And it did! Why did it take me so long to say those things aloud to people outside my college classroom? Why was I so scared to be explicit about my reasons for not wanting to classify you as a student with autism?

Still, your teacher asked me to think about labeling you so that you could be in the "integrated" class, to talk with your father about it, and to get back to her. And, so, we did think and talk. We wrote a nice letter thanking them for their time and concern, but declining the opportunity for the label. As I wrote that letter to your teacher, I thought about this quote from Baker (2002),

> The difficulty of imagining society without schools as they currently are with their baby-sitting and sorting functions or of drawing Utopian pictures of how they might be without presumptions of an ableist normativity is the difficulty of having been normalized as a schoolchild, of having a subjectivity colonized by a concern to "be able to" do something, of having been constantly examined to "prove" that one can get the point, make the point, or draw the picture of "the alternative" (n.p.)

It wasn't any individual's fault that they wanted to "change" you or "fix" you, as though you are broken or defective. We all have a hand in creating this "ableist normativity," and maybe I'm just the first mom in this school to start a conversation about why. Still, this school year, your third-grade year, has been no different—I've already been called in to talk again about classifying you as autistic.

They were all there again. This time the speech therapist told me about an assignment she does with students to help them develop eye contact. She stated that she asks the kids to tell stories in her small group. One boy, she said, was telling his story and she told him "to look me in the eye." She said to him, "The bookcase isn't listening to your story, I am. Look at me," and she presented this example as evidence of how her work was helping him develop eye contact. She says she would like to work on this with you, too. I politely declined and told her that I'm not overly concerned with your eye contact but that I did love your stories. Then I asked her, "Why is it important for students to look at you?"

Me Again

I wonder what kind of teacher I would have been if I had not had you. I remember when you were just born, in 2003, when I held you in my arms and watched the television coverage of the Iraq invasion. A mother appeared on the screen—I can't remember if she was Iraqi or American—and she spoke about the horror she felt, knowing her son was in harm's way. At that moment, I understood war in a different way than I ever had before, as a mother. I feel the same way about teaching my *Introduction to Special Education* class. I understand the construction of disability in a way I never would have before, because I still hold you in my arms while the world tries to tell me you are broken.

This semester has been an interesting one for me. Of course, as I teach this class, you and my former students are always on my mind. That can make it hard to hear my students say that some children don't belong in inclusive classrooms, or that it would be better for them to be in self-contained special education classrooms with "their kind," for "their sake." But, I let them say these things, and give those words space in my classroom, so that disability and special education does not remain silent, and so my students can be held accountable for their language.

Usually, I push them, as gently as I can, to define how they would make those distinctions. "Who is in and who is out?" I ask. And more importantly, "Why?" Sometimes, my students push each other, and this semester, for the first time that I'm aware of, I had a student with autism in my class who did the pushing. In her, I saw you, not merely because you both have autism, but rather because you both have a keen sense of justice and fairness and possibility about change in this world. Sadly, I don't think many—maybe even any—students in the class have ever had the chance to have a person with autism in their classes before (at least that they were aware of), and I hope that they realize the great injustice of that segregation on their own learning.

I've made a lot of changes to the class as my own thinking has changed. When I ask students to respond to the readings I assign in this class, I no longer ask for just written text. I ask them to draw, write poetry, create symbols, express themselves without words, and design their own methods of response. In the end, my goal is to make them see that placement in special education is arbitrary, and that giving so much power to intelligence testing neglects the multiple modes people can use to represent their knowledge and learning.

As I make my way as a researcher, I continue to explore ways to make meaning out of my experiences as a woman, a teacher, a student, a daughter, and a mother. I think about ways to use that moment of clarity in the meeting with your teachers and school personnel in my research, and not only critique the system, but also take action. My very first and last assignment in the *Introduction to Special Education* class that I teach is a paper that I call an 'Articulation.' I use this term because of the passage by Kamberelis and Dimitriadis (2005), who talk about how scholars have worked to understand and theorize "the real" (p. 123):

> Articulations are ongoing struggles to position practices with dynamic fields of force in particular ways to produce discursive-material geographies within which certain modes of thought and action are possible (p. 124).

I ask my students to articulate their understanding of special education and disability once at the beginning, and once at the end. I look for growth in the space in between. Wyatt, I write this open letter to you, but of course it's really for me. It's my own articulation to myself about how I was, am, and hope to be in this world, as I try to embrace the "ongoing struggles" of what it means to be a researcher in the field of special education. A field where words like "normed" and "objective" are passed around as Truth. It's with you, as a mom, that I see how deeply ingrained these words are, how they influence my everyday actions. So I'm trying to understand that too.

When you went with me to pick up your brother from the afterschool gardening program last Wednesday you saw Lisa, the girl you've had a crush on for two years. As you stood there looking at her, smiling, and rocking, and I saw her look up at you, I placed my hand on your shoulder and whispered in your ear, "Wy, stop rocking." As soon as I said it, I felt ashamed. I want to tell you all about those feelings, but I don't have the words for it all yet. So I will just keep asking myself questions, I guess.

But to you, I say: Wyatt, rock on.

References

Baker, B. (2002). The hunt for disability: The new eugenics and the normalization of school children. *Teachers College Record, 104*(4), 663–703.

Connor, D. (2010). Adding urban complexities to the mix: Continued resistance to the inclusion of students with cognitive impairments (or New York, New York: So bad they segregated it twice). In P. Smith (Ed.), *Whatever happened to inclusion?: The place of students with intellectual disabilities in education* (pp. 157–183). New York: Peter Lang.

Johnston, P. (2012). *Opening minds: Using language to change lives.* Portland, ME: Stenhouse Publishers.

Kamerelis, G., & Dimitriadis, G. (2005). *Qualitative inquiry.* New York: Teachers College Press.

McCloskey, E. (2012). *Taking on a learning disability: At the crossroads of special education and adolescent literacy learning.* Charlotte, NC: Information Age Publishing.

Mehan, H. (1996). The construction of an ld student: A case study in the politics of representation. In M. Silverstein & G. Urban (Eds.), *Natural histories of discourse* (pp. 253–276). Chicago: University of Chicago Press.

Chapter 11

"That's OK. They Are Beautiful Children."

Kathleen A. Kotel

Growing up, I lived across the street from a little girl with long dark hair who was a year or two older than me—and also blind. I never played with her, not because I did not want to. I did. I was never given the opportunity. Her mother did not allow or encourage her to play with the children in the neighborhood, while her older and younger brother participated in many of the neighborhood games and activities. Whenever I asked my mother about the little girl, and why she did not play with me or the other kids in the neighborhood or attend the same school that I did, she usually responded with a comment regarding her blindness. She would say something along the lines of, "Well she is blind and blind kids go to school for blind children." In doing so, she inadvertently passed on the notion that children with disabilities are not normal and do not belong in mainstream society. My mother was always quick to change the subject too. We never had a discussion about my neighbor's disability, nor did she encourage me to have a play date or a relationship with her. Her blindness was an unspoken subject, something to avoid.

I began to formulate mostly unconscious beliefs about normalcy and disability: *Being blind means one is different, not normal, not like everyone else. Being different (blind) means one lives in a neighborhood, but one doesn't play with the other children who are normal. Being different (blind) means one must attend a special school for children who are different (not normal).*

As a child I felt sorry for the little girl who lived across the street from me. I thought about how lonely she must be without any friends. I was afraid of her too, because of the unspoken barrier that surrounded her and prevented a possible friendship. I am not sure how she felt, but I can only imagine that she was lonely and isolated.

When I was in third grade, my friend's mother was a bus driver for *retarded, crippled,* and *sick* children, who attended a *special* school. Because we were off school one day, my friend and I rode the bus route with her. I remember my friend's mother preparing us for the children we were going to meet that day. She referred to all the children as "mentally retarded." She explained to us that the children were going to look, behave, and talk differently. I remember feeling apprehensive, not sure what different meant. The bus ride was extremely long, and the distances between each individual stop lengthy. The *special* school was one I had never seen before, located far away from the neighborhood where I grew up, yet many of the kids we picked up that day lived not far from me.

That experience left me with a similar impression: *Those children are not normal. They are different. They are sick, crippled, and mentally retarded. They need to be fixed and cured. They need to go to a special school far away. I might catch what they have. I need to stay away from them* The one certain thing I *caught* from that experience was a negative attitude and fear of disability.

In high school, as a senior interested in becoming a teacher, I was offered a course in child development for the first semester and the opportunity to teach in a day care program during the second semester. And, for the first time in the history of the day care program, a child with Down syndrome was enrolled. The teacher spent an entire class period explaining the genetic cause of Down syndrome and prepared us for what to expect when this little boy came to class. The teacher explained some of the stereotypical characteristics often associated with children with Down syndrome, most of which were negative. The focus was on deficits, and all that people with Down syndrome could not do. She also told us that he was most likely going to be the most loving and loveable little boy we would ever meet (another common assumption attached to children with Down syndrome).

Ready to Teach

Having very few and mostly negative experiences with people with disabilities as a child and young adult, I began my own critical analysis of my beliefs and understandings regarding disability when I had to memorize a portion of the first federal special education law in my pre-service education classes. The notion that children were now entitled to a free and public education made me question what type of educational services they had prior to the law. Why was a law needed to ensure children with disabilities would receive a free and appropriate education? I knew children with disabilities did not attend most neighborhood schools, but I had never really thought about why. Nor had I thought much about why children with disabilities were not included in any other facet of my life. I never had to critically think about my experiences or beliefs about disability—beliefs imposed upon me through my experiences and lack of open and honest discussion.

By the time I graduated from college in 1983 with a degree in elementary education, I thought of children as being of two types: *normal* and *handicapped*. Indeed, I graduated from a dual teacher education system: special education teachers and general education teachers. Though I didn't know it then, some researchers challenged the notion of a dual education system even in the early 1980s (Stainback & Stainback, 1984). Regardless of the push for inclusion, this dual system belief is still very prevalent today, perhaps especially so for children with intellectual disabilities (Smith, 2010a; 2010b).

As a new educator, I eagerly anticipated and naively assumed that students with disabilities would be placed in my classroom and I would be their teacher. My actual experience as a new teacher did not align with my desire or assumption. For the most part, children with significant disabilities were already assessed, labeled, and segregated into self-contained special education classrooms, through the typical process that Baker has coined, "the hunt for disability" (Baker, 2002).

During the third year of the thirteen years I spent teaching middle school, I was told that I was going to have a child with visual impairments in my seventh grade economics class. I met with the special education teacher, who explained to me that the student would need preferential seating and large-print textbook duplication which she would take care of. Unfortunately, at the last minute, the mother decided to transfer her daughter to a private school for visually impaired and blind children. I was very disappointed. I wondered why the mother made that particular decision. As an educator, the mother's decision seemed unnecessary to me. I was prepared to do all that I could as a teacher, to not only teach this child, but to make her feel welcome and a valued member of my class.

Another time, it was anticipated that a child with cerebral palsy, who had a companion dog, still in sixth grade, would attend the middle school where I taught the following year. Since this was the first time a child using a wheelchair and a companion dog would attend this particular school, there were many concerns, questions, and gossip amongst staff members. They spoke of allergies, biting, and distractions because of the companion dog. Many staff members openly opposed the dog attending. However, if the dog was not allowed to attend school with the boy, the boy would have been denied the support that allowed for him to be successful.

There was also lot of discussion about the mother, too. Her reputation was that she was a mother who was out to get whatever she wanted for her son, and that she would not take no for an answer. Some might perceive her actions as a loving mother who would do whatever was necessary to provide opportunities for her son, in order for him to be allowed to participate fully alongside his peers.

Once the child actually attended school, most of these concerns never materialized. There was so much speculation, worry, and debate over this situation, most of the concerns were worked out prior to the child's arrival. However, access to the outside blacktop area which was used for social activities and recess was problematic. Because there was no ramp at the door located by the cafeteria, the child had to exit the building from a different location after lunch. This meant the child had to travel outside the building around the school property. By the time the child actually reached the blacktop area, he needed to turn around and head back to the front entrance in order to get to his next class on time, allowing no time for socialization with his peers. It was not only an inconvenience in bad weather, but at times impossible for the child to move through the snow and ice. The mother went to the administrators and insisted a ramp be built at the same exit to which all the other children had access.

I remember listening to staff comments about the situation. Some respected her for her advocacy and determination, while others felt she was asking for too much, was not being reasonable, and was costing the taxpayers unnecessarily. The ramp was completed before the child left for high school; however, he was only able to use it for a few months. I remained the lunchroom supervisor for several years after the child left for high school and saw many people with and without disabilities who benefitted from this ramp—students and teachers with temporary injuries, people with achy joints who preferred ramps over stairs, people transporting goods on carts, not to mention the students who simply found the ramp a great place to socialize and play games.

The Birth of My Daughter

Fifteen years ago, I left teaching and became a mother for the first time. Fourteen years ago, I became a mother to my second child; twelve years ago, I became a mother again. When my middle child, Talia, was born, the words "Down syndrome" were attached to her identity, and my role as a mother was changed forever.

When I gave birth to my first child, my son, it was a celebration of pure joy. Phone calls were nonstop. Family and friends visited and congratulated us with flowers and gifts. The nurses and doctors congratulated us with handshakes and hugs. Every time they came to my room they would look at the baby and tell me how adorable he was. I felt like I gave birth to a king. We brought him home and simply adored him and continued to celebrate his new life.

Six months later I was pregnant with my daughter. I felt like the luckiest person in the world. I had a wonderful loving husband, a beautiful little baby boy, and now I was going to have another baby. The pregnancy, for the most part, was like my son's. I was extremely nauseous most of the time and a little tired. One day, after a routine office visit my doctor called and told me that the results of the ultrasound showed some fluid around the baby's heart, and that we should have a level II ultrasound just to make sure everything was alright. Of course this was a bit scary for my husband and me, but once we had the ultrasound and everything seemed fine we relaxed and put it out of our minds. Because I could not hold back my curiosity I asked the ultrasound technician to tell me the gender of the baby. It was a girl! I was so excited. I really wanted to have three or four children, but being as nauseous as I was, I was thrilled to know that I was having a girl and I could be done if I wanted. A healthy boy and a girl...how perfect! We didn't tell anyone we knew the gender. We wanted to keep it a surprise, but I was beyond excited. My dreams of having a girl and doing all the "girlie" things moms do with their daughters was finally going to be a reality.

The morning of my daughter's birth I woke up as usual and went about getting my son's breakfast. I didn't feel the baby moving, so I called the doctor. My due date was about three weeks away, but I felt I should just let them know she was not moving around as much as she normally did. The nurse told me to come in and the doctor would check everything out. I had a feeling I was going to have the baby that day, so I packed my bag with the camera, the pink outfit I bought for my daughter to wear home and licorice for my husband to munch on while I was in labor. I called my husband and told him to be ready, just in case.

The doctor told me everything looked fine and that I was probably in labor. He sent me to the hospital and said I would most likely have the baby that day. I remembered that once you are admitted in the hospital for labor, they won't give you anything to eat except ice chips, so I stopped at McDonald's and the vending machine for snacks. No way was I going to go through labor on an empty stomach. I called my husband again and said, "Meet me at the hospital. I think I am in labor." I was so excited to think that today was the day I was going to finally meet her. It is such a wonderful feeling knowing a baby is entering the world with nothing but pure, unconditional love waiting for them and that was how I felt, pure unconditional love for my daughter.

Once checked in, my husband arrived and the doctor confirmed I was indeed in labor. I thought, "The anticipation is over. I am going to be a mother to a little girl. All my dreams of mothering a daughter are going to be a reality soon." I know it may sound a bit cliché, but my life felt complete and I was beyond ecstatic. I was not the least bit nervous about the upcoming painful labor. I was mentally prepared for the hours to come, or at least I thought I was.

My labor with my daughter went much faster than with my son. Just a couple of hours after being admitted she was born. I was amazed. I thought I would be in labor for much longer. Once she entered the world, I waited for someone to say something like, "Congratulations" or "It's a girl." But no one did. I remember the sudden silence the moment she was born and was held in the hands of the doctor.

No one said anything.

I waited some more. Still silence.

I finally said, "Is she a girl?" It never entered my mind to ask, "Is she alright?" I don't know if anyone answered me or not, but they handed me the baby and went about with post delivery procedures silently. I held my daughter and stared at her face. She was beautiful. Soft peach colored skin, perfectly shaped eyebrows, a tiny nose, and a little bit of golden colored hair on her head. I tried to figure out who she looked like. At first, I did not see a resemblance to anyone. I looked a little longer and said, "She has lips like Brittany," a niece with very full lips. I looked at her eyes and said, "Now whose eyes do you have?" I really could not answer that. Her eyes were a bit slanted upward but I didn't think anything of it at that moment.

I knew from my son's birth that I should start nursing as soon as possible for maternal bonding reasons, so I tried. She did not latch on like she should have, so I looked around for a nurse to help me. I felt a little isolated at this point, because no one was available, even though the doctor and nurses were in the room. With my son I had eager nurses not only around me but literally in my face and available to help me with my post delivery needs, my son's care, and nursing.

I wondered why it was so quiet. No one was talking. The medical staff all seemed busy avoiding me. I saw one of the nurses watching from a distance, writing something on my chart. I don't remember what she specifically looked like, but I remember her looking serious, focused, and concerned. She did not have that joyous, excited smile that most nurses have after the birth of a baby. My husband had left the room, so he could call our family and friends with his cell phone, because the phone in the delivery room didn't work. I thought that was odd—not my husband leaving to call— but that the phone line out didn't work. Perhaps it was divine intervention preventing me from having to make two phone calls to everyone. The first one, "It's a girl!" and the second one, "She has..."

Feeling the joy of being a new mother again, and wanting to break the silence and discomfort in the room, I said to the doctor, who also did not smile, "What a great job you have, bringing beautiful babies into the world." The doctor just lifted her head up, looked at me, cracked a brief attempt at a smile, and went back to her work, saying nothing. I thought that was odd, and a bit cold, but I didn't care. I was so happy, being done with labor and holding my new baby, that I really didn't think much of it until later when I realized she knew.

After I held my daughter briefly, a nurse abruptly took her away, assuring me it was policy: "The baby needs to be seen by the neonatologist within an hour after birth in order to make sure everything is *normal*." I began to realize that her birth was very different from that of my son. With my son's birth, there were many congratulations, excitement, and smiles from all the medical staff, and I was encouraged to nurse and keep the baby with me as much as possible. No one took him away for an exam. The doctor and nurses did everything in the room, with both my husband and me there.

Now, here, I felt abandoned. From the moment Talia entered the world, whenever there was an exchange of words between the medical professionals and me, they refused to make eye contact or smile. And they took her away from me without a real explanation as to why, leaving me alone in a hospital bed after giving birth to a baby. It didn't make sense to me I should be holding my baby.

Frustrated with the hours of isolation and separation from my daughter, and the vague answers my husband gave me in response to my questions, I asked to go to the neonatology intensive care unit (NICU) to see her. I knew something was not right, and no one would talk to me. I was scared.

The NICU was a very quiet, sterile place, with intimidating professionals staring at my baby, and then at me. They all looked like scientists with lab coats and clip boards taking down data for an experiment. When I walked further into the room, they all moved away from the crib; they did not introduce themselves. They turned their backs and began to once again look busy. They lingered and hovered, but didn't speak, maintaining their emotional distance. It felt odd, detached.

When I saw my tiny baby, wrapped in a pink and blue striped flannel blanket with matching cap on her head, sleeping all alone in a glass crib, a few wires attached to her, my joy at giving birth to a new life became clouded. I was really scared now, and very confused. What is happening? Why is no one talking to me? Why is my husband acting so strangely? What is wrong?

I examined her more closely. I knew from the other's reactions that something must be *wrong*. I looked at her face, which was round and full. Her skin looked beautiful. Her lips were full and red. I then noticed the placement and size of her ears, tiny and set back. Terrified, I tried to get someone's attention, but the room began to spin, and sounds became muffled. I passed out.

Looking back, I think I tried to escape to a place of unconsciousness where I felt no fear. I woke up in a wheelchair, in the hallway, with nurses and doctors leaning over me, waving smelling salts under my nose. When the sounds of their voices came back to me, I passed out again, perhaps to avoid all the commotion of the moment, maybe to avoid the reality I was about to face.

Back in the hospital room, my husband told me the doctors were concerned about our daughter's heart. I did not know the neonatologist had talked with my husband about the possibility of a *genetic disorder*. My husband's unusual, quiet, distant behavior started to make sense to me yet I was very confused and tired.

Until the pediatrician came into the room later that evening, no one talked to me. No one came into my room to care for my post-delivery medical needs. No one offered me lunch or dinner. The emotions and room became darker as night set in. I was avoided, isolated, rejected, and had no idea why I was treated this way. My husband was quiet. I called my sister and said, "Something is wrong."

When the pediatrician walked in around 9:00 that night, she looked serious, concerned, yet compassionate. She walked over to the side of the bed and stood next to me. It was silent for what felt like a long time. We had eye contact and her head tilted down toward me. I felt safe with this compassionate gesture for a brief moment. And then she started talking. She told me she had examined my baby, that she had heart defects, and would need to have at least one open-heart surgery, possibly more, to repair them. She went on to explain that my daughter was "floppy"—had low muscle tone. I felt confused and defensive. This is not the conversation I was waiting for. This was a list of problems.

Then she asked if I had seen her eyes. Is she blind? I thought. Then it hit me. I knew. I remembered the *slanted eyes of children with Down syndrome;* I remembered Talia's eyes looked different. I could not figure out whose eyes she had when I first held her. I turned to the pediatrician and not knowing where the words came from, I asked, "Does she have Down syndrome?" She replied, with a tear rolling slowly from her eye, "I believe so, but we'll need to do genetic testing in order to confirm." I immediately said, "That's OK, they are beautiful children."

As I said this, my thoughts went in a different direction. I had visions of Talia being rejected, excluded, left out, isolated, made fun of, teased, and lonely. I thought of her at the park playing alone, other kids looking at her from a distance, pointing and giggling. She wouldn't be invited to birthday parties or play dates. She would be made fun of because of her facial features. She would be denied the opportunity to participate in activities with other children. She would be mentally retarded, and those words brought back all my childhood fears of kids with disabilities.

I was devastated. My life changed in that single instant. All my dreams turned into nightmares. I thought of my husband and son and how they would feel about having a child with Down syndrome in our family. In my mind, I made assumptions about what life would be like for us based on my previous limited experiences with people with Down syndrome—most of which were negative, with elements of isolation, segregation, and rejection. That is all I knew at that moment.

I did not sleep well for days, and often woke hoping the birth of my daughter and the disruption in my perfectly constructed life was only a nightmare. Afraid to open my eyes, I negotiated with whatever God might be handy for the opportunity to turn back the clock, to have the responsibility of mothering a child with Down syndrome and all its packaging go away. I did not want to be a mother of a child with Down syndrome. My life was supposed to be good. Mothering a child with Down syndrome was not part of my dream.

But this was no dream.

Because Talia's heart condition was very serious, she was transferred to a different hospital. The days that followed were filled with confusion, fear, and anxiety. My life suddenly turned into a world of experts, doctors, therapists and list of things to do to attempt to make my daughter as normal as possible. Our family and friends were extremely supportive in their own way. They tried to say the right things: "I'm so sorry." "You two are the perfect parents. I could never do it." "God chose you, because he knew you could do it." They were trying to be encouraging. I wish we all knew then what we know today. Her life, just like that of any other child's, is to be celebrated, not to be grieved, feared, or a reason to make us hero parents.

In spite of the fear, our friends and family came to visit and welcome Talia into the world. They took turns to be with her night and day. My father and brother-in-law, for example, went to the hospital early one morning to relieve my mother, who had been there for hours. They sat next to her crib and the nurses took her out and placed her in my dad's arms. He held her for a long time and when it was time to put her back in the crib both my brother-in-law and father were a bit perplexed as to how to do put her back in the crib—she had a lot of wires hooked up to her. These were all for monitoring purposes, not anything life-threatening, but to the non-medical person, it could be a scary sight and venture. After struggling for a bit, and not knowing how to lift her up to the crib, my brother-in-law, in his thick French accent asked, "Is there someone who can give us some professional assistance?" The nurses helped them place her back in her crib.

When Talia was in the NICU I remember feeling like a protective mother bird watching and caring for her baby in her nest, but out on a distant branch. I would make sure Talia was held and cuddled by everyone else, but I would only hold her when no one else was available. I was afraid to love her. Afraid she was going to die. Afraid of what Down syndrome meant. Afraid I would not be a good mother. I felt inadequate. And I did not want to be a mother of a child with Down syndrome. It was too scary. Too lonely. Too isolated. Too much unknown.

As the days passed, my daughter's heart condition stabilized enough to bring her home. I was afraid to leave the hospital, because it meant taking another step closer to the reality of mothering a baby with Down syndrome. It meant more responsibility. More acceptance of reality. It felt safe in the hospital, because someone else cared for her. I could escape reality. I could pretend she wasn't mine. Bringing her home meant I had to accept my role as her mother. I had to accept the responsibility of mothering this child with Down syndrome—dealing with medical needs, therapies, negative feelings, fear, and uncertainty. I felt overwhelmed. I felt alone, isolated.

I will always remember the moment I entered our house with my daughter for the first time. My 15-month-old son came around the corner, looked at her in her car seat, and said, "Ha, Tata." His love for her was pure and uncontaminated. He knew nothing other than that Talia was his baby sister. He was not infected with the negative misunderstandings, perceptions, and assumptions made and passed along by others. For him, her arrival home was a celebration. He was excited to welcome her into the world, her home, and our family. It was unconditional.

Later that day, I laid my daughter on my bed next to a window. It was spring, and the sun was shining on her while she slept. I went outside to plant some flowers, hoping to distract my overwhelming, unpleasant thoughts. In my garden, usually a place for me to escape and find peace, I thought about my old dreams of mothering—reading books, practicing ABC's, doing arts and crafts, talking with my daughter, helping her get ready for dance recitals and the prom, and all the other dreams mothers have about relationships with their daughters. I felt the sadness one feels when dreams are shattered. I felt that unwanted, lonely feeling creep in to my being again. I continued planting my flowers hoping it would go away. I am not quite sure why, or how, but in the garden my thoughts shifted.

I thought about how my daughter would need me to care for her and protect her. I assumed she would need a different kind of mothering than I had experienced as a daughter with my own mother, and I assumed it would be a different kind of mothering than my son would need in his life. But my thoughts began to bring me comfort: *I will always have my little girl with me. She will always need me. We will always be together.* We could have a relationship based on reciprocity. She would love me and I could love her.

A neighbor, a young girl in high school who babysat for my son, came over and sat with me one afternoon. She congratulated me on the birth of Talia, one of the few who did. She told me about a girl in her graduating class who had Down syndrome. She explained to me that this particular young woman was very involved in high school, was accepted by her peers. I wasn't sure if I believed her or if she was just trying to make me feel better, knowing how sad I was. Trying to change the subject, I asked her about her upcoming prom. She told me all about her dress and the young man who was taking her. Then, to my surprise, she told me that the young woman with Down syndrome was going too.

At that moment, I caught a glimpse of hope. Hope for me as a mother. Hope for my daughter as a woman. It was the first time I saw possibilities, opportunities. Going to the prom was a possibility. Maybe other things could be, too.

Childhood, Teaching, and Mothering

From time to time, I reflect back on my experiences with disability, beginning with my childhood, moving through my teaching career, and now as a mother. I cannot separate these experiences. These experiences are what shape my beliefs. I know there are many barriers that still prevent opportunities for my daughter and other people with disabilities. The other day, I was at the grocery store with my youngest child. She saw a young man with Down syndrome working there, and, excited, pointed him out to me. My first reaction was to tell her to stop pointing and talking so loudly. As I did, I realized I was telling her to stop pointing, just like my mother used to tell me.

But my youngest daughter was pointing for another reason. As a young child, I would have pointed out of curiosity, uncertainty, and fear. I was told to look away, not ask questions. My daughter was pointing to this young man out of excitement, perhaps because she saw another person with Down syndrome, perhaps because she saw a person with Down syndrome in the community, working like any other young man would. Was she reacting to and thinking about all the conversations she has heard (some intended, some not), growing up in a family with a child with a disability? Many of those conversations are about inclusion and exclusion; opportunities and their lack; peers with and peers without disabilities; and negotiating and navigating the barriers that prevent her sister from full participation in the world they share. She hears conversations that celebrate Talia's accomplishments, and ones in which we discuss future challenges or concerns. I don't know whether she was excited because she saw a young man with Down syndrome, or because she saw a young man with Down syndrome fully participating in the community, in society. I do know her experiences are what will form her beliefs.

When I think about the mothers of some of my former students, I understand better why sometimes they chose not to put their children in front of barriers that needed to be broken down; and why, at other times, they chose to advocate for their child in order to create better opportunities and understanding. My hope is that all kids play together and go to school together; that there are more open, honest conversations about disability, acceptance, and diversity; and that all teachers teach all students. My hope is that when children see people with disabilities, they will have no need to point. That's the kind of world I want my children to grow up in.

References

Baker, B. (2002). The hunt for disability: The new eugenics and normalization of school children. *Teachers College Record*, 663–703.

Smith, P. (2010a). Barriers to inclusion: Does special education work? In P. Smith (Ed.), *Whatever happened to inclusion? The place of students with intellectual disabilities in education* (pp. 61–85). New York: Peter Lang.

——(2010b). Trends for including students with intellectual disabilities in general education classrooms. In P. Smith (Ed.), *Whatever happened to inclusion? The place of students with intellectual disabilities in education* (pp. 21–37). New York: Peter Lang.

Stainback, W. & Stainback, S. (1984). A rationale for the merger of special and regular education. *Exceptional Children, 51*(2), 102–111.

Chapter 12

A New Chance to Matter

Liz McCall

When tragedy strikes, most people don't know what to say—so they throw a cliché in the general direction of the person who is floundering, drowning in grief. After my father-in-law died, everyone said to me, "Everything happens for a reason." I wanted to give them a reason to go to the hospital each time they said it. There was no space in my mind where a reason would fit; there was only space for the pain I felt.

Three years later, when my dad died, the chorus began singing that tune once again. "Everything happens for a reason" was the background music to my life. It was stuck in my head, but like all songs that get stuck there, I didn't know what came next. I asked my family, I asked my friends, I looked to my husband for the answer. They couldn't tell me; instead, they just sang along with the chorus. I wanted it to be true, that all of this had happened for a reason.

I hoped the reason would be a good one, that it would take away the pain. I waited for the reason to appear. It didn't. So I went looking—and found it waiting for me in a classroom.

*

On the first day of the first job that ever really mattered to me, the one I worked so hard for, the principal came to my classroom. I was scrubbing shelves, rearranging books, covered in sweat because schools don't have the money to run the air conditioning until the students show up, even in North Carolina, embarrassed that this would be my first interaction with the man who would be my boss. I should have looked more like a teacher, but with my tattoos exposed, wearing a tank top and shorts that I wouldn't have allowed a student to see me in, my hair in a ponytail, I must have looked more like someone who should attend school here than the new teacher expected to help students who had nowhere else to go. He was large, and looked like a man who knew what he was doing. I, on the other hand, did not look like I knew anything at all.

"Ms. Turek, I'm Carl Richards, the new principal. We haven't had a chance to meet yet."

"Hi, I'm Liz," I reached for the sweatshirt I had worn earlier that morning, hoping he hadn't noticed the wings tattooed on my back yet. "Today is my first day, too."

"Where did you work before this?" He hadn't been at my interview, had no idea that this was my first real teaching job.

"Just here. I subbed for three years while I got my teaching certificate. But this is my first classroom." I knew how that sounded: crazy. Who decides to work with the most difficult students in the county as their first job?

"This is your first job?" Incredulous. Shocked. He couldn't hide it from his face.

"Yes. But it's my dream job. This is why I went back to school. This is what I want to do. This is what I need to do." That was the truth. I had searched for years to find my place in the world, something that made the tragedy that had consumed so much of my life matter. Working with students who were outcasts because of behavior, emotional distress, and psychiatric disabilities, I had found the place where I mattered.

It wasn't the dream I had when I was five, sure I would be an astronaut or an astronomer or an architect or an archeologist. Now I see I may just have been dreaming about the letter A. By age twelve, all I wanted to be was a writer, a famous writer. I wrote rough drafts in notebooks that I hid between my mattress and box spring in case anyone wanted to read it. Adolescence brought with it endlessly clichéd poetry about suffering I had never experienced, love poems to boys who never noticed I existed, and the lies that became my best stories.—Only a year into my bachelors degree, surrounded by "real writers," I gave up the dream of paying the bills with words, told myself I was chasing a dream, not a paycheck, and graduated from college with my degree in unemployment (aka creative writing), still certain I had done the right thing. I found a gift for sales, and for a brief time I was successful in the way adults told me success should look: I brought home a good paycheck every week. Where some people dream of a paycheck, I never had, and yet I found myself settling for that and nothing more.

Each time tragedy struck my careful life, I held to the belief that if I made the right amount of money, if I could fill my house with the right things and wear the right clothes and drive the right car then I would be right. My marriage would be right. The hole my fathers left behind when they died would be filled and I wouldn't be lost anymore. I didn't tell people why I was so empty; I couldn't bear their sympathy. I couldn't bear my guilt. After all, it was my fault that they were gone. I saw that truth in everyone's eyes: my husband, his grandfather and brother, the little girls left behind when they were only five, and my grandmother as she grieved for another son. I felt responsible for my niece and nephew never knowing their grandpa.

The weight of these things, and the weight of my own missteps, held me captive. I floated from job to job, honestly thinking that the next one would be the one that would bring me fulfillment. At the end of my rope, I decided to try substitute teaching. It made no sense. My sister was a teacher, and my aunt, as well as my grandparents, but I had only briefly held any desire to be one, the desire only stemming from realizing in my last year of college that I would never find a job in my field. The desire died when my brilliant and honest grandfather told me, "You'd be a terrible teacher. Don't waste your money. Find something else you love." I listened to him, until I ran out of options and walked into my first classroom as a substitute teacher.

I was afraid; of course, I had been told that these kids were the ones that the whole school avoided. Cast off into their own classroom, not even allowed to change classes when the bell rang for fear they would intermingle with the "normal" students. I was warned by their regular teacher that they would be "an interesting bunch," and not to take what they said to me to heart. Most of all, she warned me to never let them see me cry. I almost left right then, before even looking a student in the eye. Fortunately, curiosity got the better of me and I stayed. It took no more than five minutes, and the words of a twelve year old boy to show me that I was exactly where I was supposed to be.

My first words as a teacher, or as close to teacher one can be on the first day with no training, were, "Good morning, I'm Ms. Turek. Take your seats." It was enough for that boy, who proceeded to spew a run of obscenities at me that would make a seasoned truck driver blush. I was awestruck; I never could have used such words against a teacher. Even as an adult I would struggle to repeat what he said to me, though the words are burned in my head. I didn't feel angry. More surprising, I didn't feel numb as

I had for years. The numbness had been replaced instantaneously by the realization that I understood this boy. I saw in his eyes the pain I had seen in my own eyes since my fathers died; I also saw the disconnection from reality that I watched grow so intense in the eyes of my biological father through the years of his illness. I understood these things in ways that others wouldn't be able to, because I had walked in theses shoes I had all but worn the shoes out, and still insisted on carrying them around in my backpack. I couldn't go backwards and change what had happened; I had lost the chance I had to save them. Yet, here I was, being given a new chance to matter.

I mattered because I had learned from my Dad that behind the illness, the person still exists even when they are unrecognizable. I mattered because I could see and understand the frustration in the eyes of the parents when their kids just wouldn't be who they were "supposed" to be. I too felt angry when my father wouldn't be the person he was supposed to be anymore. Their exhaustion with the struggle to help their children would never be lost on me, because I too had fought that fight for someone I loved. I wouldn't be one of the people who blamed them for the way their children were, as I had been blamed for the mistakes my father made while in the throes of mental illness. I would be for them the support I never found, and do my best to help them write a future that looked very different from my past.

*

The dream returns. It should be over by now. Six years is too long to be having the same dream over again. Dreams that don't come true die eventually, don't they?

Familiar street corners full of faces I recognize. The sun sparkles on the bay, or am I under a street lamp? Either way, I'm yelling. I'm screaming. Grabbing strangers wearing familiar faces. Begging for coins, no, I'm begging for help. The beggar on the corner no one wants to know. No one can hear me. I am alone. Always alone.

I wake up, gasping; pointless tears staining my pillow. Still alone. Except it isn't a dream; it's the nightly retelling of the nightmare I lived for two years while my father explored the depths of his mental illness. While he discovered the new and frightening abyss that consumed his mind, I stood on figurative street corners, begging for an expert to help me solve the riddle of Kevin Parmenter. I was sure that there must be help for these situations, found it impossible to believe that a twenty-four-year-old woman could be left alone to care for her father as he disappeared into his own disease. The more I was ignored by police, community mental health workers, friends, judges, attorneys, and everyone to whom I could think to talk, the easier it was to tell myself, "Of course they aren't listening to me. What do I know about mental illness?" I was wrong. Even more, they were wrong. There was one area in which I was an expert, and it was the only area that should have mattered at that time. I was an expert on my dad. But backs were turned by those who should have been helping me, and my voice was silenced. And by the time anyone heard my cries, it was too late.

*

The leaves had all fallen off the trees outside the window of our small rented house, but there was no snow on the ground. The silence of late fall in Northern Michigan was broken by the disco ring tone I had chosen for my cell phone. Seeing the number on the caller ID, I answered the phone, "Hey, Gram", the way I always did. The voice on the other end was my Grandmother, her voice still having a bright timbre that in the next few years would lose its vibrancy, become a paler version of itself.

A plane took off in my head as she spoke. I swallowed hard and made her repeat herself at least once; it might have been three times. I was too busy trying to breathe to keep track.

"Your Dad. He's at the hospital." Gram's annoyance finally cut through the noise in my head. But my ears were still flying at thirty thousand feet and I couldn't relieve the pressure in them. She kept talking.

"Gram, I can't hear anything you're saying," I interrupted her. "I'll just drive over to the hospital and find out what's going on. I'll call you after I see him." I hung up, and my husband already had the car keys in his hand. His blue eyes had turned gray—I knew he was scared. I don't remember what I told him, but the next thing I knew, Matt was driving my Jetta across town while I chewed a piece of gum, desperate to relieve the pressure in my skull.

There were so many things that could have brought my Dad to the hospital that night; little things like a cut on his hand while building one of his kayaks, or bigger things like another broken bone brought on by a sharp turn on his mountain bike. Gram had said his girlfriend had sounded scared when she called. I remembered that as we entered the emergency room, then pushed it aside. My Dad was harmless, gentle. There was a police officer standing outside his hospital room door.

The doctor stepped out of the room, and squinted at me. He and the officer exchanged glances; they knew something they weren't telling me. They seemed reluctant to speak; I thought they might refuse to let me in the room.

"What's going on?" I spoke first and they stared at me. "I'm Kevin's daughter. I'd like to see him."

The officer must have spoken; I must have ignored him. If he asked a question, I didn't answer. Instead, I entered the hospital room and there was a man there, sitting on the bed without a scratch. The man on the bed resembled my Dad. He turned and looked at me. I want to say he smiled, but it wasn't like any smile I had seen him wear before. It was wide and toothy, somehow forgetting to include his eyes. He didn't get off the bed to hug me, barely even acknowledged me.

"Dad, what's going on?" I wanted to be calm but my voice was inches from hysteria.

"I was just getting rid of some furniture, Elizabeth." It was the first time in more than ten years he had called me Elizabeth. It growled from his mouth through clenched teeth. I wasn't sure he really knew me, as if I were an acquaintance or a distant relative whom he only spoke to on holidays. I wasn't the daughter with whom he had dinner with two nights before. "I guess I got a little carried away and worried the neighbor."

"What furniture?"

"Things. Things I didn't need, things that were weighing me down. Just things. Things with bad karma. It's all just things. Why are you here?" His voice had risen from its soft baritone to a sharp tenor that hurt my ears. I was relieved when the doctor walked into the room with the officer.

"He won't let us draw blood, or give a urine sample." The officer was frigid. The doctor looked frightened.

"My Dad doesn't drink. He's never even smoked a cigarette, there's no way he's high. I'm sure he told you that, and that's why he won't get tested."

"Do you have any reason to believe he could be suicidal?" They were the first words the doctor had spoken to me and they knocked the wind out of me. It sounded like a routine question. I might have thought it was, if the doctor hadn't stayed near the door and stared at the floor as he asked it. I had to wonder what exactly they had seen at his home.

Matt and I exchanged glances, our thoughts matched like they so often did then. We were both thinking of his dad and the fear that we had missed signs of his impending suicide. The logical side of my brain, the one that can do algebra and put together boxed furniture without reading the directions, always knew it wasn't true. I couldn't have stopped him. We couldn't have. Then the writer takes over and I'm replaying that day like a movie I've seen too many times, still hoping the ending will be a happy one. It's just another sad nightmare I can't escape from.

*

It was late January, the 21st, and Matt had left the night before for a weeklong training session an hour and a half away. He wouldn't be back until Friday afternoon, which for us seemed like a long time apart, so when the phone rang at 7:30 in the morning I assumed it was him calling to say good morning. I answered the phone just as our temporary house guest, Phil, came down the stairs.

"Morning Hun. Did you sleep well?" I said into the phone, a laugh in my voice.

"I'll turn the cars on," Phil mouthed to me. "We got a good four inches of snow last night." I nodded.

"Is Matt home, Liz?" It wasn't my husband on the other end of the line. It was Cindy, his father's wife, from whom he was separated. She was rushed. I figured it was because she needed to get the girls, five-year-old twins, ready for school.

"No, he's in Lansing for training. What's going on?"

"Jim just called. He was upset about the divorce. He said he's going to kill himself. I tried to call back, but he won't answer. " Time stops here. Or it fast-forwards. "I need you to go there and check on him. He won't answer the phone. I have to get the girls to school."

Click. She hung up the phone. It was on me now. Whatever happened next would be my responsibility. I tried to call Jim's house. There was no answer. I was terrified; I knew this was too much for me to handle. I called my Mom; she said not to go alone. She told me to call the police. I called the police. I told them what Cindy had told me. They asked me if he had any weapons, and Jim's smiling face appeared in my mind, the same way it did every time I thought of him: laughing at himself, eyes squinting behind outdated aviator-style glasses, the remaining hair on-the sides of his head in desperate need of a trim. I choked out the words "Yes, he's a hunter. I suppose he has guns."

Only five minutes had passed, and I already felt too late. I rushed out the door, probably telling Phil what was going on, but I don't remember. I do know my last words to Phil were, as we each got into our cars, "If he's okay when I get there, I'm going to kill him."

No time passed on the drive to Jim's house, not even the ten minutes it normally took. I was lost in my head, thinking of all the things I would say to him when I got there and he was fine. I practiced telling him how horrible it was to scare all of us this way; I saw myself telling him how glad I was Matt wasn't home to have to handle this, I wouldn't want him to be afraid the way I was. I scolded Jim, in my mind, and then hugged him and told him how much I loved him. I drove past a packed funeral home and thought "How strange, I've never seen that before. Must be new." It was the only moment I spent outside my imagination during that drive.

I pulled into Jim's snow-packed driveway, and the police officer was there, standing outside his car waiting for me. The officer introduced himself; I can't remember his name.

"I'm his daughter-in-law; I'm the one who called. Did you already try to go inside?"

"No, Miss. Do you know where there is a key?"

"Yeah, under the grill on the back deck." I practically ran around the side of the two-story house to get the hidden key, the officer keeping pace with me. Getting the key from under the grill, I looked up and saw the steam coming from the dryer vent. I saw the blinds on the sliding glass door were open. Taking the five steps to the sliding door, I told myself there was no way Jim had left it unlocked, he was far too anal for that. But it slid easily open when I pulled on it, and I stepped my snowy boot into the kitchen simultaneously yelling Jim's name.

"Jim! Jim, its Liz!" I ran across the living room, almost tripping on one of the girl's dolls, and caught the banister at the bottom of the stairs. My foot was on the first step when the officer placed his had on my shoulder.

"Miss. Let me go up there. You go sit down in the kitchen." He was breathing heavily.

"He's up the stairs to the right." I turned and walked back to the kitchen, picking up the clumps of snow that had fallen from our shoes onto the beige carpet. Waiting for the officer to come back down the stairs, no longer truly hoping that Jim would be with him, I looked around the kitchen and wondered how I was going to tell everyone that Jim was dead.

"Miss, I'm sorry to tell you this, but your father is dead. I'm going to need to ask you a few questions."

"I know. Let me make some phone calls first." In the next ten minutes, I told a man's wife that her husband was dead, explained to the police officer who Jim was, smiled when I told him we shared a birthday, called work to let them know I wouldn't be in that day and that I wasn't sure when I'd be back. Eventually, after a series of phone calls, I spoke to my husband. I told him, the person I loved more than anything in life, that his father had shot himself.

The sound of his heart breaking has never stopped ringing in my ears.

It's been ten years.

*

I joined the doctor in looking at the floor and spoke.

"Even if he was suicidal, he would never say those words. My father-in-law committed suicide just over a year ago, and my dad thought it was a weak thing to do. He'd never admit to wanting to be weak. He doesn't look right to me. I can't see myself in his eyes." I lifted my eyes slightly, trying to gauge the reaction my dad would have to this. He should have protested, told me he would never, gotten off the bed. Reassured me that he was fine. Held me.

The man on the bed didn't react. He just sat, grinning in that bizarre way as if the world could no longer touch him.

"Mrs. Turek, we think that your father should be under observation for the next twenty-four hours. There is no space for him in the psychiatric wing here, so we'll transfer him to another hospital." I nodded yes as I kept locked eyes on my Dad, hoping to see just a little bit of him behind that blank stare. Afraid, I didn't think to protest, or even question.

*

There were four knives buried in the wall behind his kitchen table. A steak knife, a butcher knife, the filet knife he used to clean the trout we caught on childhood camping trips, and the black Bowie knife I started carrying with me that night. It was a knife I had watched my father remove slivers from his builder's hands with.

Pulling the bowie knife from the wall, I looked to my right, and saw the doors of the kitchen cabinets had been torn off their hinges. His computer desk had been relieved of the weight of the computer itself, the cords not removed from the walls but instead cut through. Shifting the knife from my right hand to the left, I looked back at the wall where it had been stuck, and wondered where the family pictures were whose places the knives had taken.

"Why are you taking that knife with you?" Matt broke the painful silence.

"I don't know. I thought maybe we'd start cleaning up the house."

It was a lie. I had no intention of cleaning the house that night. I just liked the weight of the knife in my hand. We had been led to believe the kitchen was the worst of it; it couldn't be worse than the knives, and the broken dishes, the doors ripped from their hinges. As we passed the computer desk, disabled computer with its cords cut through sitting sideways, and walked into his living room, it became clear that my father's fury had not ended here. His couches were mostly intact—except one that seemed to have been hit with an ax on the arm. Then I looked left, where the possession I prized most was kept. The piano, a baby grand reproducer, which had belonged to my Great-Grandmother, passed to my Grandmother, my Father, and next it was to have been mine.

At first glance I believed he had only crippled it, chopped off one of it's legs, causing it to rest one corner of it's body on the floor. Then I saw that the lid had been removed. The strings had been cut evenly across, one inch from the tuning pegs; the keyboard was half missing, black and white keys were scattered near the bench. The drawer that held the reproducing rolls, the irreplaceable heart of this piano, had been cut from beneath the keyboard with frightening precision. I picked a black key up from the floor, held it in my hand next to the knife.

"This makes no sense." I said to the shattered piano. The shock dug it's claws into me and with it came a strange sense of calm. I was finally able to look around the room and take it all in: the mutilated piano, the family photos missing from the walls, everything in the house that pointed towards my father's identity, to our identity as a family—it was all missing. I felt as if my father was trying to rid himself of us, as if he, too, was being lost to the chaos he had created. The blank look in his eyes seemed to make sense in this context. He didn't exist, and without him, neither did I.

"It's late, hon. Let's go home and deal with this in the morning." Matt held my hand and led me out the back door through the garage, the only place that had been untouched by whatever had taken over my father that night. It was still meticulously organized, a fragile, half-finished wooden kayak resting on sawhorses. I breathed him in deeply here, reminding myself of who he was: the smell of sawdust, and of sweat, the smell of a carpenter who took pride in his talents.

Taking the car keys from Matt, taking control back, I got into my car. I'm sure Matt noticed me put the knife under the driver's seat, but he knew better than to say anything about it. He had seen me this way before, cold and calm; I might as well have been driving away without him. It was the way I handled tragedy, attempting to protect those I loved most from the pain that I felt.

*

The hospital called the next day. I told the doctor about the pictures missing from the walls, the pile of family treasures soaked in gasoline stacked in the backyard. I tried to make him understand what he had done and failed.

"I'm sorry, Mrs. Turek. Your father is here voluntarily, and we can't make him stay just because he threw out some old pictures and got rid of some furniture."

"He didn't just get rid of some furniture!" My voice cracked. "He chopped up a priceless piano with an ax and tried to burn every family photo in the house. Why can't you see there's something wrong with him?"

"He's being released in the morning." And the doctor was gone.

*

I'm alone.
How did I get so alone?
Where did everyone go?
HELP!

*

The snow began to fly just as Thanksgiving passed. Any other year, my dad would have had his skis on as soon as he could no longer see the grass poking through, but not this year. There was no hint that he even thought about his skis. Instead, according to Grandma, he sat in her house all day talking to himself. When I asked her what he talked about, she said she didn't understand any of it. Sometimes he'd get loud and it frightened her. He wrote on yellow legal pads obsessively, and by the middle of December he was convinced that his now ex-girlfriend had stolen a gun from him. The few times that we spoke, the conversation was the kind that occurred between strangers, until my frustration with his absence would rise into my mouth and eject itself in high-pitched whining and sobbing. He'd hang up on me every time.

By the New Year, Grandma decided she couldn't take it anymore. She was uncomfortable in her own home, and she let Dad know that he would need to move back into his own apartment by the end of the month. He still held the lease on his own place; it was natural to assume he would return to living there when he left Grandma's house. She didn't tell me any of this until she had already asked him to leave, and he had been missing for three days. I hadn't heard from him either, not that I ever expected to anymore. I lied to Grandma, telling her that I was sure he was fine, that I'd find him and give her a call the next day.

It didn't cross my mind to go to his house alone. I'd been down this road before: dads who were upset and not answering phones were dead dads. That was my experience, and that experience told me that having the police meet me would be the better choice. My thoughts were full of memories of the January two years before when I had made this exact phone call to the police, in a different city for a different father. Dialing the number, I hoped I would be able to hold myself together, though the tightness in my lungs made me doubt it was possible.

"Traverse City Police."

"Yes, I'm calling because my Dad has been out of contact with us for the past three days. I need an officer to meet me at his house to check on him." I took a breath that seemed to rattle my ribcage. I heard the echo of the past in my ear—"Does he have any weapons in the house?"—and braced myself for the question.

"What is your father's name?" Relief. They didn't ask.

"Kevin Parmenter." Silence. "Hello?"

"One moment, ma'am. I'm looking in the computer to see if he's been brought in." Brought in? For what? I couldn't believe he'd be in police custody and I wouldn't have been notified. "Yes, he's here. Being held at the County Jail."

"For what? When did you pick him up?"

"Early Sunday morning. I can't tell you anything else; it's a matter of privacy."

"Why wasn't I called!" It briefly occurred to me that yelling at an officer was a bad idea, but I didn't care.

"Your father didn't request a phone call to you, Miss." He went on to tell me there was no way I would be able to speak to him, that I needed to write him a letter in care of the county jail requesting that he put me on his visitation list for Saturday. It would be the only way to talk to him. It was three o'clock on Monday afternoon.

When Matt walked in the door two hours later, I was just getting off the phone with my sister. He turned on the local news, which I could faintly hear from my office at the back of the house.

"Whoa. Hon, take a look at this guy on the news. The cops really beat the crap out of him." Matt called to me from the living room. Craning my neck out the doorway I saw my dad's swollen face on TV. Both eyes were blackened and barely open. His long, straight nose seemed askew, pushed slightly to the left, and his already full lower lip jutted from his jaw, twice its normal size.

"Matt, that's Dad." I could hear the coldness in my voice, a coldness that came to me anytime the subject of my dad came up after the night he destroyed his furniture. I had started to shut down when it came to thinking and speaking about him; I didn't even know there was a choice in the matter. Matt's blue eyes were surprised, confused. He dealt with things by ignoring reality. "What did they say?"

"Something about a high-speed chase. I don't know, I wasn't really paying attention, didn't even hear his name. Are you sure that was your dad?" I ignored the question. Of course I knew. I knew the scar on his right eyebrow, the permanent furrows in his brow, the dimple in the end of his nose.

*

That's the last clear moment I had for the next year and a half. My memories of the rest of it come in patches; they have no timeline. It's the only way I know how to write it: disconnected. I was living two lives, the one where I was attempting to salvage a marriage, and have a career. The other where I was inundated with decisions.

There were no good choices or bad choices, no right or wrong. There was just doing, walking with blinders on. I kept telling myself that I was doing the best I could, though in looking back I sometimes wonder if that was true. I always wonder.

The decisions appear as a list in my mind. I still can't wrap my head around how I made them, or why. There are blank spaces where there should be vivid memory. I wonder if I have chosen to forget, or if that is the way my mind has made it all okay. I can only put the events in order with the help of court documents, and even with those, there are holes in between that I struggle to fill in.

The first time my name appears in the arrest record is the day I bailed him out of jail. I can remember that day. I was afraid. I wanted to give them the money, and just leave. Didn't want him in my car; didn't want to be alone with him. But that wasn't a choice I was allowed to make, so I waited there in the jail. Waited to see the person that would walk through those doors, and wondered if I would recognize him at all. His first steps towards me were anxious, and our embrace was one of strangers. I don't know if we had a conversation at all; I simply took him to a motel, knowing that he had enough money to get by for at least six months. Fear was all I could feel. I lost contact with him shortly after; he moved out of the motel within the week.

Months later, a bench warrant was issued because he missed his first court date. I received phone calls from his court-appointed attorney, the only person who seemed to understand that there was nothing right about my father anymore. He asked me to call him if I spotted my dad, told me about the warrant, and told me the right thing to do: call the police and have him brought back in. At least then we would know where he was.

Two weeks later I did what I was told. I saw him sitting in a coffee shop, and called the police. I watched from across the street as they entered and he attempted to flee. I watched as they cuffed him. I felt regret, and knew I had no other choice. The attorney was right: at least I knew where he was.

I visited him weekly for the next month, maybe two. Until his trial. He was guilty, there was no question, and released with time served on the condition that he had a place to live. I refused to offer my home to him, hoping that if he stayed in the system he might receive some metal health care. It was the only hope I had. Grandma made another decision, and three days later he was living at her house again, on probation for felony fleeing. Dad knew then that I had turned him in, and he made it clear that he wanted no further contact with me. That was OK with me, and for six months I didn't visit my grandmother's home, attempting to keep my distance. Afraid what his reaction might be.

*

I got a phone call from my sister, who was in contact with my aunt. She told me Dad was scaring Grandma now, that she wanted him out of the house but didn't know how to make that happen. I knew it was time for me to step back in, though it was the last thing I wanted to do. We made an excuse to go there, something I needed to borrow from her, and Grandma sounded relieved that Matt and I would be making that visit.

I was wholly unprepared for what I encountered. I knew Dad was delusional, he had become that long before he went back to live with her. His obsessions had been left to themselves for months by now, and my heart was sure that they had only gotten worse. Bracing myself as we arrived, I had only two thoughts: protect my husband, protect Grandma.-I left myself out of that equation.

He was upstairs when we arrived. I knew because I could hear him yelling.

"Gram, who is he talking to?" I asked from the kitchen.

"No one. He does it all day. He does it at the dinner table. He does it in the shower. Sometimes he's angry, sometimes he's laughing. He never talks to me, he just talks to nothing."

"Does he know we're here?"

"I told him you were coming. I don't know if he'll come downstairs." She had aged five years in the two months I hadn't seen her. I wanted nothing more than to take this away from her, to wear it on my back. Her green eyes were dull. "I want to show you something in my bedroom."

"Matt, wait here please." I went with Grandma to her bedroom, where she continued to tell me about my dad's behavior. She thought he couldn't hear her there. We stayed, talking until I heard loud voices in the kitchen. Bolting from her bedroom, remembering my resolve to protect my husband, I turned the corner and saw Matt and my dad in the kitchen. Matt was trying to protect me.

"You need to stop, Kevin. Get some help. You're killing Liz."

"You don't know what you're talking about, Mr. Turek. You have no idea." My father, a powerful man, seemed to be challenging my husband, without really knowing who he was.

"Dad, back off." I placed myself between Matt and my dad, nose to nose with him. I looked in his eyes and saw fury. Never having seen it before, my voice became a whisper, "We're leaving now."

*

Within weeks, my dad was sent to a mental hospital, after appearing in court on a probation violation. I was relieved, hopeful that I was about to get my father back. I believed that he was finally going to get the services he needed, that I would once again see the healthy version of my father for whom I had been grieving. After a month in the hospital, he was released and moved into a halfway house run by community mental health, where he would be monitored every hour, attend group therapy, and administered his medications. They were supposed to help him rebuild his life. They failed at every turn.

I helped him move in to his new room. It was the first time since he destroyed his home that I felt like I was in a room with my dad. His eyes were still dull, but now they were dull in a way I recognized. They were dull with sadness.

"I'm so sorry, Liz. I'm just so sorry." He said it to me over and over while I helped him get settled.

"I'm just happy to see you again Dad. I've missed you." He hugged me and we both cried. I promised him I'd be there for him, that we would get through this together.

"I love you so much, Liz."

Those were his last words to me.

*

I can see him there, sitting on the worn out mattress of the lower bunk. He'd been in the half-way house just five days. His roommate would be out for the day; he would have made sure of that. He has a thin white rope in his hands, the kind we used to hang the laundry on outside in the summer. Ever the perfectionist, he worked on tying a slipknot, not a noose; the cliché would have been too much for him. I'm sure he grabbed the water pipes above him, tested to be sure they would hold his weight. He may have thought about leaving a note, but I doubt it.

He pushed the bureau in front of the door and wondered why no one had heard the noise. I imagine, when my eyes close just before sleep takes me, that as Dad stood on the cold heater in his room, that he was more afraid of living through this than he had been afraid of anything before in all the time he'd been alive.

He tied the rope around the pipe.

He tied the rope around his neck.

Chapter 13

Being an Albee

Lynn Albee

This chapter is about what it means to be an Albee. I will tell stories of my family, who take the social model to another level. There is something more powerful than having a label of autism, and that is having the label of being an Albee. And that is a very cool way to live life.

To be an Albee, you must be wild. You have to be ready for anything. When you hear about a crazy event, an Albee was most likely involved. We are a tight bunch who look after each other with extreme devotion. The lines of Autism and Albee cross over and intertwine to the point that we cannot tell the difference between having a disability and being an Albee. Maybe we all have autism?

The Albee clan includes Big Dave and Big Lynn (my parents), me, Bill, David, and Jim (my brothers). My family moved from Chicago to Galena, Illinois fifteen years ago. My parents moved the 150 miles because the private school that Bill and I were attending at the time would not allow David to enroll in the school. The pastor of the church (affiliated with the school) told my mom that "there were special schools for kids like him." My parents wanted the four of us to go to the same school. Since moving, we've racked up quite the life!

Since my brothers have grown up (and still live at home), the "Albee-ness" in the house has taken over. The bird room now has a kegerator (a special kind of refrigerator for beer kegs). The night before my wedding, my brothers and cousins came home and had a knife throwing contest in the kitchen, completely destroying the floor. Ask yourself, who *does* something like that? An Albee does, that's who! We can only get that gene from one person, and that's Big Dave.

Big Dave

Big Dave is the patriarch, the leader of the Albees. He sometimes wears eccentric outfits—a skunk hat, Zorro costume, or Dracula costume. He works out of our house as a lawyer, and spends a fair amount of time in his office. Big Dave's office has collections of cameras, pictures, court documents, and a magic 8 ball to make decisions (yes, really).

In our house, we have an additional room that used to be used as a greenhouse. Big Dave used it to breed and sell parakeets when we first moved to town. Unfortunately, only one person bought a bird, and we soon began living with as many as 20 birds. Those who are new to the Albee house might find it odd to be told to get a beer out of the kegerator in the bird room.

One particular weekend, Big Dave, my husband Brodie, and I played golf. We met up with Bill's friend Sean (the brew master at the local brewery in downtown Galena, and the only owner of any bird born from Big Dave's bird breeding endeavor). On the third hole, my dad found a cardinal feather on the tee box, and stuck it in his hat. A twosome that played through laughed, rolled their eyes, and called him "Chief."

That night, when we went out downtown, my dad continued to wear his feathered cap. We played pool, stopped at a restaurant, and then went to a bar where all of the Galena folk go. My dad insisted to everyone he encountered that (pointing to the feather) "This is rank. You call me Chief." They all laughed and rolled of their eyes, and then accepted the fact that Big Dave was out in public with a bird feather in his hat. While talking to friends that night, we heard comments about the feather in my dad's hat: "What's your dad wearing a feather in his hat for?" "I can't believe your dad's wearing that downtown, but I guess it's better than the skunk hat he wore last time I saw him." "You Albees..."

Albee Parties

It wasn't the first time I had heard the phrase "you Albee's." My family has a notorious reputation in Galena. When we first moved to the area, instead of having a housewarming party, we had a toga party. There is no such thing as a small, quiet, get-together at our house. Wouldn't you want to go to a party at the Albee house? There are magic tricks, a fully functioning train layout, a kegerator in the bird room, and most importantly, Albees!

You never know what will happen at an Albee party, and over the years, our guests have grown accustomed to that. The biggest party of the year is on Halloween. For the weeks leading up to Halloween, Big Dave decorates the yard with skulls, coffins, and headstones, while the rest of us focus on our costumes. Broken wine glasses, broken noses, and waking up to fifteen people sleeping on the living room floor are just some of the after-effects of an Albee Halloween party. Nobody likes an Albee party more than David. He invites the most people and has the best costume of the night. He is the first ready for the party, and the one still up saying goodnight to the last guests.

The Albee heritage is not just something passed along genetically. It is a way of life, a family culture that Big Dave has instilled in us. Growing up, we thought that dressing up in costumes was just something you did to express yourself. We all say what is on our mind, and we all speak in movie quotes. Some people with autism speak their mind, dress in costumes and speak in movie lines. Maybe we all have autism?

Big Lynn

My mom is the glue that keeps us all together. Level headed, she tries to keep the hot air balloon of our family from flying away. Ultimately, outnumbered by Albees, she ends up holding onto the rope for dear life as the balloon takes off.

Every year, for the Fourth of July, Big Dave sneaks out and purchases fireworks in Wisconsin. Every year, my mom says that nobody is allowed to have fireworks because it always ends badly. Every year, the police show up at the house because we set off fireworks anyway. Big Dave always spots the police car as it heads up the road, runs into the house, and hides, leaving my mom to talk to the police and clean up the mess. The police never issue a fine or ticket, probably because David has made friends with every police officer in town. While Big Lynn deals with the police, Big Dave and my brothers laugh wildly in the house and yell out the windows: "Give her a fine! Throw her in jail!" They pop their heads in and out of windows, and then hide again if they are spotted. It's ridiculous.

For as long as I can remember, my family has owned a police scanner. My dad thought it was cool to listen to the Chicago crime going on in the city. Since moving to Galena, the scanner has continued to be a useful appliance in the Albee home. My dad uses the scanner every Fourth of July.

He listens for police calls to homes that have firework activity, and rushes to hide the fireworks in a new secret hiding place (paranoid that the cops are onto his plan and going to take his fireworks).

Every Fourth, our neighbors come outside and sit on their front porch knowing that there will be a show. Like clockwork, Big Dave sets off hundreds of fireworks and giggles like a little boy. Although Big Lynn gets upset every Fourth of July because of the same antics, she plays right into them. She pretends to be mad, and I think she wishes she would sometimes be the one to play the prank on Big Dave and my brothers.

Bill

Bill is the second-oldest Albee spawn. He's an avid baseball player and coach with the ability to convince and motivate anyone to do whatever he wants.

When Bill was in high school, the MTV show *Jackass* made its debut, filled with wacky stunts submitted by viewers. So Bill took it upon himself to make his own videos to submit. He dressed up as Batman and walked the streets of Galena with David and Jim in tow, and also in Batman costumes. Once, Bill went to the high school band rummage sale and got a free drum harness from the 1970's. He took the harness and bolted it down to a broken skateboard. Donning a helmet, football pads, elbow, knee and wrist guards, Bill put the Batman suit over it all, and began filming "Batman Street-luge," rolling down some of Galena's steepest hilly streets.

While they were filming this, my mom heard on the scanner that there were a bunch of kids with a video camera rolling down Hill St. into Main St. Knowing it was my brothers, my mom said, "Lynn, go get your brothers, I don't want to be arrested for being a bad mom."

A few years ago, our grandmother (Big Dave's mom) was moving out of her house. Because she was downsizing to a condo, she got rid of a lot of furniture. Big Dave took some of the nicer pieces back to Galena, one of which was a beautiful armoire. After moving it in, Big Dave started putting things in the armoire. While opening a drawer, he found a bunch of gold-plated teeth. Big Dave had no idea whose teeth they were, but they weren't teeth of anyone alive. Instead of disposing of the gold teeth, Big Dave showed them to my brothers, and immediately, my brothers had a great idea. Using the clamps in the garage that David uses for his train creations, they put the teeth in the clamp and then took a hammer to smash the gold out of the teeth.

Big Dave saw the shattered teeth on the floor, and screamed "You left DNA in the garage! Someone is going to think you murdered someone in here! Haven't you seen CSI? That's DNA evidence!" My brothers took the gold to a pawn shop where they were awarded $165.00. They had a party, spending every dime of the tooth money. Only an Albee would do that.

Jim

Jim is the youngest Albee sibling, and an evil genius. He is the most like Big Dave, with his secretive nature and genuine sneakiness. When he was in grade school, he qualified for the gifted enrichment program. He didn't like the label of being gifted, so one year when he took his state standardized tests he filled in smiley face symbols instead of answering the questions. Nobody noticed this massive change in test score except my mom. He felt like he won one over on the school.

Jim, like Bill, is an avid baseball player. There was one particular tournament during his Little League years that stands out to me to this day. He went to my mom and dad and insisted that they buy him a bucket of chicken to bring to the baseball game. It was very hot and humid outside, and we couldn't understand why he wanted the chicken. My parents did as Jim asked, and brought him the bucket of chicken he required. As the game started, and Jim's team was in the dugout, we saw Jim passing out the chicken to his teammates. We also saw Jim with a bat on his shoulder and a golf club cover on the end of his bat. My family all started laughing and then understood why Jim did what he did. Other parents and people in the stands thought that this behavior was quite bizarre. For those in the stands who knew our family, they quickly began laughing as well. You see, *Major League* is a movie that is routinely quoted in our house. In the movie, Pedro Serrano, one of the fake Cleveland Indians players, was a follower of the voodoo religion. He believed that the only way to play well in the game was to sacrifice a live chicken. Because you can't do that on a baseball field, his teammates came up with a solution to buy a bucket of already cooked chicken for Pedro. As for the golf club cover on his bat, Jim was again quoting the movie. One of the parents in the stands looked at us, and said, "hats for bats. Keep bats warm."

No Albee can escape being an Albee. We have our inside jokes, and own language in which we converse. People with autism have inside jokes and can have their own personal language. Is this further proof we all have autism?

A Typical Albee Endeavor

A recent weekend at the Albee house proved to be indicative of a normal family gathering for our crew. This particular weekend, Jim had just graduated with his Associate's Degree, so naturally, we had a party. That night, Jim had music blaring from his three-foot-high speakers that carried throughout the entire house. On top of the music blasting through the speakers, David played his B.B. King guitar throughout the house (David has a portable amplifier that he can attach to his belt). People were in and out of the bird room, and there was laughing all night long.

The next morning, David made his usual rounds around town—it is part of his daily routine to stop where he has friends, chat for a bit, and then move on. He left the house around 5:30 AM (even though the party ended around 2:00 AM). He went to a café, had a coke, and mingled with the locals. He stopped at the VFW and chatted with veterans, and went to a store where he knows the owner to speak with customers. In addition to stopping in his favorite bars to chat, he stopped at the fire station to talk to the firemen. This weekend, the station was washing their new truck. David was able to check out the truck and learn about the detailed workings of it from the fire chief. After the stop at the station, David continued on to the brewery.

The brewery is a hot spot for David because Sean and Megan work there. That particular day, there was an open mic performance at the brewery. David called home and insisted that someone bring him his guitar and amplifier cord. I was selected, and walked into the brewery with his black Flying V guitar (different guitar than the B.B. King guitar) and was quickly greeted by Megan and David. I saw that the brewery was packed, and David was having a rum and coke at the bar, looking just like a member of the band ZZ Top: black cowboy hat, sunglasses, and a leather vest over a green striped polo shirt. His jeans were covered with dried paint from past artistic expeditions. Sean told him that he could play two songs and then make room for other players.

The man playing before David was very good. He played the guitar and sang songs by Bob Dylan and the Beatles. Megan got me a martini while David walked around to the tables, telling customers that he would be performing next. Megan and I talked in between her bringing drinks to customers.

"Lynn, did you hear David stopped down this week?"

"No, what was going on?"

"It was during the day, and we were kind of busy. I looked up from the bar and saw David wearing an ice cream bucket on his head with sheet metal on it and a cape. Then, he growled at me and said he was the Shredder [a Teenage Mutant Ninja Turtle character]. It was hilarious!"

"Oh my God, he didn't. Are you serious?"

"I'm dead serious, Lynn. Have you seen the mask? It's pretty good!"

"Yeah, he showed it to us the night we got in. It scared the dogs!"

As David's turn at the mic drew near, I got nervous for him. But that's where David and I are different. He doesn't get nervous when he performs. The Albee men don't care what anybody thinks of them. They do whatever their heart desires, with no shame attached (hence the gold teeth fiasco). He also doesn't play the guitar or sing the way you might expect. David has the uncanny ability to mimic the voice of famous musicians. I worried how people would react to his playing. When he plays at other bars, everybody knows him and will clap and cheer no matter what it sounds like. Here, there were tourists who don't know David. Would they boo him? Would they laugh at him? I got ready to jump in if need be.

David's turn approached in the brewery. David started singing "Sharp Dressed Man," by ZZ Top, and began dancing. His guitar playing was hidden by his aggressive singing and dance moves. I looked around to make sure that nobody was laughing or giving him weird looks (we Albee's have a tendency to receive weird looks when in public). I anticipated this, and thought five steps ahead. What will I do when this happens, or that happens? I think this is just part of my nature as a big sister and guardian of the Albees. Instead of seeing weird faces, I saw that the cooks, bussers, servers, and the two owners, had all stopped what they were doing to watch David perform.

When his turn was over, the crowd cheered for David, with Sean and Megan leading the yelling. David blushed and walked off stage. He looked like he had just performed a two-hour rock show. His face was red and his body was sweaty. As he walked over to me he gave me a big thumbs-up sign, and people went up to him to give him high fives and pats on the back. They gave him words of encouragement, and by the time he got to his barstool, he had a huge smile on his face. He looked at me, and said "Whooo, I really rocked! I'm ready to go home now."

People stared at us as we walked down the sidewalk—David was still in the vest, sunglasses and cowboy hat. I felt like a celebrity walking next to my brother. I heard people murmur as we walked by: "Who's that?"

"I don't know, but he must be famous."

"Look at that guy with his Gibson guitar!"

David turned to me. "They don't know anything. This isn't a Gibson." He chuckled and got in the car.

I have to wonder if other people have the same experiences when they visit their families.

David

David is the middle son, and the only Albee with the diagnosis of autism. Yet, the things he does are indicative of being an Albee. Maybe the medical field made mistakes in not diagnosing the other Albees with autism. Maybe the medical field made a mistake in diagnosing David with autism. Either way, he's an Albee.

Since as early as I can remember, David has been fascinated with all things trains, passenger and freight alike. A sitting room in our house is the train room, completely filled with an 8-foot-by-4-foot layout with four different tracks. The tracks go through mountains and stop at different stations along the way. On the wall is a bookshelf David made in shop class filled with hundreds of Amtrak engines and cars. And because the room couldn't be filled with more stuff, David's music equipment bleeds into the living room: guitars, amplifiers, microphones and microphone stands.

David has a daily routine. He gets up and makes his breakfast. He has homemade hash browns, eggs, croutons, or salad with ranch dressing. Every meal he eats is covered with ranch. He has been known to eat ranch dressing with pancakes! Part of his routine also includes eating cheddar and sour cream potato chips with ranch. To me, and the rest of my family, it's gross. We've smelled that combination for years now, and it gets nastier by the day. Unfortunately, you can't break David of this part of the routine.

Next up on David's daily routine involves his research. He works on his laptop and researches whatever musician or historical event is in his mind. Then, he makes documents to share about his recent research. Sometimes, if it involves a musician, he then goes into practicing some of that musician's music. As an Albee would, he only practices at a loud volume.

After David plays his guitar, sometimes he takes a nap to get ready for the next part of his day. He then goes out on the streets of Galena and gallivants throughout the town. He has his usual stops: the brewery, the VFW, the tattoo parlor, and the fire station. He sees the same groups of people every day, and chats with his friends about the research he has done, or what is coming up in his life. For the days leading up to a visit from other family members, David lets every one of his friends, neighbors, and community members know who is coming, when they will arrive, and what will be on the agenda for the visit. Sometimes I like coming home to visit and having a low-key weekend. David doesn't let that happen. By the time I get to town, at least five people from my high school class know I'm home and anticipate a phone call to hang out. It can be tiring work being an Albee.

Because of David's gregarious nature, he has come to know every single policeman in the city. The relationship he has with these people gives David unlimited contact with them. He will ask for rides home from them, and it's not unusual to see a cop car pull up in our driveway and have David get out with a coke in his hand. Whatever cop it is (and usually, it's the Chief of Police), they end their time together with a wave out the window. It's nice to know that if David ever needed anything, the police would always take care of him.

David has made himself a popular person in Galena. The nice thing about having a scanner in the house is that when a call comes from our house because David is having a seizure, the people on call know exactly what to expect when they get to the house. David has made friends with every single Emergency Medical Technician in the area. A friend of mine, also an EMT, has even come to the house in times of an emergency when he was not on call, just because the call on the scanner was about David. It's comforting to hear community members on the scanner say that they are on their way to the house and know the reason they are coming is because of their friendship with David. Having autism has nothing to do with these relationships. Being an Albee allows for great friendships that last a lifetime.

David's Bike Accident

Like the other Albee men, confidence and having an absence of fear oozes out of David's pores. Seeing who can out-daredevil the other is a common competition between my brothers, and this experience of David's is no different. With one exception, he is the winner.

About ten years ago, a skate park opened in Galena. There were half pipes, jumps, and bars that you could do tricks on if you had a skateboard, roller blades, or a bike. Surprise, surprise, my brothers were frequent visitors to the skate park. My mom insisted that when my brothers frequented the park, they wear their helmets. In typical Albee fashion, David was showboating at the top of a twelve-foot half pipe ramp. As he was getting ready to go down the ramp, he rolled backwards and fell off the back of the ramp, falling twelve feet. He smashed into the ground. Immediately, he was in pain and started screaming. Jim called my parents and they went to the emergency room.

David had broken his leg, wrist and hand, bit through his lip, severely bruised his occipital bone, and received stitches on his face because he sandpapered half of his face with the pavement of the park. It was beyond disgusting. Also, a few days before this accident, he had shaved his head and his eyebrows because he had seen someone do it on TV a few days before. He looked awful. He was sore, but was going to be fine. After he had been patched up, my family took him home to have him recuperate.

This is where my family differs with other families. We took pictures and compared them to previous Albee injuries. Who had the worst accident to date? I had been to the emergency room for having battery acid in my eye. Bill had been to the emergency room for being hit by a car, broken bones and stitches from sports injuries, and Jim had dislocated his arm so many times it was old hat. David had just pulled into the lead. My aunt got married a couple weeks later, and the story of David's accident was told, prompting another, "You Albees." Even at an Albee function, our stories take the cake.

Some people with autism are said to not recognize when they are in dangerous situations. Do we in our family have autism because we have put ourselves in dangerous situations like this? Is what happened to David a result of having autism or being an Albee?

David and His Costumes

David dresses in costumes every day. There are days when he is just one character, and other days when he becomes five characters. David's costumes are amazing, a form of self-expression. On any given day, David might dress up as the Joker, the Shredder (from Teenage Mutant Ninja Turtles), B.B. King, members of ZZ Top, Optimus Prime (a Transformer character), Batman, and more.

His costumes are influenced by what is important to him at the time. During the *Dark Knight* (a Batman film) phase, he dressed as the creepy, evil Joker for two years. He wore a green sport coat of Big Dave's, a purple dress shirt under the coat, and painted his face with white and red face paint. He would spray the top of his head with green hair paint and go about his rounds in town. Because David has the uncanny ability to mimic the voices of others, he was able to copy the exact mannerisms of the Joker and sound just like Heath Ledger did in *Dark Knight*.

Imagine this. You are sitting in a living room watching TV. From behind, you feel someone breathing on your neck. You turn around, and you see the Joker six inches from your face. The Joker then says, "Well, hello beautiful," running his fingers through his green hair. Then he walks away.

An hour later, the two dogs bark, running from the stairs. What's the commotion? David walks down the stairs in his Optimus Prime costume with a fully functioning helmet that turns David's voice into a robotic drone. Optimus Prime apologizes to the dogs for scaring them, and goes into the kitchen to make a salad with ranch dressing.

Later, David returns to the train room. Over a shirt and jeans, he wears a leather vest, sunglasses, a cowboy hat, and fingerless biker gloves. He grabs one of his guitars and turns the amplifier on. For the next hour, David, dressed as a member of ZZ Top, perfects his guitar playing and singing skills. When David plays, it is always a concert.

David's performance is based on research, mostly done online— musicians like ZZ Top, B.B. King, Chris Barnes, Metallica, AC/DC, Brian Setzer, Eric Clapton, or Joe Cocker, (but never Janis Joplin—she's a whiner). He listens to their music, memorizes their voices, and sometimes writes stories about them. He creates PowerPoint presentations about them, and then reads them to everyone when the story is finished.

David dresses in costumes, speaks in movie quotes, says inappropriate things at inappropriate times, and has a massive train and model collection. Yet nothing—NOTHING—of what he does is out of the norm for an Albee. While in school, teachers and students alike thought David was weird. Well, if he is weird, then my whole family is weird. David had no chance to be any different than what he is today. He grew up an Albee.

Me

I am the first born Albee. I'm also the only Albee with two X chromosomes. I have a different relationship with my brothers than they do with each other. I am called for advice and help. I've been known to lie for them and get them out of trouble with authority. I'm usually not involved in the activities, but I end up being the accessory after the fact.

Once, one of my brothers (who I will refrain from naming to protect the less-than-innocent) called me in the middle of the night. He was at a party that was busted by the police. After a few back-and-forth calls, my brother called me again but this time starting out, "Mom? Um, there is a sheriff here who wants to talk to you." I immediately put on the fake Mom hat. The sheriff got on the phone and told me (assuming I was my mom) that my brother had been at a party with some underage people in attendance, the party had been dissolved, and he needed to be picked up. I knew I couldn't wake my parents up to pick up my brother, so, I told the police officer (as my mom) that "I can't leave the house right now, I have young children at home and can't leave them. Can I send my daughter to pick up my son? She is over 21, is that okay?"

My brother and I laughed the whole way home, and only in recent years did we tell our family. Technically, I never lied to the police officer. The policeman asked, "Is this Lynn Albee?" I said yes. My mom never changed her last name to Albee when my parents got married...but he didn't need to know that.

As much as I think that living with David's autism is exciting, it has taken its toll on my family and me. Bill and I saw David's first seizure. At the dining room table, aged 5 and 3 years old, we watched our brother turn blue, watched my parents try the Heimlich maneuver, saw the ambulance arrive, saw the chaos and frenzy. We spent a lot of time with our grandparents while our parents were in and out of the hospital with David for a year.

Because I was so young when David had his first seizure, I don't remember if my life was different before that night. I do know that he is the reason that I enrolled in the Disability and Equity in Education doctoral program at National-Louis University. He is the reason I refused to get a special education teaching endorsement, knowing that if I did, I would be pigeonholed into teaching only "those kids." With a music endorsement, I get to teach everybody, including students with disabilities, and I get to do it my way.

I was a special education teacher for a year in a therapeutic day school for kids with autism. Kids deemed "too aggressive" or "too severe" were placed in my class. It was the worst and best teaching experience I have ever had. Best, because it confirmed all of the preconceived notions I had about segregated schools. Worst, because every stereotype, every label, every pathetic comment I had ever heard about people with autism was played out in that school. I hated it. So I ignored the comments and did my own thing.

I started a music program for the school. The very concept of people with autism getting music was a foreign concept; nobody in the school would acknowledge it was possible. Other teachers would only let their students come to music if they behaved appropriately that day. If they weren't behaving, they couldn't come to the one class with a universal language. Teaching in this school was like living in the twilight zone. I was the odd person out, the one with odd thinking, the one who was weird, and the one who eventually was asked not to come back.

Other teachers in the school questioned everything I did. When it came time to discuss IEP goals, I worked with students and their parents to come up with goals. I got in trouble for that with the principal, who said that I didn't really understand what this student needed, that my ideas were delusional, pie-in-the-sky dreams. The aggressiveness of my students—being bitten, hit, pinched, and kicked—none of those hurt as much as the emotional pain I experienced at the hands of teachers and administrators at this school. With every reprimand I received, I went home crying, questioning whether or not I was doing the right thing. Teaching kids with autism wasn't stressful; dealing with close-minded adults with special education endorsements was.

With all of that, I still think my students would have been more successful in their home schools. I had to go through crisis prevention training (how to do restraints) to keep this job. When I spoke up about how I thought these approaches were abusive and unethical, I was told in a mid-year evaluation that I did not understand the emotional and physical needs of a person with autism. Mind you, I was the ONLY employee in the entire school who had a relative with autism, and he never hurt me.

Having a brother who has the label of autism has made me more than just an advocate for people with disabilities. It has made me an activist. I say exactly what is on my mind. If I see things that are unethical, or wrong, I say them out loud. This has cost me jobs, and I don't see that changing anytime soon.

No matter what anybody tells me, I believe that inclusion is best, and that it is my job (as well as the job of ALL other people in education) to ensure that all kids are educated with their peers in school.

As a music teacher, I have had fantastic experiences. I have been able to teach EVERY student in the school with their peers. My students performed in a winter musical program, and every student had a valued and necessary part in the program. Taking a page from Big Lynn's book, I made all of my students say please and thank you. But taking a page from the Albee boys, I've also taught units on AC/DC and Metallica. Having David as my brother, I have grown up appreciating the eccentricities music has to offer. I am hopefully instilling that in my students.

If David wasn't my brother, would I be one of those people saying the R-word? Would I be as protective of my family? Would my family be as close as we are today? I based who I dated (and eventually married), and who my friends were, on how people interacted with David. I can see through the bullshit. I know if you like David. I know if you like my family. I know if you are worthy to come around again and join in on the chaos that is being an Albee.

Had I not grown up as an Albee, I would not be the person I am today. Am I a better teacher because of who I grew up with? You bet. But it's not because of the autism. It's because of the inclusiveness and acceptance of being an Albee.

You know the ending scene of *Little Miss Sunshine*? Where Abigail Breslin's character performs in a beauty pageant? After a grueling and troubling trip, the family finally makes it to the pageant and Abigail performs the dance her deceased grandfather taught her. To the shock of the audience, Abigail does a strip show and lap dances on stage. Her family is mortified and embarrassed by how she dances, but instead of pulling her off stage (as the pageant director demands), her entire family gets on stage and dances with her.

THAT is being an Albee.

Section 4

What's It All Mean? Reading Lives, Creating Futures

Chapter 14

What Do These Stories Tell Us about Education and Autoethnography?

Phil Smith

This chapter is a scripted performance text for an imagined symposium of the authors of the chapters in this book, following a format deployed by Denzin (2006; 2008). In order to inform, expand, and transcend this text, I asked the authors to respond briefly and conversationally to a series of questions. Their responses here are at times verbatim, sometimes, edited—but always, their answers, like the writers themselves, are provocative.

Scene: a small auditorium in a public university in the Midwest. In the front of the room is a line of 15 chairs behind some long tables. The walls are painted a bland gray, with a green chair rail encircling the walls. The lighting is poor, the acoustics worse. The air-conditioning is on, so its hard to tell that it's a bright, warm day in early summer. Somewhere out there, birds are chirping, daisies are blooming, mosquitoes are buzzing. None of that enters into the nondescript, air-conditioned stillness of the room.

(Phil opens the auditorium door, enters, and clicks on the fluorescent lights. He looks dismally at the room, and puts down a bag filled with books, paper, pen, water bottles, and laptop on the tables at the front. He sits, opens his laptop, and then gets up and puts water bottles in front of each chair. Liz pokes her head in the doorway.)

Liz: This place hasn't changed much, has it?

Phil: Liz! It's SO cool to see you! *(He goes to her and gives her a hug)*. Its been a long time since I've seen you. How's North Carolina? How's the job?

Liz: North Carolina is really nice—I love the weather. And the job—well, I'm learning new things every day.

(Michael enters the classroom, carrying two bags of food, puts them on a table at the side, and starts laying out snacks. He has a bad-boy smile and short, dark hair).

Phil: Michael! My man! What have you got for us today?

Michael: Wait'll you see—I made these killer pastries last night that are to absolutely DIE for.

(Alicia, David, and Ibby enter together, laughing, sharing some small private joke. The others wander in, as well—Erin, Kathy, Lynn, and Casey. They find places at the front, and check out Michael's pastries. Phil fiddles with some technology at the podium—Bernadette is attending by video call. Her face appears on the screen at the front. Phil pulls nametags from his bag and passes them out, and makes introductions for those who don't know each other. Students and faculty from the university come into the auditorium, and slowly the hall begins to fill. Phil rings a Tibetan prayer bell, making it sing, to call for quiet. Finally, everyone settles. Phil stands at the front.)

Phil: Thank you all SO much for taking the time to come to this symposium. We have some great guests with us this morning, all of whom have authored chapters in the new edited book, *Both Sides of the Table: Autoethnographies of Educators Learning and Teaching With/In [Dis]ability*. They've come to us from all over the country—New York, North Carolina, New Jersey, Illinois—and even from New Zealand, to share and talk with you about this book we're all doing together. *(Phil briefly introduces each of the chapter authors, talking briefly about them, and the stories they've told)*. So we thought it would be helpful, for those of you who've read the book—and I hope you all have—to talk and think about some of the common threads running through these chapters. We think that this will add some important thinking to the project, and to your understanding of it. I'm going to ask the panel a series of questions, and ask them to respond, fairly informally. So, here's the first question: given what you've written in your chapter, what do think this kind of writing and research tells us about education (understanding education as a broad socio-cultural project)? *(The group looks at each other, thinking. Erin raises her hand, tentatively).* Erin, go ahead. I don't think we need to be too formal — go ahead and just speak.

Erin: Education has to keep changing. WE — as writers, researchers, practitioners — make it be what it is. In a sense, we write it into being. And as soon as we write it, it changes. It's risky — being the subject of our own research is scary. It makes it personal, real, in a way that I hadn't thought about it being before.

Kathy: When I hear the word "research" I usually think of numbers and statistics. However, I believe stories tell more. Stories get at the truth. Stories allow for the sharing of feelings and understandings. Stories allow people to connect personally and emotionally. I get a deeper sense of what is important and how one feels, understands, and interprets life.

Casey: This kind of writing and research is a way for an author to self-reflect, to understand — to delve deeper into a particular story, and to share it with others. Sharing this form of writing connects experiences. Understanding other people's perspectives and experiences is crucial for us, to gain knowledge, and to establish a diverse, democratic learning environment.

Liz: Writing about my own experiences, and forcing myself to think about how I learned what I did, opened my mind to the realization that our students need to learn through their personal experiences. We can't expect them to see the world through our eyes, and therefore can't expect them to learn through our eyes. They need to be allowed to use their own experiences to understand the world around them. And the things we are trying to teach them need to be framed by their experiences as well.

David: It's personal. It's not neat. There are some things that should be brought into education — instead of being kept out. The research is simultaneously liberating and frightening. Education is far too complex a phenomenon to squeeze into one word. A right? A civil right? A privilege? A responsibility? A way out? A safety net? An opportunity? An equalizer? A chore? An obligation? A myth?

Michael: We need more storytelling and storylistening. We need to embed more culture (food, music, explicit examples of virtues throughout real and fictional time) into daily classroom activity. Some of us are cursed, trained to think we know more than we really do. Some of us are cursed, trained to believe we can't do more than we really can. Some of us have been trained and some of us have been nurtured.

Bernadette: Autoethnographic writing and research is real and its true and it doesn't beat around the bush. When it comes down to it, actual people and our experiences are what life and education are about. The further removed theorizing, thinking, and acting are from people's lived experiences, the greater the danger of missing out on important messages and excluding people and their insights and ways of being. Grand narratives about disability, stories removed from people's lives, ignore and marginalize disabled people and their families. Education can be a vehicle for social justice, change, and democracy. Not listening to and ignoring people's stories keeps things fucked up. *(There is laughter from the audience. Bernadette smiles.)* Autoethnographic research communicates experience from the perspectives of those who have them. Autoethnography acknowledges and values the "intelligence of experience" (Tony Booth, personal communication). It gives us space to communicate our own personal, cultural, and ethical truths.

Alicia: I think this kind of work tells us a tremendous amount about education—what people learn and how they learn it, as opposed to schooling, the sociocultural performance project by which we ostensibly educate children in the society. This kind of work enables us to understand what people have learned and experienced (materially and experientially) in their lives about ability/disability. It also tells us, I think, that there is tremendous power to be exercised in making the invisible curriculum visible and engaging with it.

Phil: OK, next question. Again, given what you've written in your chapter, what do you think this kind of writing tells us about what "counts" as research, and what the idea of research even means?

Erin: I think that research is lived, and it counts when it makes an impact. I need to connect emotionally to research to have it be meaningful. I have learned that what counts as research, much like disability, is context dependent. I think research is being "blown up" in so many exciting ways—including through the stories told in this book.

Casey: The person who experienced an event describes what happened. No one else can provide this. It was incredibly challenging, because the information was not found in a database or journal—it was inside me. You'd think that it would be easy to write about, but it is really hard to talk about personal stuff. It was pretty tough to tap into experiences that mean so much to who I am, and to express it to others. It comes from living and experiencing life.

Liz: Research demands that we look beyond what we know, find new information, and apply it to the world. If what I found inside myself in the process of writing this paper can be applied to other situations, other people's struggles, and to the improvement of any given field, then it is valid research.

David: This research will be discounted by traditionalists—it will be seen as self-indulgent, invalid, delusional or even fraudulent. Research in education has the tenor of an orthodox religion that MUST be adhered to at all costs—a sort of fundamentalist chant/rant/cant with closed ears about other ways of believing, thinking, doing, being, understanding. Plurality is a threat. Traditionalist researchers DO have a lot to lose. They are forced to reconcile that they are one of many ways of understanding—impacting everything, from questions asked, to who is involved, to methods used, theoretical frameworks for analysis.

Michael: Anything you find out is research. If I want to tell you about the Vietnam War, I can do it with a cookbook. If you want to know how to apply the quadratic formula, you can listen to a Mozart concerto. If you want to know how to discern a covalent from an ionic bond, you can make a painting. There are a gazillion ways to tell one story because stories count to a gazillion. Stories don't have both sides, they are a no-sided circle with infinite points.

Bernadette: Writing from experience is valid and powerful. Reading, writing, watching, and experiencing other people's realities and perspectives contributes to social and cultural change. Personal-social-cultural narratives dispel myths about disablement experienced by disabled people. Stories give us opportunities to engage, reflect, interpret, and think for ourselves instead of being stuck in a singular view of our cultural reality.

Alicia: I suppose the subtext of this question, in terms of thinking about what "counts" as research, is to ask, "to whom?" To the folks who successfully played by the rules of a game that regard positivist work as "real" research and critical or interpretivist kinds of work as interesting at best or dangerous at worst (and in either case, probably not "legitimate"), I don't think this work will "count" as research. It will likely be looked upon as "padding" in one's CV—an indulgence in "personal" writing that is a deviation from one's "research agenda." Experientially and materially, this is some of the most authentic writing I've ever done, and if the point of research is to better understand the world, and to engage in building a collective or shared understanding of the complexities of the world, then this work certainly "counts" as research as far as I'm concerned.

Phil: So, what do you think this kind of writing tells us about disability?

Erin: It tells us that while we talk about how disability is historically, culturally, and socially created, we create it every time we write about it. For me, disability is lived. It is a struggle, a constant questioning.

Kathy: My story exemplifies the immediate effects of labeling, and how negative assumptions are attached to that. The label of Down syndrome given to my daughter changed everything, for everyone involved. The instant that the first person suspected that she had Down syndrome, negative and fearful reactions spread throughout the hospital. I was isolated—people were afraid of and about my life experience. They assumed our lives would not be good. Talia was a baby with a disability, something to fear.

Casey: This project gave me an opportunity to express to others how disability impacts family, not just the one who has a disability. Family support is critical. My Grandma's life experience brought my family together—it strengthened us. Disability is inevitable, in all families. Disability and ability is in all of us, and it is crucial to have supports in place for each of us to be self-determined. We need to look past the label, and support one another.

Liz: I say in my chapter that I was an expert in nothing, except in knowing my father. I suppose that's true of people with disabilities of any kind. Knowing that, the people who should be writing about disability are those people intimately involved with them, and certainly those who live with the disability. They can tell us what we really need to know: what goes on inside them, and what do we need to do and know to increase their independence. No statistic or double blind study will ever tell us those things.

David: Disability is all over. It touches everyone's life. How people respond to it individually and collectively, and as a society, is important. It's really about 'ability,' about normalcy, about desirability, about citizenship, bodies, expectations, requirements, conformity, compliance.

Michael: Without being compared to an Other person, disability wouldn't exist. Those of us who think differently or communicate otherwise have a voice. Being a freak makes your voice that much more interesting. People love horror stories, scandal, tales of suffering, and myth busting. A person labeled with a disability is likely to be able to tell one story off the top of his/her/their head that encompasses all of those themes.

Bernadette: Autoethnography allows more "disabled" (and "non-disabled") people to engage with and understand each other. It makes me feel hopeful, in control of my own story. It teaches that disability, like other cultural markers of identity, is varied and complex and one of many facets of a person or family's reality and relationships. It communicates how ableism works. You get to communicate what you really think, without having to obscure it in academic jargon and support it with a whole heap of other people's thinking or research. It's creative and critical at the same time. Autoethnography is more accessible because it can take many/any forms, and can happen collaboratively between disabled and non-disabled people. You don't have to work at a university to communicate autoethnographically, you don't have to be able to speak in words. Autoethnography can create space for more people to be part of the conversation. It acknowledges multiple perspectives and truths and allows them to be expressed. It invites us to recognize and challenge destructive ways of thinking and practicing.

Alicia: Disability is everywhere. It is natural. It is ubiquitous. It pervades human existence. However, I am deeply disturbed and frightened by the omnipresence of ableism in daily life. It is a central organizing construct (unacknowledged because of its ideological nature).

Phil: Another question. Does autoethnographic work have "truthiness?" That is, does it tell us things that are meaningful, important, and valuable? Does it begin to get at the truth (small t) of the world?

Erin: Yes. *(The group laughs, and she smiles.)* Well, it does. It has truthiness, it is meaningful, and important, and is valuable. I would say there is ONLY small truth, and that large Truth is dangerous.

Kathy: Yes, autoethnography has truth. Autoethnography opens up a space of safety in which others can share. Stories not only help create better understanding for others, they also create better understanding for the people who write them. As I write, I am forced to try and understand the reactions, feelings, and thoughts of others. I understand better why people react (and reacted) as they do (and did), because I have to try and understand where they were coming from. My own personal reaction and fear was not really that much different than theirs.

Casey: Autoethnographic work does provide truth. It provides insight into other's experiences. It helps to understand how situations can vary, depending on culture and context. It allows a reader to understand that the ways each of us experience things vary, depending on beliefs, values, and culture.

Liz: Writing and sharing my story leads to someone (hopefully) reading it; that person sees themselves in the story and feels less alone, and maybe decides to share their story; their story touches another person, and they tell their story. Eventually we are led to understand that, though our circumstances may be radically different, the meat of it comes down to the same things instead of only finding the truth about ourselves, and others.

David: What is truth? That's a big question—asked by Pontius Pilate if a lapsed Catholic recalls correctly. The personal truth, the human truth, the momentary, contextualized, actual—in that instant—truth, contingent upon what's being asked, by whom. The generalizable truth is never total. We cannot replicate human actions and interactions as if we're talking about inanimate objects or controlled conditions. Controlled conditions are unnatural conditions, human inventions.

Michael: Autoethnographic work is human work. We can try to tell the story of the ocean, but we'll never be able to speak for the ocean.

Bernadette: I think that learning from truth, with a small t, is about listening to the experiences and insights of people whose experiences might be vastly different. People who live with Western cultural norms have and continue to marginalize and punish for not conforming. Not listening to, valuing, or caring about other people, their lives and circumstances, is at the root of all evil.

Alicia: Autoethnographic work comes closer to truthiness than many other genres. Strange how our dominant ideas about research tell us that Truth somehow exists outside of or independent of direct human experience, and that one's own experience is necessarily "biased," while some "neutral," "objective," "third party researcher/observer's" interpretation of our experience somehow is not? There are many, simultaneous, complexly overlapping, truths of the world, and autoethnography is a powerful genre for getting some of those truths out into the public realm for shared consideration. Autoethnography is inherently meaningful, important, and valuable, simply because I decide to write what is meaningful, important, and valuable to me, rather than someone else distilling my own experience and filtering it through their interpretations of what might be meaningful, important, and valuable to them or to their imagined audience.

Phil: What does the "doing" of autoethnographic work imply about who should be involved in research in disability studies in education, and how it should be "done?"

Erin: Why not invite everyone to the table? I wish everyone would be involved, and write about disability, because then we would have dialogue. Right now, there seems to be very little of that going on. We need more, more, more.

Kathy: I think that stories should be told by those who experience them firsthand. The thing I hoped for was to create better understanding of our experiences, with the hope that through better understanding there would be more and better opportunities for people with disabilities.

Casey: People with disabilities should be involved in research—only they can really express their personal experiences. And family members, as well as educators, need to be involved in disabilities studies research, in order to understand how society has influenced their experience. It can come in the form of journaling, interviews, blogs, forums, or poems.

Liz: Those who have a disability, or experience disability through a loved one, should be involved. I would like to see more ethnographic work done with students with emotional or psychiatric disabilities. I have yet to read a firsthand account from the point of view of a student who struggles with these disabilities. It would be so valuable to educators to be allowed to stand in the shoes of our students and see the world through their eyes.

David: The disabled and the so-called able-bodied should be involved. There should be no boundaries. It should be viewed as an art. It should dig deep, build high, stretch out—so the restrictive nature of educational research cannot contain, fails to suppress, and (reluctantly) yields to difference ways of conceptualizing dis/ability, difference, humanity. Some (plenty) good examples—but perhaps no "how-to's reduced to formulas, join the dots, checklists, rubrics. Gosh! A (w)hole book of poems on this would be SLAMming—it could rock the world of Special Dread. (*The audience laughs.*) An image I can't help but conjure: Munch's *The Scream*. Perhaps a prose poem along the lines of *When Colored Girls Consider Suicide When the Rainbow Is Enuf* by Ntozake Shange? That blew me away when I first read it. It defied categorization, and in doing so, brought a whole new experience to what was being said to how it was being said. It made me teach it in a high school class—and screen the original Channel 13 production. The kids ("LD," "BD,") got it so much more than Thornton Wilder's "Our Town." Whose reality is reflected in our research? I often ask. On another note—imagine what A PLEASURE it would be to read journals and dissertations that featured autoethnography instead of tedious, formulaic, predictable prose? Dull dull dull. No students read the journals. Only other academics interested in securing their careers. Playing the game invented by others.

Michael: Everyone has experience with ability and receiving some form of education. If you can breathe (ability), you've been alive (education)—and that is the beginning of your story.

Bernadette: Disability Studies in Education (DSE) positions itself as closely aligned to and part of the disability rights movement. Probably the most important key message from disabled activists is that there should be "nothing about us without us." That involves DSE work being led by disabled people. Currently, that's not really the situation. A lot of the research, writing, and presenting that happens is not very accessible. I think this is especially true in relation to people with intellectual disabilities. Its not impossible to make messages and knowledge accessible, it just takes more time and collaboration. We're all very good at making things more complicated than they need to be. I also don't like the word "accessible"— it's too perfunctory, one-way linear, and technical. What I mean is communicating in ways where diverse groups of people can have a conversation/dialogue and learn with and from each other. I think that autoethnography—including biography, performance, fiction, music, sound, storytelling, art, photography, comedy, parody, multimedia—is really suited to movements such as DSE when it comes to fulfilling our commitment to *action* and collaboration for social justice. There is a lot of power and potential for learning and transformation in the sharing of people's experiences and perspectives in less decontextualized ways. I think we need to be vigilant about who "our" theories (small t) come from, who is in and who do we out in the ways we develop, share and live our perspectives.

Autoethnography does away with the split between disability and impairment. It's an embodied way of communicating.

Alicia: Research is almost an inherently colonizing endeavor, although I do believe that research about disability can be conducted by nondisabled researchers respectfully, meaningfully, and as an ally. We need more autoethnographic work written by people who identify as disabled, as well as more autoethnographic work written by people who identify as nondisabled and who reflect upon their experiences of immersion in, and potentially disruption of, a powerfully ableist culture.

Phil: OK, here's the last question. What else have you learned—about yourself, about the world, about society and culture—in doing autoethnographic writing for this book?

Erin: This is the hardest writing I've ever done. I guess I like to hide behind my "methods" section, where I can "show" how I am being objective, and talk about how I categorize data. How do I categorize my life? How do I represent my son so that it's honest and doesn't invoke some sort of reaction that I (and he some day) would hate? I see my world, society, and culture reflected back at me in my interactions with my son, and let me tell you, it can be painful.

Kathy: I've learned more about perspective. After writing for this book, I understand better why people reacted the way they did—the lack of experience with disability created and perpetuated negative beliefs about disability. Shared experiences, stories, and conversations with other families that had children with Down syndrome changed everything for me. I learned how powerful unexamined beliefs are—they dominated my experience. Stories from others are what can change understanding. Stories are powerful.

Casey: This project allowed me to tap into experiences that shaped me into the person I am today. This was not always easy for me emotionally. I hid feelings and situations from myself—they were too difficult to face. I discovered the importance of supports for and within families. And I learned more about the history of disability, and how segregation remains so prevalent. I've come to realize that my experiences motivate me to be who I am as an educator.

Liz: I realized that I was hiding truth from myself. I spent years telling that story in the hardened way you, Phil, first heard me tell it. I left myself out of the story—my true self, anyway. Though this writing, I was forced to put the real me back into that situation and feel things I had refused to feel for so long. I realized that I have always been afraid of what others think about someone who has been through these things. I realized I was afraid of what I thought of myself because of what I have lived through and with. And I realized that I can't possibly be the only one who feels this way.

David: Facing fear of showing the personal—not about being gay, as I have been proactive since being a teenager, but rather my personal interpretations of lives of family members. Dealing with anxieties of the tangle, mix, mess. Of making sense. Of representing through my eyes and understanding without consulting my family members. Of fearing they may see intrusion or betrayal—a crossing of cultural boundaries. At the same time, knowing they could also see meaning, power, the ability to help others understand (some parts of) the world. Will I share it with them? Will I keep it publicly personal? Isn't this a paradox—even going contrary to DSE tenets I help to create? Is it my right, as an autoethnographer in this chapter, to involve family members who are close and not so close (but never strangers) in the portrayal of myself, thoughts, chosen career? I'm cognizant of being egotistical in writing about the self. What drives the need to push pen to paper, hands to keyboard? Having "something to say" means taking the microphone. It is very public. Of wanting to embrace life. Of shouting into the unknown: "I live(d). I am/was here. I try(-ied) to understand it as best I could." Of wanting to understand more. Of never feeling satisfied. Of knowing there's always so much to do and wondering about how we make the choices we need to, given the very real pressures of time. Of not being afraid to take risks. No risks means no new ideas, no new ways.

Michael: Autoethnographic research begins as pain. It makes you relive the best and worst moments of your life. But, Reality lies in between those moments. An autoethnographic project forces you to rediscover those moments that you never would have thought important. Yes! Autoethnographic work is economic, too! Imports and exports. Ctrl+Xs and

Ctrl+Vs. Trading and bartering. Paying penalties and reaping dividends. My world is often limited by the language I "speak." It is incredibly difficult to listen to stories in "languages" I do not speak when they are confined to words. Autoethnographic projects are "about faces," tones of "voice," textures, temperatures, twinges, and growth. Planted seeds and felled forests. Stürmen und drängen. Leap frogs and lily pads.

Bernadette: We need a new language and way of framing, making sense of and living our reality. There are heaps of terms we use that are insufficient and loaded with yucky, limiting assumptions. I think that the path to changing language is to change the ways we live, relate to and think about what we currently call and experience as "difference" and "diversity." Autoethnography (and some fiction) is a vehicle for helping us to do that. On occasion, reading, watching, or listening to an autoethnographic piece, has made me cringe. I don't enjoy watching people navel gaze, there has to be a point. Then again, if people enjoy reading it, I s'pose that's all good. To my mind, we should sustain our humility in the face of life's complexity, largeness, and unknowability.

Alicia: I have learned that continuing to engage in this kind of writing will henceforth be necessary to my continued existence on the planet. This kind of writing has enabled me to write myself out of a state of profound alienation and into one of potential connectedness with others' experiences of reality. I will continue to do the other kind of writing (traditional research, peer-reviewed, all of that). But I will continue to do this kind of writing because it is necessary to enable me to continue to meaningfully and authentically exist in the world.

Phil: (He stands, and speaks to all.) Wow. I don't know about all of you, this has been an extraordinary experience—hearing these writers talk and think about some cool ideas: autoethnography, research, education, disability. I, for one, have a lot to think about after this symposium. I want to thank our speakers this morning—let's give them a round of applause. *(The audience applauds)*. And I'd like to thank those of you in the audience for coming this morning—I hope you've learned as much as I have. I'm sure if you have any questions, our presenters would be willing to hang around for a little while to talk with you. Oh, I almost forgot: copies of the book are available for sale here at the front, and I'm sure that the authors would love to autograph your copy. Thanks again, everyone!

References

Denzin, N. (2006). Sacagawea's nickname, or the Sacagawea Problem. *Junctures, 6*, 13–33.

—— (2008). *Searching for Yellowstone: Race, gender, family, and memory in the postmodern West*. Walnut Creek, CA: Left Coast Press.

Chapter 15

Looking to the Future

Phil Smith

The lake was quiet for once—just a light breeze ruffled the water; a single loon called up the bay. My daughter Marilla and I sat in Adirondack chairs on the cabin porch, looking out over Keweenaw Bay on Lake Superior. It was early evening in late June, but this far north and west in Michigan's Upper Peninsula, the sun was still high in the sky, and wouldn't set for hours. A warm evening, with a clear sky, we looked west toward what would probably be a terrific sunset. The end of another day in paradise.

Marilla picked up her beer from the little table between us. How was she old enough to be drinking beer? And she's planning to get married. When did all *that* happen, I thought to myself? Dear god, I'm getting old.

She looked over at me. "So Dad, what's this book you're working on?"

"Weeeeeell…" Good grief, and I sound just like my father. "Hem. Uh, well, I told you about autoethnographies, didn't I?"

"Yeah," she said. "Real stories, about people's lives, told by themselves, and about what they can tell us about our culture. Sort of—sort of researching your own life, instead of researching somebody else's. Is that close?"

"Spot on, kid. Yes. It's a way of mining the data of your own life—your own experiences—to try to figure out what it means for our society, our culture. And, with luck, how to change it. So this book is a set of stories—a set of autoethnographies—by teachers and teacher educators, who either have a disability, or have someone close to them with a disability, and what that experience has taught them about disability, about education." I picked up my own beer, took a sip, and absently wiped the circle of condensation that it had left on the small green table. "And then—and then, maybe, trying to figure out what to DO about those things, too. That's the hard part. And the important part."

Marilla looked over at me. "Huh. That sounds cool. What are the stories like? Who are the people writing them?"

"Oh, the stories are awesome. They read like—I dunno, like short stories. Characters and setting, dialogue—all the structures you'd expect in a short story. And they grab you—not just intellectually, although there's a lot to them that way, too." I sat up, and looked out at the water. A kingfisher landed in the big, dead birch tree down by the water, scouting for fish. I pointed to it, and Marilla nodded.

"See, but its not just the intellectual stuff," I said. "It's the emotional stuff, too, that grabs you. Casey talks about her grandmother, what she meant to her, how she took care of her grandmother as she got older—and her grandmother had bipolar disorder, spent time in psychiatric hospital, had all kinds of medication." Another sip of beer. "Or Liz, whose father committed suicide. And Dené, working on her doctorate, who has ADHD and a learning disability, talking about what that was like. Ibby, who is a radical, autistic advocate. Just really cool stories, that make you want to get to know these people, how the perception of disability has affected their lives."

We looked together out at the lake. The sun had drifted a little farther north, a little lower in the sky, and moved out from behind a balsam tree, so that now the porch floor had a long narrow strip of golden light stretched along it. Marilla took off her glasses and rubbed her nose.

"But is all that really research, Dad?" Marilla wondered, putting her glasses back on.

"Yeah, it is, though its dangerous research, from the perspective of more traditional education and special education researchers. It calls into question what it means to know, what it means to understand, and who can do that knowing and understanding. Some of my colleagues in the disability studies in education biz—David Connor, Deb Gallagher, and Beth Ferri (2011)—have been pretty vocal about the importance of changing the paradigm of what counts in education research, especially in special education research. As have I, of course. Heck, most of my research career has been about pushing those buttons."

"So, you said that the important part was to do something about those stories." Marilla looked at me, curious. "What did you mean by that?"

"Well..." The kingfisher dove from the birch, hit the water with a splash, and came up with a small fish in its bill. It flew south, and we watched it for a moment. "Well, when the stories are done right, and are the right stories, they have a point to make. Intellectually and emotionally. And that point can be a force to not just describe the culture, but to change it, a force for social justice. Just like any good literature, any good art." I straightened up and looked at Marilla. "I'll give you an example. I read an article last week by Natalie Abbot (2011), writing about a photography project about people with disabilities. She said that the photographs change how people looked at disabled bodies. That if disability is created by social institutions, then those photographs call for different kinds of social institutions."

"Okaaay. I get that—stories can be a force for social justice. But what kind of change will these stories make? What kind of social justice will they act for? What will these stories do?"

I picked up my beer again, and looked at the brown bottle. "That's the part I've been thinking about, trying to sort out." I looked from the bottle out to the lake. What little breeze there had been had died down, and the water was now completely calm. Nothing was moving the whole nine miles across the bay to the Keweenaw Peninsula. It was so calm I could hear a truck on the state highway over on the peninsula.

"One of the things—" I started, then stopped. "As I read these stories, one of the things that keeps coming up for me is how negative the whole labeling thing is. Nothing new there, we've talked about that for a long time—how the disability label has a negative impact on people, both people with disabilities, and people without that label." I grinned at Marilla sheepishly. "And you've heard me rant about how bad special education is, how we need to get rid of it, do away with it. That it's the place in education that creates disability labels, creates stigma, creates segregation. Disenfranchises people, keeps them poor, prevents them from getting decent jobs, from being part of regular communities, poor health care. How special education is a vestige of eugenics. Blah blah blah. You've heard that whole shtick before, right?" (Smith, 1999; 2001; 2005; 2006; 2007; 2008a; 2008b; 2010; Smith & Routel, 2010).

"Right," said Marilla, and pulled on her beer. "I mean, I don't think its blah blah blah, but I've heard you go on about it before."

"OK, OK," I laughed. "You're right, its not blah blah blah. I do believe it, and I'm passionate about it." I looked out toward the lake. "OK. But special education makes that happen—it forces people to be separated from others, it creates segregation, it creates the oppression that people with disability experience. Its not—its not like special educators are bad, evil people. But special education is the tool that our culture uses to create the foundation for ableist oppression."

"So," said Marilla, "this is the part where you say we have to blow up special education, right? Start over? Do something different?" She looked at me with an air of apparent, but feigned, innocence.

"Hah!" I said, grinning. "You've been paying attention all these years."

"Well, its not like you haven't been saying this more than, I don't know, every time we talk or anything." Marilla looked at me, smiling. "But is it as simple as that? Can we just do away with special education as we know it, call it good, walk away, and everything is fixed?"

"No," I said. "Its not as simple as that. Because special education is just one part of education—and its just a small part. And I think our whole concept of education is broken, just completely messed up." I sipped my beer. Far away, almost all the way across the bay, up against the Peninsula, a boat headed home, south down the bay. I could just barely hear the sound of its motor as it skimmed across the water.

"Education? The whole thing? What do you mean by that?" She looked at me, a little concerned. She knew that I'd spent most of my adult life as an educator, in one way or another. I imagined her wondering, how could someone give up on an entire, and important, social institution—one which she planned to participate in herself, as an educator? Sometimes I wondered that myself—and how I could explain it all, to her or to me.

"Well—oh hell, hang on." I creaked my bones up out of the chair, walked across the porch, and slid open the big screen door. "Now where did I put those? Oh yes." I crossed the room and climbed the steps to the loft. Several books were on the desk, beside my laptop. I scooped them up, and headed downstairs. I grabbed another couple of beers from the refrigerator, and headed to the porch again. I opened one, and passed it to Marilla. "Here, you might need this."

"Oh, great," she said, and sighed somewhat melodramatically.

I settled back down into my chair. "That's a Smith sigh," I said, and laughed.

"No it's not, Dad." She looked at me and grinned. "Only Smith men sigh. As a woman born of a Smith man, I reject the male gendered expression of my emotional state. I'm just breathing."

"Uh huh. I see." I opened my own beer, and began paging through the books, one of which was clearly old, well-thumbed, and well-marked. "Have you heard of Ivan Illich?"

Marilla sighed—er, breathed—again, and looked at me with her Here-Goes-Dad-Into-Lecture-Mode look. "I dunno, I guess his name sounds a little familiar."

"He was a writer, thinker, educator, priest, philosopher, and mostly a radical critic of modernist, institutional, Western culture. One of his most important works was a book called *Deschooling Society* (1971). His idea was that education was a social construct that institutionalized society. Through it, society was created as a consumer culture, and education itself was the means by which learning was created and consumed. Educational personnel—teachers—become the only socially accepted producers of knowledge and learning."

I took a sip of beer. "Here, listen to this. He says:

> Half of the people in our world never set foot in school. They have no contact with teachers, and they are deprived of the privilege of becoming dropouts. Yet they learn quite effectively the message which school teaches: that they should have school, and more and more of it. School instructs them in their own inferiority through the tax collector who makes them pay for it, or through the demagogue who raises their expectations of it, or through their children once the latter are hooked on it. (p. 29)

"Hmmmm," said Marilla.

I looked out at the broad expanse of lake. Another boat headed south down the bay, probably going back to the dock in L'Anse or the marina in Baraga. "People all over the world don't go to school. Maybe they don't even want or need to go to school—their lives are rich enough the way they are. They learn without school. Illich says that most of us, whether or not we have access to schooling and the institution of education, what we really learn, we don't learn at school—we learn it almost in spite of what school does." I thumbed through the book on my lap. "He says that 'schools create jobs for schoolteachers' (p. 30)—teachers are who benefit from schooling, not students. Illich comments that 'school sells curriculum' (p. 41)—it creates the consumption of a particular kind of knowledge. He goes on to say that

> consumer-pupils are taught to make their desires conform to marketable values. Thus they are made to feel guilty if they do not behave according to the predictions

of consumer research by getting the grades and certificates that will place them in the job category they have been led to expect. (p. 41)

"Okay," said Marilla, thoughtfully. "Schools reproduce consumerist culture—maybe they *create* consumerist culture."

"Exactly," I said. "And there's more. Illich says

Everywhere the hidden curriculum of schooling initiates the citizen to the myth that bureaucracies guided by scientific knowledge are efficient and benevolent. Everywhere this same curriculum instills in the pupil the myth that increased production will provide a better life. And everywhere it develops the habit of self-defeating consumption of services and alienating production, the tolerance for institutional dependence, and the recognition of institutional rankings. The hidden curriculum of school does all this in spite of contrary efforts undertaken by teachers and no matter what ideology prevails. (p. 74)

Marilla looked over at me. "So what you're saying is that its not just special education that's broken. It's the whole institution of education that is completely messed up."

"You got it, kid. I'd read Illich a long while ago, but I started thinking about him again more recently because of the work of a famous sociologist in New York City, Stanley Aronowitz, who's written a book about his opposition to the institution of schooling as we know it today (2008). His thinking is a lot like that of Illich, although Aronowitz's concern is much more class based. He points out that our society has conflated the process of education with what goes on in schools, which he says use "mechanisms of discipline and punishment to habituate working-class students to the bottom rungs of the work world, or the academic world, by subordinating or expelling them" (p. 27).

I paused, and sipped my beer. "Aronowitz points out that schools have become corporatized: 'private corporations... are making huge profits on school systems. High-stakes testing, a form of privatization, transfers huge amounts of public money to publishers, testing organizations, and large consulting companies' (pp. 21–22). Other researchers have come to the same conclusions—Henry Giroux (2009) writes that "Public and higher education have fallen prey to forces of commercialization, privatization, and market considerations that undermine civic and critical learning while devaluing young people as a referent for a democratic and just future" (p. 8). To solve this, Aronowitz believes that we must get rid of high-stakes testing: 'schools should relieve themselves of their ties to corporate interests and reconstruct the curriculum along lines of genuine intellectual endeavor' (p. 49). Which is certainly a step in the right direction, but I don't think is quite far enough."

Marilla looked over at me. "That's not far enough? That'd be a pretty significant change all by itself, wouldn't it?"

"Well, of course it would," I said. "And tearing down the whole testing protocol and ideology on which special education—all modern education, really—is based, would be a huge thing, a wonderful thing. And I think it could be done—although it would clearly take a tremendous political shift, an ideological shift, a cultural shift, that would be, well, pretty mind-boggling to even think about how to get started."

"So," said Marilla. "Just your kind of thing." There was a twinkle in her eye.

"Yaaas, just my kind of thing. Wiseass." I smiled. "OK. So Illich, and then Aronowitz, who maybe doesn't go quite far enough. But then, more recently, I read this amazing book, by Prakash and Esteva, *Escaping Education: Living as Learning within Grassroots Culture* (2008). They extend the work of Illich, using a postmodernist perspective, and point out some truly global implications." I poked through the book some more, looking at my marginal notes.

"Listen," I said. "They note that

> the *real* price for education... is the loss of language and culture.... Schools and universities, monocultural or multicultural, do not eliminate ignorance, but make it functional, while suppressing difference and cultural diversity. (p. 10)

Schools, and the institution of education, aren't just creating and reproducing consumer culture—in doing that, they're also destroying everything else, all other cultures and their manifestations."

Looking at the lake, I went on. "Its like what happened all around us, when the Finnish miners came across the bay, here. They came after they left the mines they had been working in over on the Peninsula, when they went on strike, to establish the little farming community here that they called Aura. That means plow in Finnish, have I told you that?"

Marilla rolled her eyes. "Yes, Dad, only like a bazillion times."

"OK. Well. Anyway. They cut down a bunch of forest, pulled out the stumps, and plowed the ground. They tilled the field—including one right here where the cabin is now—and planted, oh, I don't know, probably corn.

Which is all fine, there's a lot you can eat that's made from corn. But when all you plant is corn, you're limited to what kinds of vitamins and proteins and sugars you can eat by what the corn produces. And not only that, but corn takes up from the soil only particular minerals and nutrients—which essentially eliminates those things from the soil. And because only one thing is growing there, insects and diseases that like corn infest the crop, potentially harming it. And you have to be careful of erosion, and—"

"I understand what you're saying, Dad," said Marilla. "We gain a lot by planting corn—we get lots of food. But we also lose a lot by eliminating the forest, with its wide diversity of plants and animals and soil, and the impact on the watershed."

"Exactly." I sipped my beer, and watched a pair of mergansers paddle north just off the shore, herding their collection of fuzzy, ungainly, and sometimes wayward youngsters along with them. "So what Prakash and Esteva are arguing is that the institution of education, as we've constructed it in Western, Eurocentric culture, also creates a kind of global, social monoculture, which does potential—and real—harm to the many, many microcultures that work well in extraordinary ways (ways that we, from our dominating, hegemonic standpoint can't see, don't know, and don't understand) for particular groups of people in particular contexts. And that global social monoculture does real and significant harm not just to the incredibly diverse and rich communities and cultures that are destroyed, eliminated, or forgotten—it harms *all* cultures, because we all lose the worldviews, knowledge, skills, understanding, and counter-hegemonic ideologies of those other diverse microcultures."

"OK, that makes sense. I mean, its incredibly short-sighted, but I understand what you're saying." Marilla paused a moment. "But what does that have to do with disability?"

"Well, I think that in order to create that kind of social, institutional monoculture—one based in capitalism, consumerism, positivism—you know what I mean by positivism, Marilla?"

"Yeah, yeah. It's a whatchamacallit—oh, what's that word you like—epistemology?"

"Right," I said. "God, I love that word."

"Who's that guy you're always quoting—Kincheloe?" she asked.

"Yes. With one of his colleagues, he said:

It was assumed that the natural and social worlds could be understood and improved by using reason and systematic observation; that is, the use of scientific reasoning could enhance social progress and the human condition by emulating the successes of science and scientists... (Kincheloe & Tobin, 2009, p. 515)

Marilla took another sip of beer, and burped.

"Nicely punctuated, daughter. Bring it up again and we'll vote on it."

She looked at me and grinned—it was an old family saying. She replied with the expected rejoinder: "Whadja expect, chimes?" We both laughed at our common language, our common shared history.

"Okay, positivism," said Marilla. "And?"

"So in order to create that kind of monoculture," I went on, "Western, Eurocentric, positivist, and so on, education has to—literally, is required to, as a function of what it is designed to do—sort those who can from those who can't. In fact, it *creates* categories of can and can't. Prakash and Esteva, with great irony, and tongue firmly in cheek, say—oh, where is that quote?"

I fumbled through the book for a moment. "Oh yes, here it is. They say:

Vigor and vitality require competition, profess the promoters of bell curves, standardized tests, and other marvelous measures that separate the supermen from the mental midgets... 'the survival of the fittest'... separates the grain from the chaff; the real men from the boys; the strong and able from the weak and disabled; the winners from the losers; the first from the last; the success from the failures who deserve their fate of working for McDonald's for minimum wage. The As deserve the American dream. The Ds and Fs demonstrate their incapability of dreaming it. Someone has to wash the dishes in every society; fill gasoline; collect garbage; line landfills; clean out toxic dumps; spray chemicals; fill up cancer wards... (p. 11)

Such a system, say Prakash and Esteva, is required to create "a system in which more than half of the children become human waste; dropouts or human droppings" (p. 15).

The sun was sinking lower. It was now a huge orange-red ball, directly across from us on the far side of the bay. Its light stretched like a pillar lying on its side across the still water. In the woods nearby, a hermit thrush broke the stillness, the liquid notes of its song reverberating through the balsam and cedar and birch. We admired the sky, and listened to the bird, things Marilla and I had been doing some twenty-odd years together in the North Country—first in Vermont and Maine, and now here in the Upper Peninsula.

"So what do we do?" Marilla asked.

"Hmmm?" I was pulled out of my reverie by her question. "I'm sorry?"

"What do we do to stop creating human droppings?"

"Oh. Yes." I wiped absently again at the circle of wetness my beer bottle made on the little green table between us. "Well, one thing we can do, according to Prakash and Esteva—something that I've been saying and thinking for almost 15 years now, too (Smith, 1999)—is to look for answers not at the core, not at the center, not at the mapped cartographies of social geography—but at the edges, the margins, to the people and places that are outside the boundaries of what we know or think we know."

"But what does that even mean, Dad?" Marilla asked. "I've been listening to you say that for a long time, but I'm not sure I understand what it looks like, what it sounds like, what it really means."

"Part of what I think it means, Marilla, is that we've got to stop thinking about what counts as research, and what it looks like, and who can do it, the way we've been thinking about and doing it for the last almost 100 years, ever since that way of looking at the world was created by the forces of industrialist and capitalist ideologies embedded in Eugenicist scientism. Research about disability can be—maybe should be—done by, or at least in partnership with, people with disabilities. It doesn't need to be done by white, middle-class, heterosexual, male professors in button-down shirts and tweed jackets who work at universities—dead white men, I call 'em. It doesn't need to be done in five-chapter dissertation formats—introduction, literature review, method, results, discussion."

I pulled on my beer again. "It doesn't need to be done in that kind of traditional research representation format; it maybe *can't* be done in that format. Instead, disability studies scholarship and research representation is going to look more like—*needs* to look more like—stories and songs and poems. About real people, real lives. Not objective, not neutral—it'll be subjective, research with an axe to grind, pissed off. Stories with a point to make. Stories and poems like the ones in this book I'm editing. When people understand that those kinds of stories are real, legitimate research—well, then we've truly accomplished something."

Marilla looked at me, took another pull on her beer, and wiped her mouth with the back of her hand. "So you've been saying that for a while now, right?"

"Yeah, I guess so. Saying it and trying to write it into existence for a bit now, since the last century." I looked over towards the balsam tree in front of the house, where two or seven hummingbirds (it was hard to keep track of them as they flew and buzzed and chirped) fought over the hummingbird feeder that hung from a branch of the tree. "You know I've been working to make inclusion a reality for people with disabilities, in educational and civic communities, for even longer."

"Of course, Dad. That's why you got into this work."

"Well, I've been re-thinking whether inclusion is such a good idea." I looked at her expectantly, waiting for the reaction I was pretty sure would come. I was right.

Marilla sat bolt upright, looking at me with real concern. "Whaaat?!? Rethinking inclusion? What's got into you?"

I laughed, and tried to reassure her. "I knew you'd respond that way, daughter. Don't worry—I haven't gone over to the dark side. If anything, I think I've seen an even more radical vision."

I paused, and sipped my beer. "I started thinking about this a couple of months ago, after I read a chapter by a wonderful colleague, Deb Gallagher (2010). She talked about needing to take the next step beyond inclusion, to create real belonging, because most inclusion as its done in schools doesn't work—it *can't* work, because of the ways that we've constructed education in our culture, founded on a particular brand of positivist research."

I pulled out another book from the small pile I'd brought down from the loft. "Here's what she wrote:

...once an individual disappears into an aggregate or category, genuine belonging becomes nearly impossible and all that remains is the prospect of "including" students who will undoubtedly be viewed as, for want of any other term, artificial transplants whose ersatz presence in the general education classroom will inevitably be subject to abiding doubts about their assimilative adequacy. (Gallagher, 2010, p. 36).

Well, that made sense to me. And I began to think about what the work of creating true belonging might look like, how you might go about it given the way that education is constructed, and the way that it is founded on positivist scientific research."

I paused again, sipped beer again, looked at the setting sun again. "When I read Gallagher's chapter, I was also re-reading Illich, and Prakash and Esteva. And I began to understand that creating belonging and inclusion—for people with disabilities, as well as others on the margins—in educational institutions in Western culture is impossible, truly impossible, almost by definition, given the way those institutions are constructed."

I looked over at Marilla. "And at the same time, earlier this spring, I was thinking about a presentation I was going to do at the Society for Disability Studies conference. Well, I did the presentation a couple of weeks ago out in Denver, and it seemed to be well-received, so all was good. But for me, what was really exciting about the presentation, was when one of the presenters on the panel, a terrific young scholar, Liat Ben-Moshe, spoke about the need to align the movement to abolish prisons with disability studies and the movement for deinstitutionalization of people with disabilities (Ben-Moshe, 2012).

I looked out at the sun, as it slid closer to the low hills of the Keweenaw Peninsula. I pulled out a paper stuck in one of the books, and read from it. "Ben-Moshe describes

> abolition as an ethics, not just a tactic or strategy. Abolition underscores the deep belief that life is precious and all the effects that belief necessitates about living and dying in dignity in relation to state power, living wage, accessible and affordable housing, health care, interdependence etc. Abolition thus entails much more than closing prisons or institutions. It is about creating a society free of systems of inequity, which produce hatred, violence, desperation and suffering. (Ben-Moshe, 2012)

The sun was growing increasingly red. "She describes the movement to abolish prisons as a part of a truly revolutionary politics, one opposed to liberalist politics, in which we work towards the inclusion of people with disabilities into systems that are essentially broken. And what she said just clicked for me, it all made sense to me. If you accept what Illich, and Prakash and Esteva, assert, that education as a Western, Eurocentric, monocultural social institution is not just broken, but inherently harmful, then cultural workers (critical educators, social scientists, and others) should not work toward re-jiggering or re-configuring special education; should not work toward inclusion into harmful social institutions; but rather toward re-imagining, creating afresh, the kind of educational opportunities (perhaps outside social institutions as traditionally understood by Western culture) that are not broken, not harmful."

Marilla looked at me thoughtfully. "That's really interesting, Dad."

"Yeah, I think so, too. And then she drew comparisons between the movement to abolish slavery, and the movement to abolish prisons. In both of these abolitionist movements, activists saw the harm of two social institutions that were taken for granted in American society—slavery, and prison. They didn't necessarily have a vision of what might replace those institutions, but trusted the will and work of good people to create what would need to come when they were torn down. And they also knew that we didn't have time to wait around until we created some new ways of reconfiguring our culture—that we needed to work to end slavery, dismantle prisons, now, immediately, that the evil they represented could not continue."

I sipped absently from my beer. "Ben-Moshe has this great quote: 'abolition efforts must take place while we are still enslaved' (2012). And again, that made complete sense to me. I know that, in the work of deinstitutionalizing systems for people with disabilities, that it would take continued decades, lifetimes even, to create systems of supports in communities to replace institutions for people with disabilities. But people with disabilities don't have decades or lifetimes to create those institutions—they need to get out of institutions now. Prisons, institutions for people with disabilities, separate schools and classrooms for students with disabilities, special education, schooling as an institution as we've created it in 21st century Eurocentric culture—they need to be abolished."

"So," I said, and thought for a beat. "We need to stop working towards inclusion, because including people with disabilities into the broken and harmful institution of education doesn't make sense. Instead, as Illich said, we need to figure out what it might mean to "deschool" society—to imagine and create a way for children and adults, in this silly culture within which we find ourselves, to learn and grow and teach and change in ways based on common sense, as Prakash and Esteva say. We need to do so, perhaps most especially, for people at the margins, people who have experienced tremendous oppression, people whose intersecting identities place them at enormous risk. For people with disabilities. Frank Smith (1998) reminds us that all learning is based on our relationships with each other. How can we create a way to make that happen without falling into the traps we've created using the traditional social institutional structures of dominating, hegemonic, Eurocentric culture?"

I looked at Marilla. "I think that is the real work. We need to be focused on a bigger, more important, more radical and revolutionary project. Ben-

Moshe says that project is utopian, that we can and must reclaim 'utopia as a liberatory, as opposed to derogatory position... as helpful in fashioning new ways of envisioning the world and opening up opportunities that are not closed off by readymade prescriptions' (2012)."

It was getting close to 10 pm. The sun, now brilliantly red and impossibly large, was starting to slip below the horizon, its light searing its way into our eyes. The bay was silent, almost completely calm. Marilla and I sat quietly, watching the sunset, thinking.

"So," I said. "Whadda ya think?"

"About what, Dad? asked Marilla. "The sunset, or what you said?"

"I dunno—does it matter?"

"Probably not. Its all connected, right?"

A bald eagle flew slowly and silently south, below the height of the trees, and only a few feet above the shoreline. "Wow," Marilla breathed.

"Yeah." I paused. "Native American cultures say the bald eagle is the highest power. If it's all connected, maybe that's the answer about what to do next."

"Dad, don't go all Yoda on me here, huh?"

"Oh, fine." I stuck out my tongue at her, and got up from my chair. "C'mon, kid, lets go make supper."

References

Abbot, N. (2011). "Nothing is uglier than ignorance": Art, disability studies, and the disability community in the Positive Exposure photography project. *Journal of Literary & Cultural Disability Studies, 5*, 71–90.

Aronowitz, S. (2008). *Against schooling: For an education that matters*. Boulder, CO: Paradigm Publishers.

Ben-Moshe, L. (2012). Towards abolition of the carceral: Lessons from deinstitutionalization and prison abolition. Annual Conference of the Society of Disability Studies, Denver, CO.

Connor, D., Gallagher, D., & Ferri, B. (2011). Broadening our horizons: Toward a plurality of methodologies in learning disabilities research. *Learning Disability Quarterly, 34*, 107–121.

Gallagher, D. (2010). Educational researchers and the making of normal people. In C. Dudley-Marling and A. Gurn (Eds.) *The myth of the normal curve* (p. 25–38). New York: Peter Lang.

Giroux, H. (2009). Education and the crisis of youth: Schooling and the promise of democracy. *The Educational Forum, 73*, 8–18.

Illich, I. (1971). *Deschooling society*. New York: Harper & Row, Publishers.

Kincheloe, J. & Tobin, K. (2009). The much exaggerated death of positivism. *Cultural Studies* of Science Education, 4, 513–528. doi: 10.1007/s11422-009-9178-5

Prakash, M. & Esteva, G. (2008). *Escaping education: Living as learning within grassroots culture*. New York: Peter Lang.

Smith, F. (1998). *The book of learning and forgetting*. New York: Teachers College Press.

Smith, P. (1999). Drawing new maps: A radical cartography of developmental disabilities. *Review of Educational Research, 69* (2), 117–144.

—— (2001). MAN.i.f.e.s.t.o.: A Poetics of D(EVIL)op(MENTAL) Dis(ABILITY). *Taboo: The Journal of Education and Culture, 5* (1), 27–36.

—— (2005). Off the map: A critical geography of intellectual disabilities. *Health and Place, 11*, 87–92.

—— (2006). Split------ting the ROCK of {speci [ES]al} e.ducat.ion: FLOWers of lang[ue]age in >DIS<ability studies. In S. Danforth and S. Gabel (Eds.), *Vital Questions in Disability Studies in Education,* (pp. 31–58). New York: Peter Lang.

—— (2007). Have we made any progress? Including students with intellectual disabilities in regular education classrooms. *Intellectual and Developmental Disabilities, 45*, 297–309.

—— (2008a). Cartographies of eugenics and special education: A history of the (ab)normal. In S. Gabel & S. Danforth (Eds.), *Disability and the politics of education: An international reader*. New York: Peter Lang.

—— (2008b). an ILL/ELLip(op)tical *po*—ETIC/EMIC/**Lemic**/litic *post*® uv ed DUCAT ion *recherché* repres©entation. *Qualitative Inquiry, 14*, 706–722.

—— (ed.) (2010). *Whatever happened to inclusion? The place of students with intellectual disabilities in education*. New York: Peter Lang.

Smith, P. & Routel, C. (2010). Transition failure: The cultural bias of self-determination and the journey to adulthood for people with disabilities. *Disability Studies Quarterly, 30*(1).

About the Contributors

Lynn G. Albee: Lynn G. Albee holds a BA in Music Performance and an MA in Instruction from Saint Mary's University in Minnesota. She earned her Ed.D in Disability and Equity in Education from National Louis University. Currently, she serves as the Program Director for the Master of Arts in Education program at Saint Mary's University of Minnesota. Her writing has explored the over-representation of minorities in special education, inequity in education for individuals with disabilities, and she has presented at international conferences. Albee's dissertation "Because I knew that I was right. Narrative Inquiry: A person's aesthetic of disability," tells the story of a man with an intellectual disability fighting for (and eventually winning) his right to live on campus. Albee has taught in parochial, public K-12 schools and segregated private day schools. Albee has also been an Education Specialist at the University of Minnesota, an Instructor at National Louis University and a Technology Consultant for a grant implementing Universal Design for Learning in post-secondary environments. Albee has a brother who has autism, and her experiences with him piqued her interest in the field of disability studies. As the oldest of four, Albee noticed the inequity of her education and her brother's education. As a teacher, she insisted her classrooms be inclusive. In one instance, her assertion resulted in her teaching position being terminated. She started an adapted music program for students with autism, resulting in a happier classroom and school environment. She currently teaches courses on engaging learning environments, encouraging and empowering current teachers to create classrooms that are inclusive and exciting for ALL students. Albee lives in Minnesota with her husband Brodie, daughter Madelynn, and two dogs, Oscar and Kirby.

Alicia Broderick: Alicia A. Broderick is currently an Associate Professor of Education at Montclair State University in New Jersey, USA. She is a certified special educator and holds masters and doctoral degrees in special education from Syracuse University. Despite this licensure and degree preparation, she identifies not as a special educator but as an inclusive educator and disability studies (DS) scholar. As such, she conceptualizes inclusive education as being not about disabled students, but rather about the cultural and pedagogical practices of enacting socially just education for all. The bulk of her scholarship can be described as engaging (from a DS perspective) in critique of much of the traditional lore of what is "known" about disability generally (from a traditional special education perspective), and in many cases about the specific disability construct of "autism." Much of her scholarship could be characterized as falling within either a criticalist tradition of inquiry (i.e., engaging in ideological and discursive critiques of privilege, notions of ability/disability, and other normative and exclusionary cultural constructs of schooling) or an interpretivist tradition of inquiry (i.e., aiming to construct phenomenological, narrative understandings of disability-related experience, particularly the autobiographical experiences of students labeled with significant disabilities and their families).

David J. Connor: David J. Connor is an Associate Professor in the School of Education, Hunter College, City University of New York. A "critical (special) educator," his research interests include learning disabilities, inclusive education, urban education, and race, class, and (dis)abilities in general. He is the co-author (with Beth Ferri) of *Reading Resistance: Discourses of Exclusion in Desegregation & Inclusion Debates* (Peter Lang, 2006), the author of *Urban Narratives: Life at the Intersections of Learning Disability, Race, and Social Class* (Peter Lang, 2008), and the co-author (with Susan Gabel) of *Disability & Teaching* (Lawrence Erlbaum, 2013).

dené granger: dené granger is a Ph.D. student at Syracuse University, doing work between Cultural Foundations of Education and Disability Studies. Her research interests include: the politics of language; the spaces between smart and stupid; the learning disabled identity formation and the radical potential in reclaiming the epistemology of the stupid body; embodiment, especially as it influences epistemology; and the social understanding of things like dyslexia and word blindness. You can find some of this work in an article titled "A tribute to my dyslexic body, as I travel in the form of a ghost," published in *Disability Studies Quarterly*. She identifies as a dyslexic lioness who likes to spend time gardening, discovering new little swimming holes, and running the stairs at Clark's Reservation. When she can, she also enjoys giving talks on fostering student's skills at becoming philosophers of their own education. A few times a week, you can find her training at Morningside Yoga, and sometimes you can find her teaching yoga.

Casey Harhold: Casey Harhold is a special educator, driver education school owner/instructor, and a graduate student at Eastern Michigan University. She was born and raised in Michigan. Casey is dedicated to her love for running and staying healthy, and recently ran her first marathon. Her best friend is her sister, also an educator and co-owner of their driver education school. At Eastern Michigan University, Casey was awarded the Delores Brehm Scholarship, the preeminent scholarship in special education at EMU. She has presented on inclusion at a variety of state and international conferences. In 2010, she was named a Scholar of Excellence in special education at Eastern Michigan University. Casey has also been active in the Michigan Association of Teacher Educators, Michigan Educational Association, TASH, Michigan Council of Exceptional Children, Disability Empowerment Advocacy League, the Professional Education Advisory Council at EMU, the Learning Disabilities Association-EMU Chapter, and the president of the Brehm Scholars Alumni Group.

Kathleen Kotel: Kathleen Kotel earned her doctorate in Disability and Equity in Education at National Louis University. Kathy is the mother of a child with a disability. Prior to raising her children, she taught middle school for thirteen years. Kathy is an Adjunct Professor at NLU and continues to consult with schools and parents of children with disabilities.

Bernadette Macartney: Bernadette Macartney's doctoral research explored the effects of normalizing discourses in education and society on young disabled children and their families. She is a Disability Studies in Education scholar living in Wellington, New Zealand. Bernadette is a mother of a disabled child, early childhood teacher, teacher educator, and advocate for critical and socio-cultural pedagogies as alternatives to deficit responses to disability and difference.

Liz McCall: Liz McCall graduated from Western Michigan University with a degree in writing, and did graduate work at Eastern Michigan University, in Ypsilanti, MI, where she obtained general and special education teacher certifications, concentrating on working with students with emotional disabilities. An accomplished writer, she has presented at international research conferences and maintains a blog about her life. She is fiercely attached to her dog Vedder.

Erin McCloskey: Erin McCloskey's teaching career started when she was twenty, half her lifetime ago. Though she never envisioned herself as a teacher, she taught a sculpture class and was hooked. After getting her teaching certification, she taught art in Brooklyn to students labeled as having emotional disabilities, and decided to pursue a master's degree in special education with a focus on students with learning disabilities from Long Island University in Brooklyn. She continued to teach in a variety of school settings, and a variety of age ranges. Her doctoral work explored literacy at SUNY-Albany—she received the 2010 Outstanding Dissertation Award from the AERA Disability Studies in Education SIG. She has presented widely, has published a number of papers, as well as a book about literacy and adolescence. Currently, she an assistant professor at Vassar College where she teaches classes about literacy and special education and mentors student teachers.

Michael Peacock: Michael Peacock is an educator and graduate student at Eastern Michigan University working toward master's degree in special education for children with emotional impairments. He grew up in southeast Michigan, just south of Detroit, but has lived in several states around the United States. In Seattle, Washington, he studied liberal arts at community college, after which he lived for a few months in Largo, Florida, but moved back to Michigan because he was not exactly enthusiastic about the heat and humidity Tampa Bay has to offer. He went to the other end of the continent to the University of Alaska-Fairbanks, where he studied liberal arts for a year and survived the -50°F temperatures underneath a spectacular season of the northern lights. He is fascinated with the Dada period of modern art history (avant-garde anti-war movement during World War I), an interest that brought him to the University of Iowa—home of the International Dada Archives. He lived in Iowa City for about two years and spent a few months in Minneapolis, Minnesota, before returning to Michigan to finish a bachelor's in humanities, studying art history, English, and philosophy. While he identifies as a homosexual man, and acknowledges the privileges afforded to him as a white male in the United States, his goal is to untangle the web of intersectionality. At the center of the web are the roots of prejudice and discrimination, firmly tied into a strong knot. As Stephen

Sondheim wrote, "No knot unties itself." He lives with his husband and two dogs. His other love is cooking anything from homemade macaroni and cheese to gaeng panang. At the end of the day he hopes to make his family proud.

Phil Smith: Phil is an Associate Professor and former Department Head of special education at Eastern Michigan University, where he teaches with an emphasis on inclusive education, families with members with disabilities, disability studies, and over-representation. He describes himself as being post-everything and after boundaries, but sometimes works as a critical ethnographer, poet, and visual artist. Both he and his daughter have disabilities. Phil's research interests include the representation of research; ways in which people with disabilities experience choice, control, and power in their lives; normal theory; disability and education policy; and cultural understandings of disability. He's been published widely in a variety of journals and book chapters, edited *Whatever Happened to Inclusion? The Place of Students with Intellectual Disabilities in Education* (Peter Lang, 2010), presented locally and around the country, and does training and presentations on person-centered planning, circles of support, disability rights, family support, and a host of other areas. He has worked as an inclusion specialist in schools, a service coordinator, and an independent support broker. He was also director of Vermont's Self-Determination Project, and executive director of the Vermont Developmental Disabilities Council. A transplanted Yankee, Phil now lives, gardens, hikes, and bikes in Michigan, where he watches loons, wolves, moose, and bald eagles from his cabin near Lake Superior, as well as endlessly (perseveratorily) renovating old houses.

Disability
Studies in
Education

GENERAL EDITORS: SUSAN L. GABEL & SCOT DANFORTH

The book series Disability Studies in Education is dedicated to the publication of monographs and edited volumes that integrate the perspectives, methods, and theories of disability studies with the study of issues and problems of education. The series features books that further define, elaborate upon, and extend knowledge in the field of disability studies in education. Special emphasis is given to work that poses solutions to important problems facing contemporary educational theory, policy, and practice.

To order other books in this series, please contact our Customer Service Department:

(800) 770-LANG (within the U.S.)
(212) 647-7706 (outside the U.S.)
(212) 647-7707 FAX

Or browse by series:

WWW.PETERLANG.COM